Contractual Arrangements
for Intertemporal Trade

Minnesota Studies in Macroeconomics is a series published with the financial assistance of the Graduate School and the College of Liberal Arts of the University of Minnesota.

Contractual Arrangements for Intertemporal Trade

Edited by
Edward C. Prescott
and Neil Wallace

Minnesota Studies in Macroeconomics, Volume 1

University of Minnesota Press, Minneapolis

Published by the University of Minnesota Press
2037 University Avenue Southeast, Minneapolis MN 55414.
Published simultaneously in Canada
by Fitzhenry & Whiteside Limited, Markham.
Printed in the United States of America.

Library of Congress Cataloging-in-Publication Data

Contractual arrangements for intertemporal trade.

   (Minnesota studies in macroeconomics ; v. 1)
   Bibliography: p.
   1. Demand functions (Economic theory)—Congresses.
2. Speculation—Congresses. 3. Equilibrium
(Economics)—Congresses. 4. Exchange—Congresses.
I. Prescott, Edward C. II. Wallace, Neil. III. Series.
HB801.C629 1987   332.64'4'0724   86-24888
ISBN 0-8166-1533-0
ISBN 0-8166-1534-9 (pbk.)

Contents

Contributors

Lawrence M. Benveniste, Board of Governors, Federal Reserve System
Sudipto Bhattacharya, Graduate School of Business Administration, University of Michigan
John H. Boyd, Federal Reserve Bank of Minneapolis and School of Management, University of Minnesota
Edward J. Green, Department of Economics, University of Pittsburgh
Kathleen Hagerty, Kellogg Graduate School of Management, Northwestern University
Charles J. Jacklin, Graduate School of Business, Stanford University
Edward C. Prescott, Department of Economics, University of Minnesota
Bruce D. Smith, Department of Economics, University of Western Ontario
Robert Townsend, Department of Economics, University of Chicago
Neil Wallace, Department of Economics, University of Minnesota

Preface

This volume contains most of the papers presented at a conference held at the University of Minnesota in May 1984. The conference was sponsored by the Institute for Mathematics and Its Applications, under funding provided by the National Science Foundation, and by the Finance Department of the School of Management. The organizers of the conference, ourselves and John Kareken, assembled research concerned with arrangements for carrying out intertemporal trade. Our goal was a better understanding of such arrangements.

The focus on intertemporal trade was motivated by the conjecture that such trade is special in ways that are not captured by the standard general equilibrium model, a model that does not distinguish intertemporal trade from other trade. That conjecture was partly inspired by observations that seem anomalous from the point of view of the standard general equilibrium model: the seeming incompleteness of risk-sharing markets, the existence of intermediaries, the occurrence of financial panics and runs on banks, and the relatively heavy regulation of credit markets.

The seven papers in this volume deal with various aspects of the specialness of intertemporal trade by studying environments in which such trade is more difficult to carry out than is trade in the standard general equilibrium model. Most of the papers impose difficulties in the form of private information or spatial separation linked with private information.

Ed Green studies an environment with no aggregate risk in which the consumptions and endowments of ex ante identical, infinite-lived traders are random and are private information. Subject to the implied incentive compatibility constraints and to a present-value resource constraint, Green solves for the optimal allocation and shows that it can be supported by quantity-constrained exchange of infinite-lived bonds between traders and an intermediary. Green's equilibrium displays idiosyncratic fluctuations in traders' consumptions, and their marginal utilities, in a way that is consistent with the predictions of the permanent income consumption hypothesis. In particular, individual consumption responds to individual income realizations. Since there is no aggregate risk in the model, without private information there would be no such response.

Charles Jacklin's paper is an extended comment on Diamond and Dybvig (1983), a model with preference shocks that are private information. In a generalized version of the model, Jacklin compares the outcomes achieved under the Diamond-Dybvig demand-deposit scheme with those achieved through an equity or stock market arrangement. He shows that in general the former is better, provided that there are no postrealization spot markets—in particular, no one-period credit and asset markets that operate after the preference shocks are realized.

Bruce Smith's paper is an extension of his private information, adverse selection model (Smith 1984) to an environment that allows for the existence of outside money. This allows him to study the role of a 100 percent reserve requirement against intermediary liabilities. Smith shows, among other things, that there exist settings that under laissez-faire have no (Rothschild-Stiglitz) equilibrium but that under the 100 percent reserve scheme do have such an equilibrium.

The economy studied by Bhattacharya and Hagerty is a modification of Diamond's (1982) production-exchange search model. The feature of the Diamond economy that makes Arrow-Debreu theory inapplicable is the time-consuming nature of the trade-matching process. Bhattacharya and Hagerty introduce dealers into the Diamond economy. They find that even with competition among dealers, there can still be Pareto-ordered equilibria. Moreover, because a trading externality is present, even the best of these equilibria is not ex ante efficient.

Townsend and Wallace describe an environment that has a perfect-foresight competitive equilibrium in which different private securities trade with different frequencies. The model is one in which agents, who have preferences and endowments that motivate intertemporal trade, meet pairwise over time in distinct locations. The authors show that one particular version of their model displays what they call a coordination problem: the quantities of securities that are issued in different locations and that support an equilibrium must satisfy constraints not implied by individual optimization and market clearing in each separate market at the date of issue.

Lawrence Benveniste studies the same model as do Townsend and Wallace. In that model, with its rules that limit security trades to personal IOUs and to locations that match those of the traders, some patterns of meetings among agents permit all beneficial intertemporal trade to be carried out and some do not. In particular, for some patterns of meetings, the restricted trades in personal IOUs support the allocations that would arise as equilibria if there were complete location-date contingent markets in which everyone participates before following the imposed pairwise, location-specific meeting pattern. Benveniste characterizes the patterns of meetings for which this is the case.

In the economy studied by Prescott and Boyd, two features of the production possibility sets make standard competitive equilibrium theory inapplicable: the sets are coalition specific and display increasing returns. Equilibrium in their overlapping-generations model is determined by competition among existing coalitions of the old for new young members. The resulting allocation is characterized by constant growth even though there is no exogenous source of growth. In addition, there is no tendency for economies with different initial (coalition-specific) capital endowments to regress to a common level as there is in the neoclassical growth model; nor is there any tendency for coalition (firm) size to regress toward or away from the mean size. In the Prescott and Boyd framework, a firm is an ongoing coalition and not just a subset of the commodity space as in standard general equlibrium theory.

We are indebted to John Kareken of the Finance Department and to Hans Weinberger and George Sell, codirectors of the Institute for Mathematics and Its Applications, for their help and support in arranging the conference.

E. C. P. and N. W.

References

Diamond, D. W., and P. H. Dybvig. 1983. "Bank Runs, Deposit Insurance, and Liquidity." *Journal of Political Economy* 91:401–19.

Diamond, P. 1982. "Aggregate Demand Management in Search Equilibrium." *Journal of Political Economy* 90:881–94.

Smith, B. D. 1984. "Private Information, Deposit Interest Rates, and the 'Stability' of the Banking System." *Journal of Monetary Economics* 14:293–317.

Contractual Arrangements for Intertemporal Trade

I

Lending and the Smoothing of Uninsurable Income

Edward J. Green

An economy is studied in which there is a continuum of traders who are identical ex ante. These traders, who are infinite lived, maximize expected discounted utility. They have uncertainty in their individual endowments, but there is no aggregate uncertainty. No trader is able to observe the endowment or consumption of any other trader. The optimal allocation that is incentive compatible in this environment is characterized. It is shown that the wealth of a representative trader in this environment is a random walk and that consumption at a given date is a fixed fraction of the trader's wealth at that date. The allocation can be supported by the constrained exchange of infinite-lived bonds between the traders and an intermediary. The profit-maximization problem of such an intermediary is dual to the optimization problem of the coalition of traders.

1. Introduction

During the course of its lifetime, a typical household experiences considerable fluctuation in its level of consumption.[1] Some of this fluctuation is attributable to changes in aggregate economic conditions, but a substantial part is idiosyncratic. That is, much of the fluctuation of consumption over time for each *individual* household corresponds to random variation *among* households at each particular time.[2] In a large economy, this variation among households could be eliminated (in per capita terms, at least) by pooling the consumption of households that were comparable ex ante. Such pooling would smooth the consumption of each individual household not only across random events, but also over time. Most economic agents presumably would like the variability of their consumption to be reduced in both of these respects, if this reduction could be accomplished by a means such as pooling that would not reduce their expected level of consumption.[3]

In a sense, then, the actual pattern of consumption by households is inefficient. A Pareto-superior allocation with pooled consumption would be feasible in the sense that it would require no more goods and services to be provided than are actually produced. There is a more realistic sense of efficiency, though, in which the potential existence of such a Pareto-superior allocation does not necessarily show that the actual allocation is inefficient. This alternative sense of economic efficiency is formulated by adopting a notion of feasibility that recognizes that there are constraints on how commodities can be distributed as well as on how they can be produced. In particular, incentive compatibility is a constraint on distribution in an economy where agents have incomplete information. The main question to be studied in this paper is whether idiosyncratic fluctuations such as are actually observed in consumption by households can be consistent with efficiency in this more realistic sense.

The question can be sharpened in two ways. First, one can ask whether a specific stochastic process of consumption can be represented as an efficient allocation arising in some model economy. In particular, this question arises with respect to the permanent income hypothesis of Friedman (1957). That is, can households be represented as having wealth that follows a random walk, and as consuming a constant fraction of their wealth at each date?[4]

Second, one can ask about the connection between how consumption fluctuates and how the reallocation of income is supported. The hypothetical Pareto-improving reallocation mentioned above would be achieved by providing full insurance to households against contemporaneous random variations in their income. Some such insurance actually is provided (e.g., unemployment compensation), but households depend largely on credit markets rather than on insurance markets to smooth their income over time. Income is reallocated among households not primarily in the form of insurance premiums and indemnities, but in the form of loans financed by savings. Thus one can ask whether there is a model economy in which the allocations that would be supported by competitive credit markets can be distinguished from those that would be supported by insurance markets, and in which the allocations supported by credit markets would be efficient.

I will suggest an affirmative answer to both of these questions, an answer that will be supported by the analysis of a simple model of an economy populated by infinite-lived agents who receive endowments in the form of income that fluctuates randomly and independently, who attempt to maximize their expected discounted utility, who observe their own income as it is received, and who cannot communicate this information to others.[5] These assumptions about agents' endowments are intended to capture some of the economically significant features of more realistic but more complicated models, such as those that posit unobservable insurance risks or unobserved levels of effort in labor supply. This model is described in Section 2 of the paper.

In this model economy, there are two constraints on the feasibility of allocations. First, an allocation certainly would not be feasible if its implementation required information in excess of what was available in the whole economy. The statistical independence of agents' endowments implies that even if they could pool their information, they could not discover anything about their future incomes. Thus, an agent's expected utility cannot be improved by having his net trade at any date depend on any information beyond the history of his own previous and current income. Rather than considering arbitrary net trades, then, we can restrict our attention to those net trades that are consistent with this informational restriction. These informationally constrained net trades, which can be thought of as being implemented by decentralized contracts, are described in Section 3.

Second, feasible allocations are constrained by the need to implement contracts on the basis of agents' unverifiable and unfalsifiable reports of their past and current incomes, rather than on the basis of actual observations. That is, incentive compatibility is a constraint on the feasibility of net trades in this environment.[6] This constraint is formulated in Section 4, and the problem of efficient allocation is stated there.

The characterization of the optimal contract is outlined in Section 5 and is accomplished in sections 6–10. This contract can be described by imputing to each agent a credit balance that fluctuates over time. The credit balance is the expected discounted present value of the agent's future net trade. The agent will elect to increase his credit balance at dates when he receives a unit of endowment and to reduce his balance at dates when he receives nothing. An agent who increases his balance must forgo some current consumption relative to an agent with an identical history who reduces his balance, but he will have a better prospect of future consumption. That is, agents make a choice at each date between current consumption and saving.

In Section 11, the time-series behavior of agents' wealth and consumption is compared with the rough empirical generalizations mentioned above. Given the parametric form of the model (including the specification of each agent's endowment as an i.i.d. stochastic process), an agent's wealth is a random walk. There is a fixed constant that approximately determines each agent's consumption at each date as a proportion of his wealth at that date.

Section 12 deals with the relationship between efficiency and competition in the model economy. This discussion is based on a duality theorem for welfare maximization and cost minimization that is proved in Section 7. Because the solutions of these two optimization problems coincide, the unique symmetric, efficient allocation of the model economy is perfectly competitive in a sense suggested by Ostroy (1980). Specifically, the contract that supports this optimal allocation can be interpreted in terms of the constrained trading of infinite-lived, fixed-rate bonds between each agent and a competitive intermediary. The form of this endogenous credit constraint is significantly different from the kind of rationing that has typically been imposed as an exogenous specification in previous models of credit allocation.

2. The Economy

This section describes the theoretical model that is used to examine formally the questions that have been posed in the Introduction. The model specifies the endowment, tastes, and technology of an economy composed of many households. These households are infinite lived, and they consume a single, perishable, composite commodity at each date. Each household is exposed to endowment risk: that is, the amount of the commodity received as endowment by a particular household is not known beforehand. The subjective opinion (shared by all households) about this quantity (about the amount of commodity to be received by the particular household i on the particular date t) is described by representing the quantity as a random variable defined on a sample space K having probability measure k. (E_k will denote statistical expectation with respect to this measure.) In other words, the theory treats households as Bayesian agents, and the elements of K are sample points or "possible states of the world." For simplicity, it is assumed that each household will receive either no endowment or else one unit of endowment at each date. These random endowment quantities are identically and independently distributed, both across households and across dates. The mean of their distribution (i.e., the probability that one unit of the good is received in endowment), which will be denoted by p, is strictly between 0 and 1. Consequently the variance of the distribution is strictly less than 1.

If there were n households, then the variance of per capita endowment would be less than $1/n$. In the present theory, it is supposed that the population is so large that this variance is negligible. In fact, the theory concerns an idealized economy in which, although the endowment of each individual household is uncertain, the per capita endowment is p units with certainty.[7] To reconcile this idealization mathematically with the statistical independence of the endowments of households, the population of households is represented as a set H with a nonatomic measure h. (For mathematical convenience, h is normalized so that $h(H) = 1$. E_h denotes the integral over the population with respect to h.) If households were assumed to receive their endowment only at a single date, then this desired mathematical consistency would be assured by a theorem of Judd (1985). However, because the endowment of a household in this model is a stochastic process rather than a single random variable, the present theory actually requires that endowment distributions of households at a given date be independent conditional on endowments already received before that date and that conditional population averages be equal to the corresponding conditional expectations. An example from Feldman and Gilles (1985) suggests that the construction used by Judd cannot simply be iterated to guarantee the consistency of these conditional statements. Nevertheless, the assumptions of the model are in fact consistent with set theory, including the axiom of choice. (The proof of consistency will be presented in a forthcoming paper.) A precise mathematical statement of the assumptions is now presented, following which the tastes of the households and technology of the economy will be specified.

The Endowment

The endowment is a function $Y:H \times K \times N \to \{0,1\}$. $Y(i,\theta,t)$ represents the amount of the consumption good that household i receives in endowment at date t, if the true state of the world is θ.

For any household, the set of sample points at which its endowment takes prescribed values at finitely many specified dates is an event (i.e., is a measurable subset of K). Formally, for any finite set F, let $\#F$ denote the number of elements of F. If i is a household, and if F and G are disjoint, finite subsets of N, then define the event $K_{i,F,G}$ to be the set of sample points θ such that $Y(i,\theta,t) = 1$ for $t \in F$ and $Y(i,\theta,t) = 0$ for $t \in G$. Then the fact that the endowment of household i is a Bernoulli process is expressed by

$$k(K_{i,F,G}) = p^{\#F}(1 - p)^{\#G}. \tag{1}$$

Also, the fact that the endowment of a household is independent of finite initial histories of the endowments of any finite set of other households is expressed by the statement that, if $i_1, \ldots, i_n$ are distinct households and if for $j \leq n$ the sets F_j and G_j are finite disjoint subsets of N, then

$$k\left(\bigcap_{j \leq n} K_{i_j,F_j,G_j}\right) = \prod_{j \leq n} k(K_{i_j,F_j,G_j}). \tag{2}$$

Equation (2) will not be used explicitly in the paper. However, it is assumed that each household will revise its expectations concerning its future endowment by conditioning its prior beliefs on its own past history alone and ignoring information that might be gained from observing the equilibrium behavior of other households. Equation (2) implies that, if each household has the capacity to observe only finitely many others, then conditioning on such observations would not cause any change in beliefs. Similarly, the efficiency concept to be formulated here supposes that the net trade offered to a household at any date will depend only on the past history of the household itself. The statistical independence expressed by (2) assures that these restrictions are consistent with the efficient use of information by the coalition of all households.

Measurable subsets of K are interpreted as events about which Bayesian households have subjective beliefs. Mathematically, though, the population H of households with the normalized measure h is also a probability space, and the expectation $E_h[Y(i,\theta,t)]$ is the per capita endowment received at date t in state of nature θ. It has already been mentioned that this quantity is assumed to be p with certainty. In fact, the stronger assumption is made that, in every state of nature θ, the function $Y(i,\theta,t)$ from $H \times N$ to $\{0,1\}$ is mathematically a Bernoulli process on H. The economic content of this assumption, combined with assumption (2), is that each household understands perfectly the pattern of endowment distribution that will occur in the economy and regards itself as being indistinguishable from other households in its endowment prospects, but that each household is behind a "veil of ignorance" regarding the relationship of its own endowment to the economy-wide pattern.

To state formally the assumption that Y is a Bernoulli process on H for every θ, subsets $H_{\theta,F,G}$ of the population are defined that are analogous to the events $K_{i,F,G}$. If θ is a state of nature (i.e., if $\theta \in K$), and if F and G are disjoint, finite subsets of N, then define the subset $H_{\theta,F,G}$ to be the set of households i such that $Y(i,\theta,t) = 1$ for $t \in F$ and $Y(i,\theta,t) = 0$ for $t \in G$. Then, for every $H_{\theta,F,G}$,

$$h(H_{\theta,F,G}) = p^{\#F}(1 - p)^{\#G}. \tag{3}$$

Consumption, Production, and Preferences

The households in H can collectively transform and reallocate their endowment Y. Their ability to do so, and their preferences among the allocations that might result, are now described.

An allocation is any function $Z: H \times K \times N \to R$ (R denotes the real numbers) such that the mean of the subjective probability distribution of every household concerning its income at each date, and the aggregate endowment in every state of nature at each date, are well defined and finite. That is, Z satisfies two measurability conditions:

For every $i \in H$ and $t \in N$, $Z(i,\theta,t)$ is integrable w.r.t. k, (4)

and

For every $\theta \in K$ and $t \in N$, $Z(i,\theta,t)$ is integrable w.r.t. h. (5)

A commodity bundle is a function $C: K \times N \to R$ such that, for every t, $C(\theta,t)$ is integrable as a function of θ. If Z is an allocation, then $Z(i,\theta,t)$ is a commodity bundle for almost every i. An allocation is feasible if the discounted present value of aggregate consumption is, almost surely, equal to that of the endowment. That is, Z is feasible if

$$\sum_{t \in N} [\beta^t E_h Z(i,\theta,t)] = (1 - \beta)^{-1} p \text{ for almost all states } \theta. \tag{6}$$

Equation (6) describes a constant-returns technology that allows β units of consumption at time t to be transformed into one unit of consumption at time $t + 1$, or vice versa. It is assumed that $0 < \beta < 1$. This technology is available to the coalition of all traders, but no individual trader is able alone to transform consumption available at one date into consumption at another date. This technology has been introduced primarily to simplify the analysis by characterizing technical feasibility in terms of equation (6) alone, rather than being required to introduce a separate constraint at each date.

If Z is an allocation, then $Z - Y$ is a net trade. Net trades belong to the same linear space of functions as do allocations. However, when one of these functions is considered as a net trade, it is called feasible if it is the difference between a feasible allocation and the endowment. Equivalently, net trade B is feasible if $\Sigma_{t \in N} [\beta^t E_h B(i,\theta,t)] = 0$ for almost all states θ. Note that, if B is a net trade, then $B(i,\theta,t)$ represents the amount that trader i borrows at time t in state θ.

All traders share the same preferences concerning their own consumption. These preferences are derived from maximization of the expected discounted value of a temporary-utility function of consumption. If consumption (at a time and in a state) is x, then the temporary utility of consumption is given by the CARA function $W : R \rightarrow R$ defined by

$$W(x) = -e^{-rx}, \tag{7}$$

where $r > 0$ is the coefficient of absolute risk aversion. The utility of a commodity bundle is the discounted expected value of W. Formally, let Y_i denote the commodity bundle that trader i receives in the allocation Y. That is, for all t and θ, $Y_i(\theta,t) = Y(i,\theta,t)$. Then the discounted expected utility to i of receiving a consumption bundle C in net trade is the utility $U^i(C)$ defined by

$$U^i(C) = E_k \left[\sum_{t \in N} \beta^t W(Y_i(\theta,t) + C(\theta,t)) \right]. \tag{8}$$

Until this point, the model described here has been essentially a version of the model of competitive exchange under uncertainty that was originally introduced by Arrow (1964). In that model, traders are assumed to have common information about the state of nature. In particular, it is assumed that the disposable income of every trader is publicly observable at the time of its receipt. Under this assumption of public information, it is feasible and efficient for all the traders to pool their income and redistribute it evenly among themselves. By agreeing to do so, they fully insure themselves against the idiosyncratic risks that they face. By (1) and (3), and the strict concavity of W, this full-insurance allocation is the unique core allocation under complete information.

In contrast, in addition to the assumption that traders do not observe their disposable income until the time of its receipt, it is also assumed here that each trader's transitory income is directly observable by him alone. Thus the insurance arrangement just described is unworkable, because under it traders would have incentive to deny that they had received disposable income when in fact they had received it. In this environment of incomplete information, the traders need to design an allocation that, besides being feasible in the materials-balance sense, can be implemented on the basis of traders' disposable-income reports that are potentially subject to misrepresentation. The characterization of the efficient symmetric allocation that is subject to these constraints, and that of the contract that implements it, are the tasks of this paper.

3. Net Trades Specifiable by Contracts

Since traders are anonymous and their consumption bundles in the endowment are i.i.d. random processes, it is natural to consider allocations that assign each trader a net trade that is a function of that person's own endowment, that allow borrowing in each state and at each date to depend only on disposable income received in that state and by that date, and that treat all traders symmetrically. Such an allocation is completely specified by the consumption bundle (or the net consumption bundle) that it assigns to a representative trader. Consumption bundles of this sort, or contracts, are now defined. In this section, the unobservability of income before its receipt is taken account of while the privacy of this observation is temporarily ignored.

Define the space S of deterministic income streams by $S = \{0,1\}^N$. A contract is a function $\Gamma : S \times N \to R$ that is consistent with the temporal structure of the trader's observation of his own income. $\Gamma(\sigma,t)$ is what the trader borrows at t if his income stream to date has been $\langle \sigma_0, \sigma_1, \ldots, \sigma_t \rangle$. [For convenience, denote this finite sequence (which is of length $t + 1$) by $\langle \sigma \rangle_{t+1}$. Let $\langle \sigma \rangle_0$ denote the empty sequence.] Then the temporal-structure requirement on Γ is that, for all income streams σ and τ and for all dates t,

$$\langle \sigma \rangle_{t+1} = \langle \tau \rangle_{t+1} \Rightarrow \Gamma(\sigma,t) = \Gamma(\tau,t). \qquad (9)$$

A contract Γ defines a net trade Γ^* by

$$\Gamma^*(i,\phi,t) = \Gamma(\langle Y(i,\theta,0),Y(i,\theta,1),\ldots\rangle,t) \tag{10}$$

for all i, θ, and t.

Actually, the feasibility of Γ^* and the expected discounted utility that it will yield each trader can be determined by considering Γ alone. To do this, consider the probability measure on income streams that is induced by the consumption bundle that a trader i receives in the endowment, according to (1). Give the product topology to $S = \{0,1\}^N$ and define s to be the unique Borel probability measure that assigns probability p to $\{\sigma|\sigma_t = 1\}$ for every t and that makes these events independent. The operator E_s denotes the integral with respect to s. Now, Γ^* is a feasible net trade if

$$\sum_{t\in N} [\beta^t E_s \Gamma(\sigma,t)] = 0, \tag{11}$$

because the integral of Γ over S is equivalent to the population average of Γ^* over H $a.s.$ by (3). The discounted expected utility U^i of the net-trade consumption bundle assigned to trader i by Γ^* is constant for almost all i by (1), and this constant $U(\Gamma)$ is defined by

$$U(\Gamma) = E_s\left[\sum_{t\in N} \beta^t W(\sigma_t + \Gamma(\sigma,t))\right]. \tag{12}$$

4. Incentive Compatibility and the Coalition's Optimization Problem

In the formulas above, the consumption bundle received by a trader in the endowment has been treated as an argument of the contract Γ. Actually, though, a trader's borrowing is supposed to be a function of his report about his income, rather than of the income itself. For the formulas correctly to describe the equilibrium, then, the trader must decide to report truthfully at each date. Contract Γ is incentive compatible if truth is always the trader's utility-maximizing report.

Formally, define a reporting plan to be a measurable function $\pi:S \to S$ that satisfies the same temporal-structure requirement as does a contract. That is,

$$\langle\sigma\rangle_{t+1} = \langle\tau\rangle_{t+1} \Rightarrow (\pi(\sigma))_t = (\pi(\tau))_t. \tag{13}$$

If trader i follows reporting plan π, then at date t he will receive net trade $\Gamma(\pi(\sigma),t)$ if his true endowment is σ. Define the contract $\Gamma \circ \pi$ by $\Gamma \circ \pi(\sigma,t)$

$= \Gamma(\pi(\sigma),t)$. Then Γ is incentive compatible if truth is the best reporting plan; that is, if P is the set of reporting plans, then

$$U(\Gamma) = \max_{\pi \in P} U(\Gamma \circ \pi) > -\infty. \qquad (14)$$

Now the optimal credit contract can be defined. It is the contract Γ that maximizes $U(\Gamma)$ subject to the feasibility constraint (11) and the incentive compatibility constraint (14).

5. Characterizing the Optimal Contract: An Overview

Sections 6–10 are devoted to characterizing the optimal contract and establishing its optimality. An overview of this fairly lengthy argument may be helpful before launching into the details of its proof.

First, the proof requires some understanding of incentive compatibility. One definition of incentive compatibility is that truth-telling is an optimal solution of the infinite-horizon stochastic programming problem defined by a contract. The variational and transversality conditions for the optimality of truth-telling are studied in Section 6. The variational condition, to be called temporary incentive compatibility (t.i.c.), will play an important role throughout the proof.

The credit balance of a trader is introduced in Section 7. The feasibility constraint (11) can be interpreted as stating that each trader must initially have a credit balance of zero. Therefore, the coalition's optimization problem is an instance of finding the incentive-compatible contract that maximizes expected discounted utility subject to a constraint on the trader's initial credit balance. The dual to this problem is finding the incentive-compatible contract that minimizes the initial credit balance required for the trader to attain a specified level of expected discounted utility. It will be shown that a solution to the dual problem is also a solution to the primal problem.

At any point, the trader's credit balance is the expected discounted value of the future borrowings to which that trader is entitled. Thus, when the dual problem is viewed as a stochastic, dynamic, cost-minimization problem for the coalition, the credit-balance process can be used to define a cost function that satisfies an inequality resembling the functional equation of dynamic programming. This is shown in Section 8. The operator defining the functional inequality is called the t.i.c. operator.

Temporary incentive compatibility suggests a finite-dimensional version of the dual problem. This temporary dual problem is used in Section 9 to characterize the minimum fixed point of the t.i.c. operator that could possibly be the cost function of a feasible contract. A contract that actually does have this as its cost function is constructed in Section 10. By duality, this contract is also the solution to the primal utility-maximization problem of the coalition.

6. Temporary Incentive Compatibility

Suppose that, beginning at date 1, the coalition could observe the income of each trader, but that income at date 0 were private information. That is, $\Gamma(\sigma, t)$ would depend on the trader's report of σ_0 but on the actual values of subsequent disposable income. If telling the truth at date 0 would be optimal for the trader, then Γ will be called temporarily incentive compatible (t.i.c.) at $\varnothing$ (the trader's history prior to date 0). More generally, given any finite history $\langle\sigma\rangle_t$, Γ will be called t.i.c. if, had he previously reported $\langle\sigma\rangle_t$ as his income and were he to be constrained to report his income truthfully after date t, the trader would voluntarily give a truthful report at date t no matter what income he actually received then.

Formally, define (σ, t) (the node at $\langle\sigma\rangle_t$) by

$$(\sigma, t) = \{\langle\tau^0, \tau^1\rangle \in S^2 | \langle\sigma\rangle_t = \langle\tau^0\rangle_t = \langle\tau^1\rangle_t \text{ and } \tau_t^k = k \text{ for } k = 0, 1\}. \quad (15)$$

Also, for every finite history $\langle\sigma\rangle_t$, define $V(\Gamma, \sigma, t)$ to be the trader's expected utility from consumption determined by Γ beginning at date t, discounted to date t. Formally, letting $E_s[|\langle\ \rangle_t]$ denote conditional expectation with respect to history before date t, define

$$V(\Gamma, \sigma, t) = E_s\left[\sum_{n\in N} \beta^n W(\sigma_{t+n} + \Gamma(t+n)) | \langle\ \rangle_t\right](\sigma). \quad (16)$$

[Note that τ in (16) is the variable of integration for E_s.] Finally, define Γ to be t.i.c. at (σ, t) if, for all $\langle\tau^0, \tau^1\rangle \in (\sigma, t)$,

$$W(k + \Gamma(\tau^k, t)) + \beta V(\Gamma, \tau^k, t + 1)$$

$$\geq W(k + \Gamma(\tau^{1-k}, t)) + \beta V(\Gamma, \tau^{1-k}, t + 1). \quad (17)$$

The characterization of the optimal contract requires three results about temporary incentive compatibility. First, if Γ is t.i.c. at the initial node $(\sigma, 0)$ and is incentive compatible after date 0, then Γ is incentive compatible. Second, if Γ is t.i.c. at every node and if the present discounted value of sanctions imposed under Γ in the distant future approaches zero uniformly, then Γ is incentive compatible. Third, if Γ is t.i.c. at (σ, t), then in event (σ, t) the trader will borrow more at date t if he has not received income at that date than if he has. These three results are now stated formally and proved.

Define a contract to be (σ,t)-incentive compatible $[(\sigma,t)$-i.c.] if, having received income stream $\langle\sigma\rangle_t$ before date t and having reported this truthfully, the trader would thereafter have no incentive to lie. Formally, Γ is (σ,t)-i.c. if

$$V(\Gamma,\sigma,t) = \max\{V(\Gamma \circ \pi,\sigma,t)|\langle\pi(\sigma)\rangle_t = \langle\sigma\rangle_t\}. \tag{18}$$

Note that incentive compatibility as defined in (14) is $(\sigma,0)$-incentive compatibility.

LEMMA 1. Γ is (σ,t)-i.c. if and only if it is t.i.c. at (σ,t) and is both $(\tau^0,t + 1)$-i.c. and $(\tau^1,t + 1)$-i.c., where $\langle\tau^0,\tau^1\rangle \in (\sigma,t)$.

PROOF. This is an instance of Bellman's (1957) principle of optimality. Q.E.D.

Typically, optimal policies in infinite-horizon dynamic problems can be characterized in terms of a variational condition like (17) if a transversality condition, stating that events in the remote future will have negligible consequences for present decisions, is satisfied. Equation (19) below is the transversality condition for the trader's problem of choosing the optimal reporting rule in response to a contract.

LEMMA 2. If Γ satisfies

$$\lim_{t\to\infty}[\inf_{\sigma\in S} \beta^t V(\Gamma,\sigma,t)] = 0, \tag{19}$$

then Γ is incentive compatible if and only if it is t.i.c. at every node.

PROOF. Temporary incentive compatibility at every node is an immediate consequence of Lemma 1 if Γ is incentive compatible. To prove the converse, a contradiction will be obtained from the assumption that Γ is t.i.c. at every node but that $U(\Gamma \circ \pi) > U(\Gamma)$. First it will be shown that, if any π satisfies this inequality, then there is a π that satisfies it and that involves truthful revelation except at finitely many nodes. The application of t.i.c. at these exceptional nodes will lead to the contradiction.

Define reporting plan π^n by specifying $(\pi^n(\sigma))_t$ to be equal to $(\pi(\sigma))_t$ if $t < n$ and to σ_t if $t \geq n$. By (12) and (16),

$$U(\Gamma \circ \pi^n) = E_s\left[\sum_{t<n} \beta^t W(\sigma_t + \Gamma \circ \pi(\sigma,t))\right] + \beta^n E_s V(\Gamma,\pi(\sigma),n). \tag{20}$$

Considering the right-hand side of (20) as $n \to \infty$, the monotone convergence theorem applies to the first expectation and the bounded convergence theorem applies to the second. Taking these limits yields

$$\lim_{n\to\infty} U(\Gamma \circ \pi^n) = U(\Gamma \circ \pi). \tag{21}$$

In π'', there is misrepresentation of income in at most 2^n nodes. Thus, by (21), it can be assumed without loss of generality that the number of nodes where π involves misrepresentation is already finite, and in fact that π has been chosen so that this number is as small as possible.

That π possesses this minimality property will now be contradicted. Choose σ and t so that t is as large as possible subject to $(\pi(\sigma))_t = 1 - \sigma_t$. Then define π' to be equal to π except that $(\pi'(\sigma))_t = \sigma_t$. Because π is t.i.c. at (σ,t), $U(\Gamma \circ \pi') \geq U(\Gamma \circ \pi)$. This is a contradiction, because π' involves misrepresentation at one fewer node than π does.   Q.E.D.

Temporary incentive compatibility has an intuitively appealing consequence—that traders with identical past histories will currently borrow amounts that are inversely related to their current levels of disposable income.

LEMMA 3. *If $\langle \tau^0, \tau^1 \rangle \in (\sigma,t)$ and Γ is t.i.c. at (σ,t), then $\Gamma(\tau^0,t) \geq \Gamma(\tau^1,t)$ and $V(\Gamma,\tau^1,t + 1) \geq V(\Gamma,\tau^0,t + 1)$.*

PROOF. Because $W(1 + x) = e^{-r}W(x)$, (17) is equivalent to

$$(-(e^{-r}))^k[W(\Gamma(\tau^1,t)) - W(\Gamma(\tau^0,t))]$$

$$\leq (-1)^k\beta[V(\Gamma,\tau^0,t + 1) - V(\Gamma,\tau^1,t + 1)]. \quad (22)$$

Adding the instances of (22) for $k = 0,1$ together yields

$$(1 - e^{-r})[W(\Gamma(\tau^1,t)) - W(\Gamma(\tau^0,t)] \leq 0. \quad (23)$$

This implies that $\Gamma(\tau^0,t) \geq \Gamma(\tau^1,t)$, because W is increasing. Then $V(\Gamma,\tau^1,t + 1) \geq V(\Gamma,\tau^0,t + 1)$, or (17) would fail for $k = 1$.   Q.E.D.

7. A Duality Theorem for Credit Balances

The trader's credit balance at a node is the discounted expected value at that node of the future payments specified by the contract, conditional on the past history. Formally, define the stochastic process B of credit balances by

$$B(\Gamma,\sigma,t) = E_s\left[\sum_{n \in N} \beta^n \Gamma(\tau,t + n)|\langle \ \rangle_t\right](\sigma). \quad (24)$$

Note that, besides specifying the balance of the representative trader at the beginning of the contract, $B(\Gamma,\sigma,0)$ also is almost surely the aggregate discounted cost of fulfilling the contract for all traders. Thus the initial balance defines a constraint in the coalition's primal problem of writing an efficient contract, and it serves as the objective function in the dual to that problem. It is now shown that a solution to the dual problem is a solution to the primal problem as well.

LEMMA 4. *If* $U(\Gamma^*) = u^*$ *and* $B(\Gamma^*,\sigma,0) = b^*$, *and if* Γ^* *solves the dual problem*

P_8: *minimize* $B(\Gamma,\sigma,0)$ *subject to* Γ *incentive compatible and*

$$U(\Gamma) \geq u^*,$$

then Γ^* *also solves*

P_π: *maximize* $U(\Gamma)$ *subject to* Γ *incentive compatible and*

$$B(\Gamma,\sigma,0) \leq b^*.$$

PROOF. In the proof, reference will be made to the amount that a trader with disposable income k needs to borrow to achieve temporary utility w. Denote this amount by $g(k,w)$. Formally, g is defined by

$$W(k + g(k,w)) = w. \tag{25}$$

Solving (25) yields

$$g(k,w) = -r^{-1} \ln(-w) - k. \tag{26}$$

Suppose that Γ^* does not solve P_π. It must be shown that it does not solve P_8 either. That is, either Γ^* is not incentive compatible or else there exists an incentive-compatible contract Γ' such that $U(\Gamma') > u^*$ and $B(\Gamma',\sigma,0) \leq b^*$.

Since Γ^* solves P_8, thought, it must be incentive compatible. Consider the other possibility, then. By Lemma 1, Γ' is t.i.c. at $(\sigma,0)$ and it is $(\tau^k,1)$-i.c. for $k = 0$, 1, where $\langle \tau^0,\tau^1 \rangle \in (\sigma,0)$. For each $n \in N$, define Γ^n to be the contract that yields a temporary utility level n^{-1} less than Γ' at date 0 to a trader who receives a unit of disposable income, regardless of what the trader reports, and that is identical to Γ' thereafter. That is,

$$\Gamma^n(\sigma,0) = g(1,W(1 + \Gamma'(\sigma,0)) - n^{-1}) \tag{27}$$

and for $t > 0$,

$$\Gamma^n(\sigma,t) = \Gamma'(\sigma,t). \tag{28}$$

For every n, Γ^n has the property that $B(\Gamma^n,\sigma,0) < b^*$, and $\lim_{n \to \infty} U(\Gamma^n) = U(\Gamma')$. Consider n sufficiently large so that $U(\Gamma^n) > u^*$. If Γ^n is incentive compatible, then Γ^* does not solve P_8. Because Γ^n is $(\tau^k,1)$-i.c. for $k = 0$, 1, since it is identical to Γ' after date 0, it is sufficient to prove that it is t.i.c. at $(\sigma,0)$. It satisfies (17) for $k = 1$ by construction.

To show that (17) holds for $k = 0$, its equivalent (22) will be established. Note that, by (25) and (27),

$$W(\Gamma^n(\tau^k,0)) = -e^{-r[-r^{-1}\ln(-(W(1+\Gamma'(\tau^k,0))-n^{-1}))-1]}$$
$$= e^r[W(1 + \Gamma'(\tau^k,0)) - n^{-1}]. \tag{29}$$

Hence

$$[W(\Gamma''(\tau^1,0)) - W(\Gamma''(\tau^0,0))] = e^r[W(\Gamma'(\tau^1,0)) - W(\Gamma'(\tau^0,0))]. \quad (30)$$

By (28) and (30), Lemma 3 implies that (22) must hold of Γ'' for $k = 0$ since it holds of Γ'.   Q.E.D.

8. A Cost Function for Contracts

Lemma 4 suggests the following question: Given a level u of welfare, what is a lower bound on the initial credit balance required to guarantee u using an incentive compatible contract? A lower bound $f_\mu(u)$ is characterized in this and the following two sections, and then a contract that achieves this lower bound is constructed for every $u \in R_-$. In particular, the contract that achieves utility level $f_\mu^{-1}(0)$ must be the efficient, incentive-compatible contract by Lemma 4.

Given a contract Γ, say that a function $f: R_- \to R_\infty$ is a cost function for Γ if, for every node (σ,t),

$$f(V(\Gamma,\sigma,t)) = \inf\{B(\Gamma,\tau,n)|V(\Gamma,\tau,n) \geq V(\Gamma,\sigma,t)\} \quad (31)$$

and for all $u \in R_-$,

$$f(u) \geq f_0(u) = -r^{-1}(1 - \beta)^{-1}[\ln(1 - \beta) + \ln(-u)] - p. \quad (32)$$

LEMMA 5. *For every incentive-compatible contract Γ, there is at least one cost function f_Γ.*

PROOF. $f_0(x)$ is the expected discounted cost of providing utility level x to a trader if incentive compatibility is not required—that is, if the trader can be fully insured. Under the incentive-compatibility constraint, then, providing a utility level at least as great as u must have an expected discounted cost of at least $f_0(u)$. In particular, the infimum in (32) must be at least $f_0(V(\Gamma,\sigma,t))$. Therefore, the function f_Γ defined by $f_\Gamma(u) = \inf\{B(\Gamma,\tau,n)|V(\Gamma,\tau,n) \geq u\}$ (where the infimum over the empty set is infinite) satisfies both (31) and (32).   Q.E.D.

It is standard to solve discounted infinite-horizon optimization problems by using "backward induction" to converge from an arbitrary candidate for the cost function to the cost function of the optimal decision rule. As usually formulated [e.g., by Denardo (1967)], this method relies heavily on the boundedness of the cost function. Since the cost function here is unbounded, this method has to be modified. However, the basic idea is the same. Given some cost function f, it is assumed that for any utility levels v_0 and $v_1 < 0$, there is a contract Γ such that $V(\Gamma,\tau^k,1) = v_k$ and $B(\Gamma,\tau^k,1) = f(v_k)$ for $k = 0, 1$, where $\langle \tau^0,\tau^1 \rangle \in (\sigma,0)$. If $W(k + \Gamma(\tau^k,0)) = w_k$, then the expected discounted cost $B(\Gamma,\sigma,0)$ of Γ would be equal to

$$b(w,v) = (1 - p)[g(0,w_0) + \beta f(v_0)] + p[g(1,w_1) + \beta f(v_1)]. \tag{33}$$

The expected discounted utility $U(\Gamma)$ would be equal to

$$u = (1 - p)[w_0 + \beta v_0] + p[w_1 + \beta v_1]. \tag{34}$$

By (22), Γ would be incentive compatible if for $k = 0,1$,

$$(-(e^{-r}))^k[w_1 - w_0] \geq (-1)^k \beta[v_0 - v_1]. \tag{35}$$

Now, letting $\geq$ denote the pointwise-comparison partial ordering on functions, let $F = \{f | f \geq f_0\}$. For $f \in F$, define Tf by

$$[Tf](u) = \inf\{b(w,v) | w \text{ and } v \text{ satisfy (34) and (35) for } k = 0,1\}. \tag{36}$$

The following three facts about T can be established by standard arguments.

LEMMA 6. *(a) $T:F \to F$. (b) $Tf_0 \geq f_0$. (c) If Γ is an incentive-compatible contract and f_Γ is the cost function for Γ defined in the proof of Lemma 5, then $Tf_\Gamma \leq f_\Gamma$.*

9. The Minimum Fixed Point of T

Motivated by the functional form of f_0, cost functions of the form

$$f(u) = c - r^{-1}(1 - \beta)^{-1} \ln(-u) \tag{37}$$

will now be considered. Define $x_k = w_k/u$, $y_k = v_k/u$, $q_0 = (1 - p)$, and $q_1 = p$. Then (33) is equivalent to

$$b(w,v) = \sum_{k=0,1} q_k[-r^{-1} \ln(-ux_k) - k + \beta(c - r^{-1}(1 - \beta)^{-1} \ln(-uy_k))]$$

$$= -[r^{-1} - \beta(r^{-1}(1 - \beta)^{-1})] \ln(-u) - p$$

$$+ \beta c - r^{-1} \sum_{k=0,1} q_k[\ln(x_k) + \beta(1 - \beta)^{-1} \ln(y_k)]. \tag{38}$$

Noting that $r^{-1} + \beta(r^{-1}(1 - \beta)^{-1}) = r^{-1}(1 - \beta)^{-1}$, (38) can be written as

$$b(w,v) = j(c,x,y) - r^{-1}(1 - \beta)^{-1} \ln(-u), \tag{39}$$

where

$$j(c,x,y) = \beta c - p - r^{-1} \sum_{k=0,1} q_k[\ln(x_k) + \beta(1 - \beta)^{-1} \ln(y_k)]. \tag{40}$$

Moreover, the constraints (34) and (35) respectively are equivalent to

$$1 = \sum_{k=0,1} q_k[x_k + \beta y_k] \tag{41}$$

and

$$(-(e^{-r}))^k[x_1 - x_0] \geq (-1)^k \beta[y_0 - y_1]. \tag{42}$$

Thus, for f of form (37), Tf is defined by

$$[Tf](u) = \inf\{j(c,x,y) - r^{-1}(1 - \beta)^{-1} \ln(-u)$$

$$|x \text{ and } y \text{ satisfy (41) and (42) for } k = 0,1\}. \tag{43}$$

By (43), $[Tf](u)$ is the solution of a convex minimization problem. The next lemma states the properties of the solution.

LEMMA 7. *There are x^* and y^* that are the minimizing values that define $[Tf](u)$. These are constants that do not depend on c or on u. $0 < y_1^* < y_0^* < \beta^{-1}$.*

The function $j(c,x^*,y^*)$ is a contraction mapping in c. By (43), Lemma 7, and the fixed-point theorem for contraction mappings, there is a fixed point f_μ of T that is of form (37) and that is the limit of the increasing sequence of functions $\langle T^n f_0 \rangle_{n \in N}$. This and Lemma 6 imply:

LEMMA 8. *For every incentive-compatible contract Γ, $f_\mu \leq f_\Gamma$.*

10. The Optimal Contract

It is now clear how to define the optimal contract Γ. First, define $V(\Gamma,\sigma,t)$ recursively by

$$V(\Gamma,\sigma,0) = f_\mu^{-1}(0) \tag{44}$$

and

$$V(\Gamma,\sigma,t + 1) = y_{\sigma_t}^* V(\Gamma,\sigma,t). \tag{45}$$

Next, define $\Gamma(\sigma,t)$ by

$$\Gamma(\sigma,t) = g(\sigma_t, x_{\sigma_t}^* V(\Gamma,\sigma,t)). \tag{46}$$

Note that, by (46) and the bounds on y^* stated in Lemma 7, the hypothesis (19) of Lemma 2 holds. From (19) and (46), it follows that the stochastic process M defined by

$$M(\sigma,t) = \sum_{n<t} \beta^n W(\sigma_n + \Gamma(\sigma,n)) + \beta^t V(\Gamma,\sigma,t) \qquad (47)$$

is a bounded martingale. Applying Doob's martingale convergence theorem (Breiman 1968, Theorem 5.23) to M shows that (16) holds.[8] Then Lemma 2 implies:

LEMMA 9. Γ *is incentive compatible.*

A parallel argument shows that (24) holds, so that:

LEMMA 10. Γ *is feasible.*

Finally, by (44), $B(\Gamma,\sigma,0) = 0$. Therefore, Γ solves P_δ. By Lemma 4:

THEOREM. Γ *solves the coalition's optimization problem* P_π.

11. The Time-series Behavior of Consumption and Wealth

In this section, it is shown that the optimal contract Γ can be supported by the issuance of infinite-lived bonds. This representation of the contract provides a characterization of the stochastic processes of consumption and credit balances for the representative consumer.

To simplify notation, define $V_0 = V(\Gamma,\sigma,0)$ and define three stochastic processes X, Y, and Z on S by

$$X(\sigma,t) = x^*_{\sigma_t} \qquad (48)$$

$$Y(\sigma,t) = y^*_{\sigma_t} \qquad (49)$$

$$Z(\sigma,t) = -r^{-1} \ln(Y(\sigma,t)). \qquad (50)$$

By induction using (45), it is seen that

$$V(\Gamma,\sigma,t+1) = \left[\prod_{u\leq t} Y(\sigma,u)\right] V_0. \qquad (51)$$

By (44), the initial credit balance is zero. By (37), this means that

$$B(\sigma,0) = c - r^{-1}(1 - \beta)^{-1} \ln(-V_0) = 0. \qquad (52)$$

Again using (37), (51) and (52) imply that

$$B(\sigma,t+1) = f_\mu(V(\Gamma,\sigma,t+1)) = (1 - \beta)^{-1} \sum_{u\leq t} Z(\sigma,u). \qquad (53)$$

Since Z is an i.i.d. sequence of random variables, (53) shows that the credit balance of the representative trader is a random walk. The trader's consumption at node (σ,t) is $\sigma_t + \Gamma(\sigma,t)$. Using (26), (45), and (51), this can be evaluated to be

$$\sigma_t + \Gamma(\sigma,t) = \sum_{u < t} Z(\sigma,u) - r^{-1} \ln(-X(\sigma, t)V_0). \tag{54}$$

Friedman (1957) has suggested that a household will attempt to consume the annuitized value of its "permanent income" at every date. That is, the preferred consumption of the household will be the amount of interest that its wealth earns at the market rate. Equations (53) and (54) show that the traders in the model economy fit this description closely. To see this, recall that β^{-1} is the marginal rate of transformation of income from one date to the next: in other words, $\beta^{-1} - 1$ is the interest rate in the economy. For β close to 1, Taylor's theorem shows that this interest rate is approximately equal to $1 - \beta$. According to the permanent income hypothesis, then, $(1 - \beta)B(\sigma,t)$ should be equal to $\sigma_t + \Gamma(\sigma,t)$. By (53) and (54), the difference between these quantities is $r^{-1} \ln(-X(\sigma,t)V_0)$. This difference is thus an i.i.d. sequence of random variables with finite variance. Asymptotically, the difference will be negligible relative to the credit balance, since the latter is a random walk, which has a variance that tends to infinity. Thus it is a good approximation to say that the representative trader consumes the annuitized value of his wealth at every date.

12. The Optimal Contract as an Outcome of Competition

Comparing (53) and (54) also leads to a characterization of the trader's credit balance and consumption in terms of holding and trading infinite-lived bonds. To discuss below some issues that are raised by this characterization, let us assume that traders are allowed to buy and sell bonds only through an intermediary. At every date u, the trader pays $\sigma_u + r^{-1} \ln(-X(\sigma,u)V_0)$ to the intermediary, and the trader receives $Z(\sigma,u)$ bonds in return. At every date t thereafter, each of the bonds pays one unit of consumption. Thus the discounted value at date t of the proceeds to be received at t and future dates from the trader's bond transaction at date u is $(1 - \beta)^{-1}Z(\sigma,u)$, and the sum of these values for all dates prior to t is $B(\sigma,t)$.

There is a clear sense in which this long-term relationship between traders and the intermediary is competitive. To begin with, the intermediary earns zero profits. No competing intermediary could successfully bid traders away by offering an alternative long-term contract. By construction of the optimal contract Γ, any contract that would provide higher levels of utility to traders must require the intermediary offering it to provide a subsidy. In particular, then, the optimal contract defines a no-surplus allocation in the sense of Ostroy (1980).

It remains an open question whether the optimal allocation is supported by a system of Walrasian prices. In fact, it is difficult even to formulate this question. The price system in question would be a continuous linear functional on some linear topological space of commodity bundles. In this paper, no topology on commodity bundles has been defined. A price system supporting the optimal allocation would have to be an incomplete-markets system, because the allocation in which every trader is fully insured (consuming p units of income at every date with certainty) is the only Walras equilibrium with complete markets. The events on which a trader's consumption is contingent in the optimal allocation are defined in terms of his own endowment, however, so there would have to be a vast array of contingent commodities—defined for sufficiently many events to make the endowment of every trader measurable.

Whether or not there exist supporting prices in principle, the interpretation of the optimal contract as a long-term relationship between traders and an intermediary suggests that the allocation would in fact be supported by a set of market institutions that might include rationing of credit by the intermediary in some circumstances. Rationing typically has been described as a constraint on the total amount of debt that a trader would be allowed to owe.[9] Since a trader's credit balance determined by the optimal contract is a random walk, that sort of constraint is not imposed. Rather, the *rate* at which a trader increases his debt is bounded. A trader may owe so much interest on his existing debt that it will exceed the amount of new debt that he issues. In this case, he will make a net payment to the intermediary even if he has received no income.

13. Conclusion

The problem of optimal incentive-compatible allocation has been studied in a simple model of an economy where traders have private information about their endowments. This optimal allocation has been characterized in sufficient detail to describe the stochastic process of a representative trader's consumption and wealth. This stochastic process has the properties described by the permanent income hypothesis. The contract that supports the optimal allocation is competitive in the sense that no other incentive-compatible contract could guarantee traders equally high utility unless it provided them with a subsidy.

Several questions have not been resolved, though, even in the context of this highly simplified model. One of these questions concerns whether the imposition of incentive compatibility as a constraint will affect the characterization of efficient production as well as of efficient allocation. Recall that in the model economy there is a technology that can transform consumption from one date to the next at exactly the same rate as the traders' rate of pure time preference. Since the aggregate endowment is the same at every date, this technology would not be used if agents were fully insured. Since full insurance cannot be provided here, though, it is possible that the optimal incentive-compatible allocation requires a technological transformation of the aggregate endowment.

Since the stochastic process of traders' consumption in the optimal allocation resembles the consumption of actual households, one might also study whether the optimal allocation could be supported by market institutions that would resemble actual institutions of intermediated credit. When the optimal allocation has been interpreted in this paper in terms of intermediated credit, the intermediary has been described as offering a very limited choice to traders. There is a fixed quantity of bonds that a trader is allowed to buy at a single date and a fixed quantity that he is allowed to sell, and he must make exactly one of these two permissible transactions. It is plausible, though, that traders could be induced to make these choices from a constraint set that looks more like a budget set, or like some other contract that is observed in actual financial markets. In particular, it would be of interest to know whether the optimal allocation could be supported by the intermediary charging a spread between bid and ask prices on bonds, or whether there must be explicit quantity rationing of credit.

Finally, the model studied in this paper is severely restricted: there is no aggregate uncertainty, there is no private information about future endowments, and traders are always able to honor contracts that require them to make arbitrarily large payments. I hope that the analysis developed here will also be applicable to more realistic models that do not incorporate these stringent simplifying assumptions.

Notes

1. Much of the research reported in this paper was done while I was a visiting fellow at the Institute for Advanced Studies, Hebrew University of Jerusalem. I would like to thank Jacques Cremer, Christian Gilles, Arnold Kling, Robert E. Lucas, Jr., Julio Rotemberg, and Neil Wallace for their comments on earlier drafts.

2. This equivalence is implied by the ergodic theorem of probability theory.

3. On the surface, this statement may seem inconsistent with the choice of consumers to make occasional large expenditures on commodities such as medical care and consumer durables. The theories of human capital and of household production resolve this dilemma by treating these expenditures as investment rather than as consumption.

4. This statement is suggested by Friedman's (1957) permanent income hypothesis. Obviously, since actual households have a lower bound on their feasible consumption, the description is not literally true. The sense in which it is an approximation has been clarified by Yaari (1976), Schechtman (1976), Bewley (1977), Hall (1978), and others. Statistical tests of the random-walk hypothesis using data on consumption, beginning with Hall (1978), have had mixed results [cf. Shapiro (1984) and the work cited by him]. However, the characterization given here is intended only as a highly stylized contrast between the performance of actual economies and what would be expected in an environment with complete information.

Jovanovic (1983) and Scheinkman and Weiss (forthcoming) have shown that, in an environment with aggregate uncertainty as well as purely individual uncertainty, allocations that resemble those derived here on the individual level may also involve business-cycle phenomena on the aggregate level. The present paper may be viewed as providing an explanation of the restrictions on market structure that they assume.

5. Radner (1981) and Rubenstein and Yaari (1983) have studied incentive problems in environments where there are infinite-lived agents who maximize asymptotic-average utility and where there is imperfect information. Their results can be restated to apply also to the specific kind of incomplete information that is assumed here. Because the agents have no time preference, it is possible for agents in noncooperative equilibrium to achieve the best utility levels that would be possible if they were to act cooperatively under complete and perfect information. In contrast, when traders maximize discounted utility, they are unable to attain the same utility levels that they could if information were complete. The model studied here is essentially identical to that of Townsend (1982), except that Townsend imposed an exogenous finite bound on the length of contracts. There is some work in a similar spirit in monetary economics, including Gale (1982, chap. 6) and Bewley (1983).

6. See Harris and Townsend (1981).

7. Roy Radner has emphasized in discussion that full insurance is not possible in an economy with finitely many traders who have statistically independent endowments, because with positive probability all would simultaneously suffer a loss. However, traders who were ex ante identical would pool their endowments, and by doing so they would greatly decrease their individual exposure to risk.

8. A bounded martingale converges both almost surely and also in the function space L^1. That is, if $M(\sigma,t)$ is a bounded martingale, then it converges almost surely to a random variable $M^*(\sigma)$, and $M(\sigma,t) = E_s[M^*|\langle \ \rangle_t](\sigma)$.

9. For example, Friedman (1957) suggests that a household can borrow only to the extent of its nonhuman wealth.

References

Arrow, K. 1964. "The Role of Securities in the Optimal Allocation of Risk Bearing." *Review of Economic Studies* 31:91–96.

Bellman, R. 1957. *Dynamic Programming*. Princeton, N.J.: Princeton University Press.

Bewley, T. 1977. "The Permanent Income Hypothesis: A Theoretical Formulation." *Journal of Economic Theory* 16:252–92.

———. 1983. "A Difficulty with the Optimum Quantity of Money." *Econometrica* 51:1485–1504.

Breiman, L. 1968. *Probability*. Reading, Mass.: Addison-Wesley.

Denardo, E. 1967. "Contraction Mappings in the Theory Underlying Dynamic Programming." *SIAM Review* 9:165–77.

Feldman, M., and C. Gilles. 1985. "An Expository Note on Individual Risk without Aggregate Uncertainty." *Journal of Economic Theory* 35:26–32.

Friedman, M. 1957. *A Theory of the Consumption Function*. New York: National Bureau of Economic Research.

Gale, D. 1982. *Money: In Equilibrium*. Cambridge: Cambridge University Press.

Hall, R. 1978. "Stochastic Implications of the Life Cycle-Permanent Income Hypothesis: Theory and Evidence." *Journal of Political Economy* 86:971–87.

Harris, M., and R. Townsend. 1981. "Resource Allocation under Asymmetric Information." *Econometrica* 49:33–64.

Jovanovic, B. 1983. "Micro Uncertainty, Fluctuations of Averages, and the Efficiency of the

Business Cycle in an Economy with Idiosyncratic Exchange." Working paper, Department of Economics, New York University.

Judd, K. 1985. "The 'Law of Large Numbers' with a Continuum of IID Random Variables." *Journal of Economic Theory* 35:19–25.

Ostroy, J. 1980. "The No-Surplus Condition as a Characterization of Perfectly Competitive Equilibrium." *Journal of Economic Theory* 22:65–89.

Radner, R. 1981. "Monitoring Cooperative Agreements in a Repeated Principal-Agent Relationship." *Econometrica* 49:1127–48.

Rubenstein, A., and M. Yaari. 1983. "Repeated Insurance Contracts and Moral Hazard." *Journal of Economic Theory* 30:74–97.

Schechtman, J. 1976. "An Income Fluctuation Problem." *Journal of Economic Theory* 12:218–41.

Scheinkman, J., and L. Weiss. "Borrowing Constraints and Aggregate Economic Activity." Forthcoming.

Shapiro, M. 1984. "The Permanent Income Hypothesis and the Real Interest Rate: Some Evidence from Panel Data." *Economics Letters* 14:93–100.

Townsend, R. 1982. "Optimal Multiperiod Contracts and the Gain from Enduring Relationships under Private Information." *Journal of Political Economy* 90:1166–86.

Yaari, M. 1976. "A Law of Large Numbers in the Theory of Consumer's Choice under Uncertainty." *Journal of Economic Theory* 12:202–17.

II

Demand Deposits, Trading Restrictions, and Risk Sharing

Charles J. Jacklin

This paper explores the role of demand deposits in risk sharing. Demand deposits coupled with restricted trading opportunities are shown to provide greater risk sharing than equity shares that are traded freely. Trading restrictions allow the achievement of allocations using demand deposits superior to those obtained using equity shares—with or without trading restrictions. The removal of the trading restrictions, however, eliminates the advantage of demand deposits. In this case, demand deposits and equity shares are shown to provide identical risk-sharing opportunities.

1. Introduction

In recent papers, Diamond and Dybvig (1983) and Bryant (1980) develop models of banking to explore bank runs and their prevention.[1] Although the focus of these papers is bank runs, both identify the demand deposit as a mechanism that facilitates risk sharing. Bryant (1980) characterizes the demand deposit as providing "insurance" for an otherwise uninsurable event. Diamond and Dybvig (p. 402) state that "banks issuing demand deposits can improve on a competitive market by providing better risk sharing. . . ." These authors raise an important issue—the role of demand deposits in risk sharing. But, given they are primarily concerned with modeling bank runs and deposit insurance, they do not fully explore this very important issue.

The purpose of this paper is to explore in depth the role of the demand deposit in risk sharing. Diamond and Dybvig demonstrate in their model that demand deposits allow greater risk sharing than direct investment in the underlying technology. For their model, I show that dividend-paying equity shares provide the same risk-sharing opportunities as demand deposits but do not introduce the possibility of a bank run. This result only requires that a market exist for the ex-dividend shares. I also show that equity shares cannot be used to achieve the same allocation as demand deposits for a large

26

class of economies. The fact that they can in Diamond and Dybvig's environment follows directly from the extreme nature of their assumed preference structure. I show for fairly general preference structures that demand deposits provide opportunities for risk sharing beyond those provided by equity shares—whether the firm issuing the shares pays dividends or not.

Trading restrictions are, however, an essential element of the story. Demand deposits facilitate risk sharing because markets are incomplete. Hart (1975) demonstrates that, in a sequence of market settings, adding a spot market at a point in time may not even weakly increase the space of (explicitly or implicitly) marketed claims and thus may make everyone worse off. The economy modeled here provides an example of this phenomenon. The risk-sharing opportunities provided by demand deposits disappear if certain trading opportunities are introduced. The demand deposit allows risk sharing because it is a mechanism by which individuals of different types each self-select an allocation that is designated for that individual's type. For self-selection to take place, the alternative allocations must be incentive compatible. Additional trading opportunities may eliminate potential risk sharing because, after the introduction of the new trading possibilities, the alternative allocations may no longer be incentive compatible. If they are not, individuals of all types do not self-select and the mechanism breaks down.

In Section 2, I review Diamond and Dybvig (1983) and demonstrate that trading in the equity shares of a dividend-paying firm results in the same allocation achieved using demand deposits. In Section 3, I modify the preference structure assumed by Diamond and Dybvig and show that in this case the use of demand deposits allows greater risk sharing than does trading in the shares of a firm. The role of trading restrictions is developed in Section 4. I demonstrate that the equilibria in the economies discussed in sections 2 and 3 no longer exist if trading restrictions are relaxed or if trading in a new asset is introduced. Section 5 contains conclusions and suggestions for future research.

2. Risk Sharing Using Equity Shares in the Diamond/Dybvig Model

Diamond and Dybvig (1983) show in their model that demand deposits improve on the risk sharing achieved in a competitive market for the underlying technology. In this section, I show that trading in the shares of a dividend-paying firm achieves the same allocation as demand deposits—without incurring the risk of a bank run.

To begin, let us review their model and results. The main features are discussed below.

Production Technology

All investment in the production of the single good in the economy occurs at $T = 0$ (designate time as $T = 0,1,2$). The production process is infinitely divisible. Any portion of the production can be interrupted at $T = 1$ and immediately yield a total return equal to the initial investment, but then no additional return occurs in period 2. Otherwise, if the production process is not interrupted at $T = 1$, at $T = 2$ it yields a total return per unit invested of $R > 1$. R is a constant known to all at $T = 0$.

Individuals can store the good at no cost. This storage is not publicly observable.

Preference Structure

There is a continuum of individuals of total measure one. At $T = 0$, all individuals are identical. Their types are unknown to themselves as well as others. Types are independently and identically distributed. A person is of type 1 with probability t and of type 2 with probability $1 - t$.[2] At $T = 1$, each individual learns his own type but learns nothing regarding the types of others. Either he is of type 1 and dies at the end of period 1 or he is of type 2 and lives through the end of period 2. Furthermore, preference for consumption in periods 1 and 2 (where c_T indicates consumption in period T) is assumed to have the utility representation

$$\mu(c_1, c_2, \theta) = \theta u(c_1) + (1 - \theta)\rho u(c_1 + c_2)$$

where θ is a random variable equal to 1 if the individual is of type 1 and 0 if the individual is of type 2 and where $1 \geq \rho > 1/R$ and $u : R_{++} \to R$ is twice continuously differentiable, increasing, strictly concave, satisfies the Inada conditions $u'(0) = \infty$ and $u'(\infty) = 0$, and has relative risk aversion $cu''(c)/u'(c) > 1$ everywhere.

In addition, it is assumed that type is unobservable and that there exists no credible way of revealing one's type. That is, traditional insurance contracts tied to the observation of one's type are ruled out.

At $T = 0$, individuals are assumed to maximize the expectation of their state-dependent utility function $\mu(c_1, c_2, \theta)$ where c_{ik} represents consumption in period i for an individual of type k and where

$$E_\theta(\mu(c_1, c_2, \theta)) = tu(c_{11}) + (1 - t)\rho u(c_{12} + c_{22})$$

since $E_\theta(\theta) \equiv t$.

Endowments

Each consumer receives an endowment of one unit of the good in period 0 (and none at any other time).

Demand Deposit Contracts

A *demand deposit* is defined as a contract that requires an initial investment at $T = 0$ in exchange for the right to withdraw per unit of investment (at the discretion of the depositor and conditional on the bank's solvency) either r_1 in period 1 or $R(1 - r_1 f)/(1 - f)$ in period 2, where R is the total return on the two-period technology and f is the proportion of individuals who withdraw in period 1. Of course, the depositor who attempts to withdraw after the bank runs out of funds gets nothing. If r_1 is greater than 1, then the demand deposit provides insurance against being of type 1 since in that case the type 1 individuals get some benefit from the two-period production process even though they die before the process comes to fruition. However, if that is the case, there is the potential for a bank run since if more than $1/r_1$ of the individuals choose to withdraw their funds in the first period the bank runs out of funds.

Given this specification, Diamond and Dybvig show that using demand deposit contracts leads to two possible Nash equilibria. The first of these achieves socially optimal risk sharing. The other equilibrium is interpreted as a bank run. All depositors wish to withdraw all of their funds from the bank in the first period. Unfortunately, given the demand deposit contract, the bank does not have sufficient funds to meet the withdrawal demand, and consequently the bank fails. Type 1 depositors who are able to withdraw their funds before the bank fails receive their optimal allocation, and type 2 depositors who are able to withdraw their funds before the bank fails receive an amount less than their optimal allocation. Remaining type 1 and type 2 depositors, who do not withdraw before the bank fails, receive nothing.

Socially Optimal Risk Sharing

The socially optimal allocation is found by solving the following constrained optimization:

$$\max_{c_{11}, c_{12}, c_{21}, c_{22}} tu(c_{11}) + (1 - t)\rho u(c_{12} + c_{22})$$

subject to

$$(c_{11} + c_{21}/R)t + (c_{12} + c_{22}/R)(1 - t) = 1$$

and

$$c_{ik} \geq 0$$

for $i = 1, 2$ and $k = 1, 2$.[3] If demand deposits are to offer a social improvement, individuals must not be able to achieve their optimal allocation by directly investing in the production technology. Directly investing, an individual can be assured of the choice between either one unit of the good in period 1 or R units of the good in period 2. Therefore, if demand deposits are to have a role in the economy, the social optimum must be an improvement over this allocation. To assure that this is the case, Diamond and Dybvig assume that the coefficient of relative risk aversion is greater than 1 everywhere. Given this assumption, the social optimum is characterized by:

$$c_{12}^* = c_{21}^* = 0$$

$$c_{11}^* > 1$$

$$c_{22}^* = R(1 - c_{11}^* t)/(1 - t) \tag{1}$$

where the * indicates optimality and $c_{22}^* > c_{11}^*$.

Review and Discussion of Results

Diamond and Dybvig show that by setting $r_1 = c_{11}^*$, the socially optimal allocation can be achieved as the superior symmetric Nash equilibrium using demand deposits. This equilibrium allocation results if the late diers conjecture that only the early diers will withdraw their funds in period 1. If late diers believe that everyone else will withdraw their funds in the first period, then they also want to withdraw theirs, and the bad equilibrium—a bank run—obtains. They also show that giving the bank the ability to suspend the convertibility of deposits ensures that only the good equilibrium allocation is a Nash equilibrium outcome.

Optimal Risk Sharing Using Equity Shares

Consider a firm that has access to the two-period technology and raises an amount of capital, C, by issuing shares (with a price of 1) at $T = 0$. Having purchased the shares of the firms, at $T = 0$ the shareholders also decide the firm's production policy and declare a per-share dividend, D, payable at $T = 1$ to the shareholder of record at $T = 0$. Thus, each share represents the right to a dividend of D at $T = 1$ and liquidating dividend of $R(C - D)$ at $T = 2$.

At $T = 1$, the shareholders receive their dividends and a market in the ex-dividend shares opens. All individuals now know their own type, so there are potential gains from trade. The type 1 individuals want to trade their ex-dividend shares for additional period 1 consumption goods. The type 2 individuals are indifferent between period 1 and period 2 consumption. Thus, if the price of ex-dividend shares is less than $R(C - D)$, they are willing to trade the period 1 consumption goods they received as a dividend for additional ex-dividend shares [which represent the right to $R(C - D)$ units of period 2 consumption].

Suppose that, instead of investing in demand deposits at $T = 0$, all individuals invest in this firm (i.e., $C = 1$). If the per-share dividend, D, is set at tr_1 and at $T = 1$ trading takes place in the ex-dividend shares, the social optimum obtains.

The price of the ex-dividend shares is determined by market clearing and is $r_1(1 - t)$. By (1), we know that $R(C - D) = R(1 - tr_1) > r_1(1 - t)$. Therefore, the type 2 individuals are willing to trade at this price. The fraction t of the total population who are of type 1 will trade their rights to $tR(1 - tr_1)$ in liquidating dividends for $(1 - t)r_1t$ in current consumption. Thus, each type 1 individual nets tr_1 in dividends plus $((1 - t)r_1t)/t = (1 - t)r_1$ from the sale of ex-dividend shares, giving each type 1 a total of r_1 in period 1. Each type 2 individual receives $R(1 - tr_1)$ in liquidating dividends plus $(tR(1 - tr_1))/(1 - t)$ in additional liquidating dividends from his ex-dividend share purchase, netting each type 2 individual $(R(1 - tr_1))/(1 - t)$ in period 2 consumption. This allocation is, of course, the social optimum.

One question remains. Will the firm pay a dividend of tr_1 at $T = 1$? The answer is yes. At $T = 0$, all the shareholders are identical. Thus, the social optimum coincides with each individual's optimum. Therefore, at $T = 0$ the shareholders unanimously agree to declare a dividend of tr_1 payable at $T = 1$.[4] At $T = 1$, individuals know their types and no longer agree on the dividend policy. However, having declared the dividend at $T = 0$, at $T = 1$ the firm has no choice but to pay the dividend.

This analysis requires that individuals can only invest in the shares of the firm. Similarly, Diamond and Dybvig must assume that individuals can only invest in demand deposits. In Section 4, I show that introducing additional investment and trading opportunities can eliminate the equilibria in both cases and thus reduce risk sharing.

3. Improving Risk Sharing with Demand Deposits

In the last section I showed that, in the context of Diamond and Dybvig's model, demand deposits cannot improve on the allocations achieved with a competitive market for a dividend-paying firm. This is not generally true. In this section I show that, with a different, yet quite reasonable, preferable structure, demand deposits do improve on competitive markets—even those with dividend-paying firms.

Let us consider a modification of the economy modeled by Diamond and Dybvig. This new economy retains the same initial endowment and two-period production technology but has a different preference structure and a revised definition of a demand deposit.

Smooth Preferences

Assume that all individuals live in both periods and have preferences that are smooth in period 1 and period 2 consumption. Types now reflect differences in time preferences. Type 1 individuals prefer more consumption in the first period than do type 2 individuals. Types are still independent, and the ex ante probabilities of being type 1 and type 2 are still t and $1 - t$, respectively.

Formally, preferences have the utility representation

$$\mu(c_1, c_2, \theta) = \theta U(c_{11}, c_{21}) + (1 - \theta) V(c_{12}, c_{22})$$

where θ is an indicator variable for type 1 and $U(.,.)$ and $V(.,.)$ are twice continuously differentiable, increasing, strictly concave, and satisfy the Inada conditions. Further, let

$$U_1(c_1, c_2)/U_2(c_1, c_2) > V_1(c_1, c_2)/V_2(c_1, c_2)$$

for all values of (c_1, c_2).

Type is still unobservable, and there is still no credible way of revealing one's type. Consequently, there is no opportunity to construct traditional insurance contracts against being of a particular type.

At $T = 0$, individuals are assumed to maximize the expectation of their state-dependent utility function $\mu(c_1, c_2, \theta)$, where

$$E_\theta[\mu(c_1, c_2, \theta)] = tU(c_1, c_2) + (1 - t)V(c_1, c_2)$$

since $E_\theta(\theta) \equiv t$.

Demand Deposits

Since we are now concerned with the potential for risk sharing using demand deposits and not with modeling bank runs, we use a definition of demand deposits that assumes that bank runs are avoided somehow. The definition would need to be expanded if this possibility were allowed.

Define a demand deposit as a contract that requires an initial investment at $T = 0$ in exchange for the right to withdraw per unit of investment (at the discretion of the depositor and conditional on the bank's solvency) either:

$$x_1 \text{ in period 1 and}$$

$$x_2 \text{ in period 2}$$

or

y_1 in period 1 and

y_2 in period 2.

As part of the definition, assume that trading in demand deposits is prohibited. The last assumption is discussed in Section 4.

At first glance, this contact bears little resemblance to the usual definition of a demand deposit. However, one's intuition may be improved if the contract is viewed as implicitly representing two financial instruments. The first is a direct investment in the two-period technology, and the second is a contract quite similar to a demand deposit. To see this, consider the following: in this economy, regardless of type, optimally there is a minimal amount everyone would consume in the second period. At $T = 0$, that amount can be assured for the second period by a direct investment in the two-period technology. Having assured themselves of this second-period income, type 1 individuals will want to consume all of their remaining wealth in the first period. On the other hand, type 2 individuals will want to consume a portion of their remaining wealth in each of the two periods. Since types are not known at $T = 0$, a contract that allows investors the option of taking all their return at $T = 1$ or taking a portion of their return in each period can facilitate risk sharing. The second instrument represented in the definition of a demand deposit does exactly this.

So, the demand deposit defined here represents two contracts. The first requires an investment of x_2/R at $T = 0$ and guarantees a return of x_2 at $T = 2$. The second requires an investment of $1 - x_2/R$ at $T = 0$ in exchange for the right to either

x_1 in period 1 and

0 in period 2

or

y_1 in period 1 and

$y_2 - x_2$ in period 2.

The second contract is similar to the usual definition of a demand deposit. Furthermore, if $1 - x_2/R < x_1$, a bank run could potentially arise with this second contract.

Demand Deposits vs. Trading in Equity Shares

To compare the extent to which demand deposits and trading in equity shares allow risk sharing, we must compare the allocations that can be obtained using the two mechanisms. Simultaneously, we can investigate whether the allocations obtained are efficient. My approach is to characterize an upper bound and then demonstrate the conditions under which the bound can be achieved by each mechanism.

At $T = 0$, all individuals are essentially identical. Therefore, subject only to the resource constraint, the ex ante efficient allocation is found by solving the following maximization:

$$\max_{c_{11}, c_{12}, c_{21}, c_{22}} tU(c_{11}, c_{21}) + (1 - t)V(c_{12}, c_{22})$$

subject to

$$(c_{11} + c_{21}/R)t + (c_{12} + c_{22}/R)(1 - t) = 1.$$

The assumed Inada conditions guarantee an interior solution to this problem, and smoothness guarantees that the solution is unique. The optimal allocation satisfies the budget constraint and the following first-order conditions:

$$U_1 = V_1,$$

$$U_2 = V_2, \text{ and}$$

$$U_1/U_2 = R.$$

To simplify the analysis, assume that individuals cannot store the good. Allowing private storage complicates the analysis without changing the general nature of the results.

The optimal allocation gives all individuals of the same type identical two-period consumption streams. Further, there is an implicit aggregate production decision made in the optimization. If the total endowment is invested in the two-period production process at $T = 0$, the period 1 consumption must be obtained through the liquidation of a portion of the original investment. Given this implicit decision, we can characterize the social optimum as a point in an Edgeworth's box.

Consider figure II-1. The dimensions of the Edgeworth's box are determined by the aggregate production choice. The axes represent consumption in the first and second periods. The lower left-hand corner is the origin from the perspective of type 2 individuals, and the upper right-hand corner is the origin from the perspective of type 1 individuals. The curves C_1C_1' and C_2C_2' are indifference curves for type 1 and type 2 individuals, respectively. The optimal allocation is represented in figure II-1 as point 0. Notice that this is a point of tangency for the two indifference curves. From the first-order conditions we know that the slope of the indifference curves at point 0 is $-R$.

The use of the Edgeworth's box is helpful because it allows us easily to identify three alternative characterizations, represented by figures II-1 through II-3, of the social optimum. I now discuss these three characterizations.

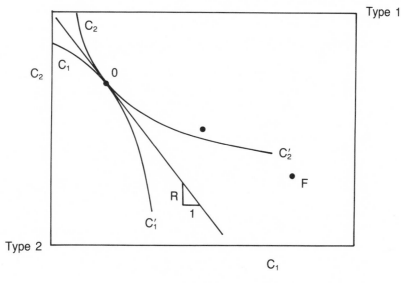

Figure II-1

Two properties of the social optimum are of interest. The first is whether the social optimum represents an incentive-compatible allocation. An allocation is incentive compatible if individuals of each type prefer their own allotment to the allotment of the other type. That is, the social optimum represents an incentive-compatible allocation if

$$U(c_{11}^*, c_{21}^*) \geq U(c_{12}^*, c_{22}^*)$$

and

$$V(c_{12}^*, c_{22}^*) \geq V(c_{11}^*, c_{21}^*)$$

where the * indicates optimality.[5]

In figure II-1, the point 0 represents an incentive-compatible allocation. This is seen by noting that an allocation that gives individuals of each type the other type's allocation, represented by point F, moves neither type into their preferred set. On the other hand, in figure II-2 the point 0 represents an allocation that is not incentive compatible. In that figure, reversing the allocations moves the type 2 individuals into their preferred set.

The second property of the optimal allocation that is of interest is whether the line tangent to the two indifference curves at the social optimum passes through the identical endowment point. In figure II-3, the tangent line does pass through this point (designated E). The identical endowment point represents an allocation that allots individuals of both types the same two-period

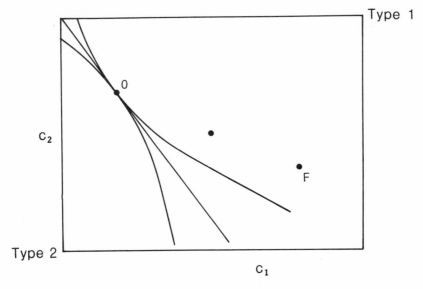

Figure II-2

endowment (as happens with equity shares). That is, type 1 individuals receive the same amount of endowment in each period as do type 2 individuals. Note, however, that the amount received may vary from period 1 to period 2. We shall see that, if the social optimum has this property, both demand deposits and equity shares can be used to achieve the optimal allocation.

First, let us consider incentive compatibility, which is of interest because types are not observable. If demand deposits are to be used in achieving the optimal allocation, individuals of different types must self-select the allotment that is designated for their type. If the optimal allocation is not incentive compatible, individuals do not self-select appropriately. Thus, we have the following theorem:

THEOREM 1. *Assume that demand deposits cannot be traded. Then, demand deposits can be used to achieve the social optimum subject only to the resource constraint if and only if this optimum is incentive compatible.*

PROOF. Let $(c_{11}^*, c_{21}^*, c_{12}^*, c_{22}^*)$ be the social optimum. If this allocation is incentive compatible, then it can be achieved using demand deposits by setting the terms of the demand deposit so that

$$x_1 = c_{11}^*,$$

$$x_2 = c_{21}^*,$$

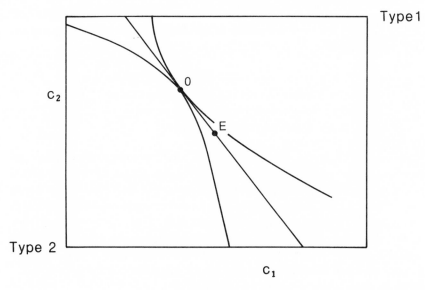

Type 1

C_2

Type 2

C_1

Figure II-3

$y_1 = c_{12}^*$, and

$y_2 = c_{22}^*$.

Since demand deposits cannot be traded and the good cannot be stored, an individual can only choose between two consumption streams, (c_{11}^*, c_{21}^*) and (c_{12}^*, c_{22}^*). If the social optimum is an incentive compatible allocation, type 1 individuals prefer the first allotment and type 2 individuals prefer the second. Thus, individuals self-select appropriately and the social optimum is achieved.

On the other hand, if the social optimum is not incentive compatible, both types prefer the same allotment. Ex ante optimality requires that individuals of one type take an allotment that is dominated. Types are not observable, so there is no way to force individuals of that type to select the dominated allotment. Thus, in this case the ex ante optimum cannot be achieved using the demand deposits.   Q.E.D.

Notice that I ignore the possibility of bank runs in the case where the social optimum is incentive compatible, because the focus of this work is on potential risk-sharing opportunities. Bank runs can be avoided in this case by using suspension of convertibility as in Diamond and Dybvig (1983).

Theorem 1 characterizes the allocations that are achievable using demand deposits, the key factor being whether the allocation is incentive compatible. If trading in equity shares is used instead, the key factor becomes whether the tangent line at the social optimum passes through the identical endowment point. The following two theorems characterize this dependency and distinguish between the risk-sharing capabilities of demand deposits and equity shares.

THEOREM 2. *Equity shares can be used to achieve the socially optimal allocation subject to only the resource constraint if and only if the tangent to the two indifference curves at the social optimum passes through the identical endowment point.*

PROOF. (If.) Suppose that at $T = 1$ all individuals invest their initial endowment in the equity shares of a firm that has access to the two-period production technology and that every shareholder in the firm is treated similarly. Thus, all the investors do is transform their equal initial endowments into rights to identical two-period endowments. That is, everyone has the right to the same dividend stream over two periods. The magnitude of the dividend payable at $T = 1$ is determined and declared at $T = 0$. Assume that this dividend decision reflects the implicit aggregate production decision made in the social optimization. That is, the total dividend is equal to $tc_{11}^* + (1 - t)c_{12}^*$.

At $T = 1$, investors learn their own type and receive a period 1 dividend. A market in the ex-dividend shares opens at this time, and because people now have different preferences, there are potential gains from trade. Each individual has the right to the same two-period dividend stream represented by point E in figure II-3. The competitive equilibrium from this point is the social optimum. We can verify this by seeing that, for a relative price of period 2 to period 1 consumption of R, all individuals maximize their utility by trading from point E to point 0.

All that remains to proven for the first part of the proof is that the firm does indeed choose the dividend policy that leads to this allocation in equilibrium. The dividend decision is made at $T = 0$, when all individuals are identical. We have seen that the assumed dividend decision leads to the ex ante optimal allocation. Therefore, at $T = 0$ all shareholders unanimously agree on this policy.[6]

(Only if.) Essentially, this part of the proof demonstrates that, if the tangent line to the social optimum does not pass through the identical endowment point, then the social optimum is not a competitive equilibrium from that point. Consider figure II-4. Suppose that the social optimum is a competitive equilibrium from point E. Then the equilibrium relative price must be minus the slope of the line $E0$. However, if this were the relative price and individuals had traded to point 0, the price would not be equal to either type's marginal rate of substitution. Therefore, both types would still wish to trade. This contradicts the premise that point 0 represents a competitive equilibrium from point E.   Q.E.D.

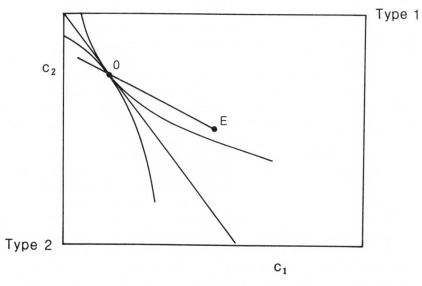

Figure II-4

Thus, we can summarize the difference between demand deposits and equity shares in their abilities to facilitate risk sharing as follows: if demand deposits cannot be traded and the social optimum is incentive compatible but the line tangent to the two indifference curves at the social optimum does not go through the identical endowment point, then demand deposits can be used to achieve the social optimum but trading in equity shares cannot.

These results can be viewed in terms of individual vs. coalition incentive compatibility. Since demand deposits cannot be traded, they can be used to achieve any allocation that is individually incentive compatible (i.i.c.). That is, individuals must self-select the withdrawal stream designated for their own type.

On the other hand, the final allocation achieved using equity shares is a competitive equilibrium and thus represents an element in the core of the economy starting at $T = 1$ with identical two-period endowments. By definition, all elements of the core are not only i.c.c. but also coalitionally incentive compatible (c.i.c.). That is, for all elements of the core there does not exist a coalition of individuals each of whom can be made better off by following a strategy specified by the coalition and then redistributing the coalition's total allocation. (A *strategy* designates a trading rule in the case of equity shares and a withdrawal rule in the case of demand deposits.)

In both the demand deposit and equity economies, the same objective function (i.e., ex ante expected utility) is being maximized; therefore, demand deposits can generally achieve greater risk sharing than equity shares traded in competitive markets since, in the demand deposit economy, the same objective function is being maximized over a less constrained set.

The necessity of restricting trade in the demand deposit economy, which is also apparent from this interpretation, can be seen by contrasting this economy with the equity one. At $T = 1$ in the equity economy, all individuals have the right to identical two-period dividend streams. Having learned their types, they trade from these identical streams. Clearly, every individual has the same amount of wealth at $T = 1$. In the deposit economy, on the other hand, no trade is allowed. Thus, each individual must consume whichever withdrawal stream that person chooses. The two possible withdrawal streams are constructed to be incentive compatible—that is, all those persons of type 1 prefer one stream whereas all those in type 2 prefer the other, given that they cannot trade ex post. Since no ex post trade is allowed, these two withdrawal streams do not necessarily represent the same amount of wealth where wealth is defined as the value in a world where ex post trade is allowed. So, using the deposit contract can accomplish potentially greater risk sharing than using the equity contract because allocations are not restricted to being of equal wealth across types. For example, individuals could be insured against being type 1 to a greater extent (than in an equity world) with a deposit contract that offered two incentive-compatible withdrawal streams (given no ex post trade) where the stream preferred by type 1 individuals represented more wealth than the stream preferred by those in type 2.

Note that such insurance never takes place in the environment analyzed by Diamond and Dybvig. Even if trading in demand deposits is prohibited, demand deposits do not improve on a competitive market in a dividend-paying firm because, in their model, the social optimum is always a competitive equilibrium from identical endowments. The social optimum has this property because of the assumed preference structure. In their model, type 1 individuals only have utility for consumption in period 1. Hence, their marginal rate of substitution of period 2 consumption for period 1 consumption will be infinite. On the other hand, consumption in period 1 vs. that in period 2 is a perfect substitute for type 2 individuals. Therefore, the marginal rates of substitution for the two types are not equalized at the social optimum. This preference structure allows the competitive price of period 2 consumption in terms of period 1 consumption to be any number between 0 and 1. The competitive price in this range is determined solely by the ratio of the aggregate endowments in periods 1 and 2. As a result, the social optimum can always be achieved as a competitive equilibrium from identical endowments.

The above discussion should also clarify the nature of the trading restrictions imposed in the deposit economy. Not only is trade in the deposit contract prohibited, but also any type of trade or credit market that effectively circumvents this trading restriction. For example, a one-period credit market at $T = 1$ (using demand deposits as collateral) is ruled out. The key is not actually the total prohibition of such credit markets—rather, it is required that such markets be sufficiently inefficient to preclude effective circumvention of the restriction on the trading of deposits.

I have shown that neither mechanism considered achieves perfect risk-sharing in this economy unless the optimal allocation is incentive compatible. Now consider how these mechanisms compare when the optimal allocation is not incentive compatible. In the problem at hand, this means we wish to perform the following optimization:

$$\max_{c_{11},c_{12},c_{21},c_{22}} tU(c_{11},c_{21}) + (1 - t)V(c_{12},c_{22}) \tag{3}$$

subject to

$$(c_{11} + c_{21}/R)t + (c_{12} + c_{22}/R)(1 - t) = 1; \; U(c_{11},c_{21}) \geq U(c_{12},c_{22})$$

and

$$V(c_{12},c_{22}) \geq V(c_{11},c_{21}).$$

Restricting attention to nonstochastic allocations, we see that the following theorem distinguishes between the risk-sharing properties of demand deposits and equity shares when the social optimum is not incentive compatible.[7]

THEOREM 3. *If demand deposits cannot be traded and the social optimum subject only to the resource constraint is not incentive compatible, demand deposits can be used to achieve the optimal nonstochastic, incentive-efficient allocation, but equity shares cannot.*

PROOF. (Demand deposits.) Let $(\hat{c}_{11},\hat{c}_{21},\hat{c}_{12},\hat{c}_{22})$ be the solution to (3) with the choice variables restricted to being nonstochastic. This allocation is incentive compatible by construction. Therefore, by an argument similar to that of Theorem 1, this allocation can be achieved through the use of demand deposits.

(Equity shares.) We have seen that equity shares can only achieve allocations that are competitive equilibria from identical endowments. Suppose $(\hat{c}_{11},\hat{c}_{21},\hat{c}_{12},\hat{c}_{22})$ is a competitive equilibrium. Since the Inada conditions hold for U and V, we know that $\hat{c}_{ik} > 0$ for $i = 1, 2$ and $k = 1, 2$. If one of the incentive compatibility constraints is binding, at the constrained maximum the marginal rates of substitution of the two types are not equalized. Therefore, there are potential gains from trade. This contradicts the premise that the constrained optimum is a competitive equilibrium. Q.E.D.

4. The Need for Trading Restrictions

Thus far, I have assumed that demand deposits cannot be traded. Furthermore, I have stated that adding assets may introduce problems in the economies examined. In this section I show that if demand deposits can be traded, optimal risk sharing is guaranteed in neither Diamond and Dybvig's economy nor the economy with smooth preferences described in Section 3. This breakdown in risk sharing happens because the social optimum is no longer a Nash equilibrium if individuals have additional trading opportunities.

In the Diamond and Dybvig Model

The equilibrium in the Diamond and Dybvig model has the following flaw: if ex post trading is possible and new assets can be introduced, on the margin individuals have no incentive either to invest in the shares of a dividend-paying firm or to deposit their funds in the bank. Consider an individual who either invests directly or in a marginal firm or bank (sufficiently small so as not to affect prices in equilibrium) that offers only the right to R units of the good at $T = 2$ for each unit of investment at $T = 0$. Assuming that prices do not change, an individual is better off investing in this "deviant" firm or bank. If at $T = 1$ the individual is of type 2, he or she can just hold onto the shares or withdrawal rights and receive $R > (R(1 - tR_1))/(1 - t)$ at $T = 2$. On the other hand, if the individual is of type 1, the shares or withdrawal rights can be sold for $((1 - t)r_1)/(1 - tr_1) > r_1$.[8] In either case, the person is better off.

This unraveling problem is a result of the preference assumptions of Diamond and Dybvig. Since type 1 individuals have no utility for period 2 consumption, marginal rates of substitution are not equalized across types at the social optimum. Failure to equalize marginal rates of substitution allows the unraveling problem to exist. Diamond and Dybvig do not address this point; presumably, they assume it away implicitly. This flaw results from marginal rates of substitution not being equalized at the social optimum.

In an Economy with Smooth Preferences

If preferences are smooth and demand deposits can be traded costlessly, the only allocations that can be achieved are competitive equilibria from equal endowments. This assertion holds regardless of whether equity contracts or demand deposits are used in the economy. In this subsection, this assertion is proved and an example illustrating the theorem is provided.

For the remainder of the section, let preferences be as described in Section 3—smooth and representable by functions that satisfy the Inada conditions in both arguments. These assumptions are sufficient to assure that the social optimization has an interior solution and that at the social optimum the marginal rates of substitution are equalized across types. Having made these assumptions, consider figure II-5, which is an Edgeworth's box representation of the socially optimal allocation between type 1 and type 2 individuals. First notice that the social optimum, represented by point 0, is individually incentive compatible. This is seen by noting that an allocation that gives each type the other type's optimal allocation, represented by point F, moves neither type into that individual's preferred set. However, with ex post trading, individual incentive compatibility is not the appropriate incentive compatibility concept. For example, a group of individuals could form a coalition, have some individuals select the inappropriate withdrawal strategy, redistribute their total allocation, and all be better off. In particular, for the situation depicted in figure II-5, a group of type 2 individuals could form a coalition and, having agreed to divide the total allocation equally, each achieve any point along the line $0F$. Part of this line falls in their preferred set. Thus, all the individuals in the coalition can be made better off than they were at point 0. Unless they are restricted from forming coalitions, coalition incentive compatibility is the appropriate concept of incentive compatibility in this situation.

Note, however, that the set of all coalitionally incentive compatible points is defined to be the core of the economy. Furthermore, Aumann (1964)

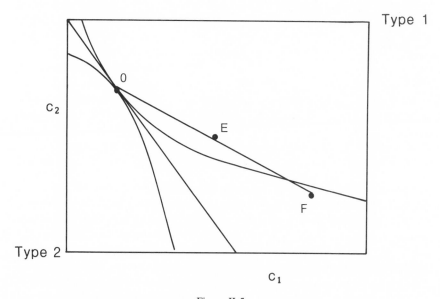

Figure II-5

proves that, in an economy with a finite number of types (for which there exists a continuum of individuals of each type), the core of the economy collapses to the set of competitive equilibria. Thus, the formation of coalitions can be thought of as occurring through the process of trading. The following theorem shows that allowing trade in demand deposits makes them equivalent to equity shares.

THEOREM 4. *If demand deposits can be traded costlessly, equity shares and demand deposits are equivalent risk-sharing mechanisms.*

PROOF. First, it is easy to see that the use of deposit contracts can achieve any allocation that can be achieved using equity contracts. The deposit contract just needs to specify the two alternative withdrawal streams to be final allocations achieved in the equity economy for individuals of type 1 and type 2. Since these allocations represent a competitive equilibrium, there are no gains from further trade if everyone self-selects appropriately. Furthermore, neither type has any incentive to misrepresent its type since both withdrawal streams represent the same amount of wealth and thus could be used to achieve the same set of possible allocations through trade.

Now, it is shown that if trade in demand deposits is allowed, then the best allocation that can be achieved using demand deposits is the allocation achieved using equity shares. The possibility of ex post trade affects each type's choice of withdrawal stream. To be consistent with the optimal liquidation decision, we know that the one-period gross return from holding demand deposits from time 1 to time 2 must be R. Thus, being able to compute what prices will be in the market at $T = 1$, everyone will prefer the allocation that offers the greatest wealth. This constrains the bank to offering withdrawal streams representing the same amount of wealth. Given that each withdrawal stream offers the same amount of wealth, either stream could be achieved through trade in the equity economy. Thus, any allocation achieved in the deposit economy can also be achieved in the equity economy. Q.E.D.

The following example demonstrates how the deposit equilibrium breaks down if coalitions can form costlessly (or if frictionless trade takes place).

EXAMPLE. Let preferences be smooth and trading be costless and unrestricted. Assume that each individual believes all other individuals act myopically (i.e., they do not consider potential trades in choosing their withdrawal strategy). Then, unless the optimal allocation is a competitive equilibrium from equal endowments, all the individuals of one of the two types will find it in their best interest to choose the inappropriate myopic allocation. They will do so by believing that they will always be able to achieve a Pareto-improving allocation by making a finite number of unconditional trades with any arbitrary group of individuals (i.e., the type mix of the group does not matter).

Consider figure II-6. A deviant type 2 individual wishes to trade from point β to point γ. Note that, using point Z as the origin, β has coordinates (c_{11}, c_{21}) and γ has coordinates $(c_{11} - a, c_{21} + Ma)$. Thus, the deviant type 2 individual wishes to trade a units of first period consumption for Ma units of second-period consumption.

Notice that the tangent line at point a has slope $-R$ and that $R > M$. Therefore, by the smoothness of preferences, we know that there exists δ_1, $\delta_2 > 0$ such that

$$(c_{11} + \delta_1, c_{21} - M\delta_1) \gg_1 (c_{11}, c_{21})$$

and

$$(c_{12} + \delta_2, c_{22} - M\delta_2) \gg_2 (c_{12}, c_{22})$$

where $\gg_i$ indicates strict preference for type i. Now, let δ be defined to be $\min(\delta_1, \delta_2)$. It is clear that the deviant individual, to succeed in moving from point β to point γ, need only make at most $a/\delta < \infty$ Pareto-improving trades with individuals of either type who have chosen their myopic allocation.

Theorem 4 raises severe doubts as to the viability of demand deposits in a frictionless economy in which all individuals have smooth preferences. Equity contracts could always be used to obtain the same equilibria. For

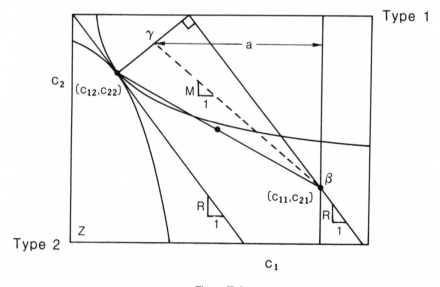

Figure II-6

demand deposits to have an important social role, trade in deposits must be prohibited or costly. This includes the prohibition of a frictionless credit market at time 1, since such a market effectively circumvents any restrictions on the trading of demand deposits. Note, however, that at $T = 0$ everyone in the economy would agree to such restrictions because they allow all individuals to improve their ex ante expected utility.

5. Conclusions

This paper has attempted to clarify and add support to the social role for demand deposits identified by Bryant (1980) and Diamond and Dybvig (1983). That trading restrictions are necessary for the existence of a social role for demand deposits in models of the type examined here is a principal contribution of this paper. This result is similar to the result in the taxation literature (Hammond 1979, 1983), which shows that whenever the optimal taxation policy is nonlinear it is vulnerable to resale. Whenever frictionless markets exist, individual incentive compatibility of a mechanism is not sufficient to guarantee truthful revelation of types.

Notes

1. I would like to express my appreciation to Sudipto Bhattacharya for the many insights he provided in our discussions of this and related work. I would also like to thank Ben Bernanke, Milt Harris, Ed Prescott, Ed Robbins, Neil Wallace, and Bob Wilson for helpful comments on earlier drafts of this paper. All remaining errors are, of course, mine.

2. Although there are problems with the law of large numbers when there is a continuum of i.i.d. random variables, Feldman and Gilles (1985) and Judd (1985) have demonstrated that these problems can be alleviated by imposing sufficient regularity on the mathematical structure.

3. Social optimality is used interchangeably with ex ante expected utility maximization of a representative individual. Note that at $T = 0$ everyone in the economy is identical.

4. If we assume that the firm is valued as a discounted dividend stream and that the appropriate discount factor for the second period is R (the rate of transformation), this dividend policy is not necessarily value maximizing; nonetheless, it is unanimously agreed upon by all shareholders. This should not be surprising. Given the preference structure, individual's marginal rates of substitution are not set equal to the marginal rate of transformation in equilibrium. Thus, the (marginal) rate of transformation is not necessarily the appropriate discount factor.

5. If storage were allowed, the constraints would be

$$U(c_{11}, c_{21}) \geq U(c_{12}(1 - S_1), c_{22} + S_1 c_{12})$$

and

$$V(c_{12}, c_{22}) \geq V(c_{11}(1 - S_2), c_{21} + S_2 c_{11})$$

for all S_1 and S_2 between 0 and 1.

6. Note further that, given smooth preferences and the premises of Theorem 2, this dividend decision is also value maximizing (ex post).

7. The use of lotteries may offer improvements to the allocations considered here. See Prescott and Townsend (1984) for a discussion of the use of lotteries to improve incentive-constrained allocations.

8. Recall from Section 2 that the price of an ex-dividend share, which pays $R(1 - tr_1)$ at $T = 2$, is $r_1(1 - t)$. Therefore, the price of a share, which pays R at $T = 2$, is $(r_1(1 - t))/(1 - tr_1)$.

References

Aumann, R. J. 1964. "Markets with a Continuum of Traders." *Econometrica* 32:39–50.

Bryant, J. 1980. "A Model of Reserves, Bank Runs, and Deposit Insurance." *Journal of Banking and Finance* 4:335–44.

Diamond, D. W., and P. H. Dybvig. 1983. "Bank Runs, Deposit Insurance, and Liquidity." *Journal of Political Economy* 91:401–19.

Feldman, M. and C. Gilles. 1985. "An Expository Note on Individual Risk without Aggregate Uncertainty." *Journal of Economic Theory* 35:26–32.

Hammond, P. 1979. "Straightforward Individual Incentive Compatibility in Large Economies." *Review of Economic Studies* 46:263–82.

――――. 1983. "Multilateral Incentive Compatibility in Continuum Economies." Working paper, Economics Department, Stanford University.

Hart, O. D. 1975. "On the Optimality of Equilibrium When Markets Are Incomplete." *Journal of Economic Theory* 10:418–43.

Judd, K. L. 1985. "The 'Law of Large Numbers' with a Continuum of IID Random Variables." *Journal of Economic Theory* 35:19–25.

Prescott, E. C., and R. M. Townsend. 1984. "General Competitive Analysis in an Economy with Private Information." *International Economic Review* 25:1–20.

III

Private Information, the Real Bills Doctrine, and the Quantity Theory: An Alternative Approach

Bruce D. Smith

Recent developments in the theory of economies with private information permit a reexamination of the issues raised in the "real bills-quantity theory" debate. A model is developed here in which there are banks, in which fiat money is present, and in which agents possess private information. Two regulatory regimes are then considered. In the first, banks are essentially unregulated; in the second, banks face 100 percent reserve requirements. Issues related to existence and optimality of equilibrium are addressed, and problems with existence are given an interpretation in terms of the "stability" of the banking system. Existence (stability) problems that arise under laissez-faire banking can be rectified by a 100 percent reserve requirement. However, unless there is private information regarding access to investment opportunities, better ways can typically be found to accomplish this. Finally, it is shown that, even in the presence of 100 percent reserve requirements, banks are not simply "money warehouses." Bank deposits and money bear different (real) return streams, even under 100 percent reserves.

1. Introduction

One of the longest continuing discussions in economics has involved the role that financial intermediaries (banks) play in allocating resources and expediting the undertaking of "monetary" transactions.[1] This discussion has most often manifested itself in the debates between adherents of the "real bills doctrine" and of the "quantity theory." The first of these positions has often been interpreted as an advocacy of "unfettered private intermediaries" (Sargent and Wallace 1982, 1212), and the second as an advocacy of 100 percent reserve requirements—or, more generally, of legal restrictions on intermediaries that restrict their ability to "create money." As argued by Sargent and Wallace (1212), these two views constitute "a useful way to

48

organize the discussion of . . . issues" related to the theory of money and banking.

In fact, the two views suggest very different interpretations of the roles played by banks in the process of resource allocation. Smith (1776), for instance, clearly views banks as institutions that help to overcome economic frictions. On the other hand, Simons (1948) suggests that allowing investment to be intermediated through banks is destabilizing and results (at times) in socially suboptimal levels of investment. Thus, adherents of the real bills doctrine have stressed the economic benefits of banking, whereas quantity theory advocates have stressed problems introduced by banks.

Both of these aspects of banking have been addressed by recent developments that emphasize the presence of private information and its implications for financial intermediation. In particular, Boyd and Prescott (1984) discuss the role of intermediaries in efficiently allocating investment funds when borrowers know more than lenders about investment opportunities. Diamond and Dybvig (1983), Jacklin (1983), King and Haubrich (1983), and Smith (1984) emphasize the role of intermediaries in creating insurance opportunities for lenders under private information, with all of these efforts but King and Haubrich also focusing on "stability" problems that arise for an unregulated banking system because of the frictions created by the presence of private information. Diamond and Dybvig (1983) and Smith (1984) go on to discuss some regulatory responses to this instability. Thus, recent developments would seem to provide an opportunity to reexamine the questions raised in the real bills-quantity theory debate.

However, existing models are not really equipped to do this for at least two reasons. One is that none of the models mentioned contains money, so that questions concerning the role of banks in a (potentially) monetary economy cannot be addressed. The second is that several of the models mentioned do not predict whether or not problems will arise in banking. In particular, Diamond and Dybvig (1983) and Jacklin (1983) construct models with multiple equilibria. Some result in Pareto-optimal allocations, whereas in others "bank runs" arise. Hence, whether stability problems will arise under laissez-faire banking is not a question that these models can address.

This paper is an attempt to examine some of the questions involved in the real bills-quantity theory debate in the context of a model with private information. This seems appropriate, for several reasons. In particular, recent reexaminations of this debate, employing models that are essentially free from underlying economic frictions, conclude that there is no obvious reason to regulate banking. This is hardly surprising, of course, since in full information, complete markets settings there is nothing special about the activity of banking.[2] Arguments that intermediation is special (e.g., a special candidate for regulation), then, require some departure from such settings.

A simple method of introducing private information into a model of banking is therefore pursued below. In particular, the model synthesizes two features emphasized by Simons (1948) and Smith (1776), respectively. One is that each individual who makes a deposit with a bank has a probability distribution over future withdrawal dates that is not known ex ante by the bank. The second is that, even so, if banks behave prudently, inflows of funds will match outflows of funds based on considerations of the law of large numbers (Smith 1776, 289). In addition, banks (and all agents) are endowed with a simple investment opportunity that generates a nonstochastic return stream.

The paper then investigates two different banking arrangements for economies with the features described. In one arrangement, banks are unrestricted in terms of behavior (with two inessential exceptions discussed below). In the other, banks are forced to hold 100 percent reserves of a safe, noninterest-bearing government liability against deposits. Several questions may then be raised regarding the two regimes. First, following Sargent and Wallace (1982), one might ask whether equilibria under one regime dominate, in any sense, equilibria under the other regime on the basis of some welfare criterion. This, of course, presupposes existence of an equilibrium in each case. Second, one could ask questions related to the existence of an equilibrium under either regime. Third, one could ask whether any economic interpretation could be placed on the failure of an equilibrium to exist with unregulated banking. Fourth, there are government interventions that produce an equilibrium when one otherwise fails to exist. Different interventions may be Pareto-compared. What kinds of interventions seem socially desirable?

The analysis permits some conclusions to be drawn on these questions and suggests what types of considerations are important when the analysis is inconclusive. Some of the results obtained are as follows:

1. Under the conditions outlined, when an equilibrium exists under each of the two regimes, either may be "socially preferred." The 100 percent reserve regime seems most desirable when there is private information regarding access to investment opportunities.

2. Under either regime, a Nash equilibrium (which is the equilibrium concept imposed) may fail to exist. Existence fails when no bank can structure deposit interest rates in such a way that its competitors are deterred from bidding away its most profitable depositors. Competition among banks for deposits was universally viewed as the reason for instability of the banking system before 1933. Hence, failure of an equilibrium to exist may be given an interpretation in terms of the "stability" of the banking system. When no equilibrium exists under laissez-faire banking, the banking system is unstable.

3. For some economies with no Nash equilibrium, an equilibrium can be caused to exist by imposing 100 percent reserve requirements. This can also be accomplished by imposing an interest rate ceiling.
4. Given the interpretation of nonexistence as "banking instability," and given that the two regulatory interventions in (3) above produce stability, one might attempt to Pareto-rank the two interventions. There is some presumption in the model in favor of interest rate ceilings.

In addition, there are economies where fiat money fails to have value under either the laissez-faire banking regime or under a regime where all banking is prohibited. Nevertheless, some such economies do have equilibria with valued fiat money under a 100 percent reserve regime, indicating that in such a regime banks are not simply money warehouses. In particular, it will be shown that even under a 100 percent reserve regime, bank deposits and money bear different rates of return. Moreover, if there is private information regarding access to investment opportunities, more productive investors may prefer the 100 percent reserve regime to laissez-faire banking.

The scheme of the paper is as follows. To introduce the essential aspects of the model and to develop the incentives that exist for banks to form, Section 2 presents a version of the model under full information. Section 3 introduces private information and examines the behavior of an (essentially) unregulated banking system. Section 4 describes how an equilibrium in the banking system is determined under 100 percent reserve requirements. Section 5 then develops some of the results outlined above under the assumption that all agents have access to the same investment opportunities. Section 6 relaxes this assumption, permitting investment opportunities to vary across agents and thus permitting uncertainty on the part of banks about an agent's characteristics both as a depositor and as someone in whom the bank might invest. Section 6 then derives additional results under this assumption, and Section 7 concludes.

2. The Model under Full Information

The Model without Banking

The format of the paper is to examine the simplest possible monetary economy with private information. To introduce fiat money (which can potentially be valued in equilibrium), the economy will be given an overlapping generations structure. Thus, let time be discrete and indexed by $t = 0$, $1, \ldots$. At $t = 0$ there is an initial old generation, which is endowed with the entire aggregate stock of fiat money, M. This stock will then be held constant through time. At $t = 1$, this generation disappears. At $t = 0$, there is also an initial young generation that becomes old at $t = 1$, and so on.

No further description will be required of the initial old generation. However, in order to introduce private information, each young generation will need to display some heterogeneity among its members. Although this section does not deal explicitly with private information, to introduce the economic setup let each young generation consist of three types of agents, indexed by $i = 1, 2, 3$. Each generation is "large" (so that the population is infinite at each date), with proportion θ_i of type i agents. Type 1 and 2 agents face similar economic circumstances, whereas type 3 agents play a much different role in the analysis. Hence, we discuss these types separately.

All young agents of type i ($i = 1,2$) begin their first period of life with one unit of the single consumption good. However, whereas endowments of the good are received at the beginning of the first period, consumption of the good can occur only at the end of the first period or at any time during the second period. Since endowments are not received by young agents at a time when consumption can occur, then, these agents have two options. One is to trade their endowment for money held by the current old and then to use this money later to purchase the good themselves. Money acquired at the beginning of an agent's first period of life can be spent either at the end of that period or when old.

The second option facing these agents is to place the good in "storage" at the beginning of the period, which yields the gross rate of return $Q_1 <$ 1 if the good is removed from storage at the end of the same period and the return $Q_2 > 1$ if the good is removed from storage in the second period. (Returns to storage are zero thereafter). For the present, type 1 and 2 agents are assumed to have access to the same storage technology.

Let C_j denote consumption in period j for any agent, where $j = 1$ denotes youth and $j = 2$ denotes old age. It is assumed that type 1 and 2 agents possess identical utility functions given by $U(C_1, C_2) = U(C_1 + C_2)^3$ with $U'' < 0$. Thus, these agents are indifferent regarding the timing of consumption. In the absence of other considerations, then, they would simply consume when old to maximize the returns on their investments.

Suppose there is a random shock, however, specific to each individual, so that in one state of nature a type i agent ($i = 1,2$) is forced to consume when young.[4] The other possibility is that one can consume when old. Moreover, at the beginning of an agent's life, each agent has a probability distribution over which date he will be forced to consume in. In particular, a type i agent faces ex ante probability p_i of being forced to consume when young, where the values p_i are time invariant and obey $p_1 < p_2$. For the purposes of this section, each agent's type is publicly known.

Type 3 agents, who are less interesting, are introduced for technical convenience (see below). These agents live two periods with certainty and have preferences given by $V(C_1, C_2) = C_1 + C_2$. The other difference between them and agents of other types is that these individuals receive their endowment of a single unit of the good at the end of their first period of life. Investment in the storage technology can occur only at the beginning of an agent's youth, so these agents have no access to a storage technology.[5]

Having described the economic environment, let us now consider two different trading arrangements in which risk sharing (the operation of a financial intermediary) is prohibited. The first is one where $M = 0$, so that monetary transactions are also prohibited. Then all agents face autarky, so that, in particular,

$$C_{i1} = Q_1 \text{ with probability } p_i \tag{1a}$$

$$C_{i1} = 0 \text{ with probability } 1 - p_i \tag{1b}$$

$$C_{i2} = Q_2 \text{ with probability } 1 - p_i \tag{1c}$$

$$C_{i2} = 0 \text{ with probability } p_i, \tag{1d}$$

where C_{ij} is the consumption of type i agents in period $j (i = 1,2)$. The autarky arrangement yields expected utility levels $U_i^A \equiv p_i U(Q_1) + (1 - p_i)U(Q_2)$; $i = 1, 2$.

Now consider an economy in which $M > 0$. Let the consumption good be the numeraire, and let S_t denote the number of goods purchasable with a unit of money (the inverse price level) at t. Now young agents with $i = 1, 2$ face a nontrivial portfolio selection problem when young. In particular, they may choose to place a fraction $\lambda_i \in [0,1]$ of their goods in storage and to use the remainder $1 - \lambda_i$ to purchase money from the current old. Hence, if a young type i agent acquires $1 - \lambda_i$ units of real balances when young, his consumption is given (for $i = 1,2$) by

$$C_{i1} = \lambda_i Q_1 + (1 - \lambda_i) \text{ with probability } p_i \tag{2a}$$

$$C_{i1} = 0 \text{ with probability } 1 - p_i \tag{2b}$$

$$C_{i2} = \lambda_i Q_2 + (1 - \lambda_i)(S_{t+1}/S_t) \text{ with probability } 1 - p_i \tag{2c}$$

$$C_{i2} = 0 \text{ with probability } p_i. \tag{2d}$$

Hence, type i agents ($i = 1,2$) select $\lambda_i \in [0,1]$ to maximize

$$p_i U(\lambda_i Q_1 + 1 - \lambda_i) + (1 - p_i)U[\lambda_i Q_2 + (1 - \lambda_i)(S_{t+1}/S_t)],$$

taking the sequence $\{S_t\}_{t=0}^{\infty}$ as given. The optimal choice of λ_i; $i = 1, 2$ along with (2) then dictates consumption for type i agents. In the sequel, only steady states are considered. Since the economy does not vary over time, $S_{t+1}/S_t = 1$ in steady state. However, in places the notation S_{t+1}/S_t will be retained for clarity.

The Model with "Banks"

The object of this section is to demonstrate the incentives that exist in the economy just described for intermediaries to form. However, for such incentives to be present, it is necessary that $p_1Q_1 + (1 - p_1)Q_2 > 1$. In fact, it is henceforth assumed that $p_2Q_1 + (1 - p_2)Q_2 > 1$. The assumption of public knowledge of the type of each agent is still retained at this point.

The model is now augmented to contain a set of agents who act as bankers, with there being free entry into the activity of operating a bank. All banks have access to the storage technology described above, plus they can also acquire real balances if so desired. In addition, banks can borrow from (or lend to) type 3 agents at the end of the first period.[6] Since type 3 agents supply their entire endowment of the good elastically at a gross rate of return equal to unity, so long as banks do not wish to borrow more than the total endowment of type 3 agents they will face an intertemporal (gross) rate of interest equal to one.

It remains to describe bank behavior. It is assumed that banks announce gross rates of return R_{ij} to be paid to type i agents who withdraw their deposits at age j; $i, j = 1, 2$. Since individual types are publicly known, this is informationally feasible. A Nash equilibrium concept can then be imposed, so that a vector of announcements $(R_{11}, R_{12}, R_{21}, R_{22})$ is an equilibrium if no bank has an incentive to announce a different vector of state contingent payoffs on deposits, given the announcements of other banks and given the equilibrium sequence $\{S_t\}$.

Consider, then, the situation faced by type 1 and 2 agents when banks are present. These agents can place any nonnegative fraction of their goods in storage, in bank deposits, or they may acquire real balances. Let λ_{i1} be the fraction of goods deposited in a bank by a type i agent (each agent need deal only with one bank), λ_{i2} be the fraction of real balances held by a type i agent, and λ_{i3} be the fraction of the portfolio held in storage, with $\lambda_{ik} \in [0,1]$; $i = 1, 2$ and $k = 1, 2, 3$. Then, consumption for a type i agent is given by

$$C_{i1} = \lambda_{i1}R_{i1} + \lambda_{i2} + \lambda_{i3}Q_1 \text{ with probability } p_i \qquad (3a)$$

$$C_{i1} = 0 \text{ with probability } 1 - p_i \qquad (3b)$$

$$C_{i2} = \lambda_{i1}R_{i2} + \lambda_{i2}(S_{t+1}/S_t) + \lambda_{i3}Q_3 \text{ with probability } 1 - p_i \qquad (3c)$$

$$C_{i2} = 0 \text{ with probability } p_i. \qquad (3d)$$

The values λ_{ik}; $k = 1, 2, 3$ are then chosen to solve the problem

$$\max p_i U(\lambda_{i1}R_{i1} + \lambda_{i2} + \lambda_{i3}Q_1)$$
$$+ (1 - p_i)U[\lambda_{i1}R_{i2} + \lambda_{i2}(S_{t+1}/S_t) + \lambda_{i3}Q_2] \qquad (4)$$

subject to $\Sigma_k \lambda_{ik} = 1$, and $1 \geq \lambda_{ik} \geq 0 \; \forall \; k$. Then denote the optimal choice of the vector $(\lambda_{i1}, \lambda_{i2}, \lambda_{i3})$ by $(\lambda_{i1}, \lambda_{i2}, \lambda_{i3}) \equiv \Phi_i[R_{i1}, R_{i2}, Q_1, Q_2, (S_{t+1}/S_t)] \equiv [\Phi_{i1}(\;), \Phi_{i2}(\;), \Phi_{i3}(\;)]$.

Having described the portfolio choices of type 1 and 2 agents, we can now characterize an equilibrium for this economy. First, in light of the fact that there are large numbers of agents, banks face no uncertainty here. Therefore, in light of the assumption that there is free entry into banking, the equilibrium return vector must be such that banks earn zero profits. Here it should be noted, then, that banks can borrow from (and lend to) type 3 agents at a gross rate of interest of unity, subject to one restriction that is now imposed: for each withdrawal made from a bank by an agent only one period after making a deposit, the bank must remove one unit of the good from storage. This may be viewed as a legal restriction on the amount of indebtedness incurred by any bank. The reason for imposing this restriction is as follows. Given the linear preferences possessed by all agents and the linearity of bank objective functions, in equilibrium banks must either face a gross intertemporal rate of return of one, or of Q_2. In the absence of the requirement that one unit must be taken out of storage for each withdrawal by individuals of age 1, the first situation (a unitary rate of return) would obtain if $\Sigma_{i=1}^2 p_i \theta_i Q_2 \leq \theta_3$ and the latter would obtain otherwise. Now it is a matter of considerable technical convenience here to have banks face an intertemporal rate of return of one. In particular, if they faced Q_2, to guarantee a nontrivial role for banking here it would be necessary to impose $cU''(c)/U'(c) < -1$.[7] This would preclude setting up examples in which it is possible to produce closed-form solutions for equilibrium values. However, if $\Sigma_{i=1}^2 p_i \theta_i Q_2 \leq \theta_3$ held, and if banks faced no borrowing restrictions, no units would ever be withdrawn from storage after only one period. Then there would be no private information problem here. In light of these two considerations, then, it seems reasonable to impose a borrowing restriction on banks. Any such restriction would suffice. The assumption that one unit must be taken out of storage for each withdrawal is attractive, then, since under a restriction to be imposed shortly, it prevents banks from increasing, simply by their presence, the discounted present value of the aggregate wealth of any generation. This is important, as such a result would derive entirely from the presence of type 3 agents, who are introduced only to simplify the analysis. Thus, this assumption prevents banks from altering the aggregate set of resource-feasible allocations for this economy. Finally, a borrowing restriction on banks is not unattractive, since in practice the amount of bank borrowing is closely monitored.

Given our assumption on bank borrowing, then, the zero profit conditions on return pairs offered to type i agents are

$$p_i R_{i1} + (1 - p_i) R_{i2} = p_i Q_1 + (1 - p_i) Q_2; \; i = 1, 2, \tag{5}$$

where the fact that banks can borrow from type 3 agents at a zero net rate of interest has been used in (5). This requires that banks not wish to borrow more than type 3 agents can lend. Formally, the latter condition may be written as

$$\sum_{i=1}^{2} \theta_i p_i (R_{i1} - Q_1) \Phi_{i1} \leq \theta_3. \tag{6}$$

A parameter restriction is imposed below that guarantees satisfaction of (6). Hence, it will be treated as not binding in the discussion that follows.

As argued above, any equilibrium return pair (R_{i1}, R_{i2}) must earn zero profits. It must also solve the problem

$$\max W_i[R_{i1}, R_{i2}, Q_1, Q_2, (S_{t+1}/S_t)] \tag{7}$$

subject to (5), where

$$W_i[R_{i1}, R_{i2}, Q_1, Q_2, (S_{t+1}/S_t)] \equiv p_i U[R_{i1} \Phi_{i1}[R_{i1}, R_{i2}, Q_1, Q_2, (S_{t+1}/S_t)] + \Phi_{i2}(\ )$$
$$+ Q_1 \Phi_{i3}(\ )] + (1 - p_i) U[R_{i2} \Phi_{i1}(\ ) + \Phi_{i2}(\ )(S_{t+1}/S_t) + \Phi_{i3}(\ )Q_2]. \tag{8}$$

The reason for this is easy to see. If (6) is not binding and all banks announce (R_{i1}, R_{i2}) pairs that solve (7) subject to (5), then no bank has an incentive to offer a different set of (R_{i1}, R_{i2}) pairs. In particular, if (R_{i1}^*, R_{i2}^*); $i = 1, 2$ is a pair of announcements solving (7) subject to (5), the only way in which a bank can attract type i depositors [i.e., offer them a pair (R_{i1}, R_{i2}) such that $W_i[R_{i1}, R_{i2}, Q_1, Q_2, (S_{t+1}/S_t)] > W_i[R_{i1}^*, R_{i2}^*, Q_1, Q_2, (S_{t+1}/S_t)]$ is to offer an (R_{i1}, R_{i2}) pair satisfying $p_i R_{i1} + (1 - p_i) R_{i2} > p_i Q_1 + (1 - p_i) Q_2$. But, of course, such an offer loses money and so will not be made. Hence any arrangement with all banks offering (R_{i1}^*, R_{i2}^*); $i = 1, 2$ constitutes a Nash equilibrium.

It is also easy to see that this is the only Nash equilibrium for a given $\{S_t\}$ sequence. In particular, suppose to the contrary that (R_{i1}, R_{i2}); $i = 1, 2$ is a Nash equilibrium with $(R_{i1}, R_{i2}) \neq (R_{i1}^*, R_{i2}^*)$, and with (R_{i1}, R_{i2}) satisfying $p_i R_{i1} + (1 - p_i) R_{i2} = p_i Q_1 + (1 - p_i) Q_2$. Then clearly $W_i[R_{i1}^*, R_{i2}^*, Q_1, Q_2, (S_{t+1}/S_t)] > W_i[R_{i1}, R_{i2}, Q_1, Q_2, (S_{t+1}/S_t)]$ for some i. Thus, there exists for this i a vector $(\hat{R}_{i1}, \hat{R}_{i2})$ with $W_i[R_{i1}^*, R_{i2}^*, Q_1, Q_2, (S_{t+1}/S_t)] > W_i[\hat{R}_{i1}, \hat{R}_{i2}, Q_1, Q_2, (S_{t+1}/S_t)] > W_i[R_{i1}, R_{i2}, Q_1, Q_2, (S_{t+1}/S_t)]$, and such that $p_i \hat{R}_{i1} + (1 - p_i) \hat{R}_{i2} < p_i Q_1 + (1 - p_i) Q_2$. This offer attracts all type i agents and earns a profit. Hence, the hypothesized arrangement is not an equilibrium, giving the desired contradiction.

It is not difficult to see, then, that since $p_i Q_1 + (1 - p_i) Q_2 > 1 \ \forall \ i$, and since banks can offer return vectors obeying $R_{i1} = R_{i2}$, that both money and storage are dominated here by bank deposits. Hence, $\Phi_{i2} = \Phi_{i3} = 0$ for this economy. Therefore (R_{i1}, R_{i2}) solves

$$\max\ p_i U(R_{i1}) + (1 - p_i)U(R_{i2})$$

subject to (5). This optimization problem yields first-order conditions that can be manipulated to obtain

$$\frac{p_i U'(R_{i1})}{(1 - p_i)U'(R_{i2})} = \frac{p_i}{1 - p_i}, \tag{9}$$

or $R_{i1} = R_{i2}$. Hence in equilibrium $R_{ij} = R_{ij}^* = p_i Q_1 + (1 - p_i)Q_2$. Thus, under full information, banks provide full insurance. Finally, it remains to impose parameter restrictions that imply (6). In light of the fact that $R_{ij}^* = p_i Q_1 + (1 - p_i)Q_2$, (6) is implied by

$$p_2 \theta_2 [p_2 Q_1 + (1 - p_2)Q_2 - Q_1] + p_1 \theta_1 [p_1 Q_1 + (1 - p_1)Q_2 - Q_1]$$

$$= (Q_2 - Q_1) \sum_{i=1}^{2} p_i \theta_i (1 - p_i) \le \theta_3. \tag{10}$$

It remains to explain the role played by type 3 agents here, since their presence is clearly somewhat artificial. Type 3 agents, then, add to the analysis in two important ways. One is that banks obviously act so as to provide insurance for "investors." Clearly, $Q_2 > Q_1$ must hold for there to be an insurance motive here. However, if there were no agents of type 3 in the model, there would be no opportunity for banks to borrow at gross rate of interest one. Then, as is easily verified, banks would not provide the complete insurance derived above. This provision of complete insurance greatly simplifies subsequent analysis, so that the presence of type 3 agents is helpful in this respect.

Second, considerable attention has been devoted to equilibria that display "bank runs" in models of the type considered here.[8] Suppose that a bank could not observe whether agents had to consume at the end of their initial period and hence could not make individual payments contingent on this event. In the absence of type 3 agents, banks could still offer the rate of return pairs (R_{i1}^*, R_{i2}^*) (or their analog when they cannot borrow from type 3 agents). However, now "run equilibria" could occur in the following way. If all agents conjecture that all other agents are planning to make withdrawals at the end of their initial period, banks may be bankrupted. Hence, those who do not attempt to withdraw at this time earn a zero rate of return. Thus, all agents will withdraw at the end of their initial period, causing a run.

Now consider the model with type 3 agents present. If the claims of depositors take precedence over the claims of type 3 lenders on banks, a run cannot occur. To see this, notice that for every agent who does not make a withdrawal at the end of the initial period, one unit of the good remains in storage. Since (as is easily verified) $R_{i2}^* < Q_2$, and since depositor claims on the bank enjoy a preferred status, a bank can always pay off depositors who do not make "premature" withdrawals. Thus, no agent has an incentive to make such a withdrawal, and no run can occur. Then, notice that bank debts to type 3 agents are always honored in equilibrium.[9]

One final point about type 3 agents is worthy of note. It was assumed above that once a unit was placed in storage, its ownership could not be transferred. However, it is reasonable to ask what would happen if type 1 and 2 agents who learn they must complete their consumption at the end of their initial period could sell their investment to type 3 agents (who are the only agents that could make such a purchase). The answer is that this does not affect any of the above analysis if

$$(p_1\theta_1 + p_2\theta_2) > \theta_3. \tag{11}$$

To see this, notice that type 3 agents would not give up more than Q_2 units of current consumption for a claim to a unit in storage. If asked to give up exactly Q_2 units for a claim to a unit in storage, type 3 agents (in per capita terms) would supply any amount of current consumption in the interval $[0,\theta_3]$. Finally, if asked to surrender less than Q_2 units for such a claim, the aggregate (per capita) supply of current consumption by type 3 agents would be θ_3. Type 1 or 2 agents who were willing to sell such claims, however, would obviously not surrender them for less than Q_1 units of current consumption. At Q_1 units of current consumption per unit in storage, the aggregate supply of such claims could take any value in the interval $[0, p_1\theta_1 + p_2\theta_2]$, and at any amount greater than Q_1 the supply of such claims would be $p_1\theta_1 + p_2\theta_2$. Then the supply of and the demand for claims to future consumption are as depicted in figure III-1. Under assumption (11), the equilibrium price of a unit in storage would be Q_1, as shown, so that type 1 and 2 agents would not benefit from being able to sell such claims. Of course, type 3 agents would benefit from being able to buy them at this price, but this would not affect the arguments above regarding the incentives for banks to form. Henceforth, then, to maintain maximum simplicity, the assumption that units already in storage are not transferable is retained.

To summarize, then, there is an incentive for banks to form here in order to provide a source of insurance for investors. We may now direct our attention to provision of such insurance under private information.

3. Private Information and Laissez-Faire Banking

Description

In this section the operation of an (essentially) unregulated banking system under private information is considered. Two minor restrictions are imposed

Figure 1

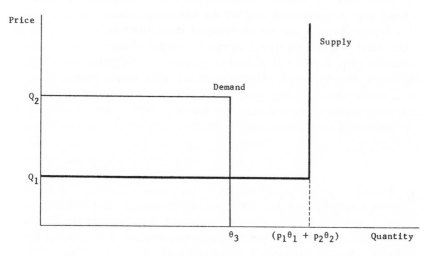

Figure III-1

on banks, however. One is the borrowing restriction discussed above: for each unit withdrawn, a unit of the good must be removed from storage. A second is a technical condition imposed to simplify the analysis, which is that banks are not permitted to lose money on any deposit payoff pair, or

$$p_i R_{i1} + (1 - p_i)R_{i2} \le p_i Q_1 + (1 - p_i)Q_2; \ i = 1, 2 \quad (12a)$$

if type i deposits are held only by type i agents. If agents of both types were to make the same types of deposits (in their population proportions), then the relevant condition would be

$$(\theta_1 p_1 + \theta_2 p_2)R_1 + [\theta_1(1 - p_1) + \theta_2(1 - p_2)]R_2$$

$$\le (\theta_1 p_1 + \theta_2 p_2)Q_1 + [\theta_1(1 - p_1) + \theta_2(1 - p_2)]Q_2. \quad (12b)$$

This is a standard assumption in private information settings of the type now described.[10]

The economy has all of the features described in Section 3, except that now each agent's type is unobservable ex ante. Thus, depositors are possessed of private information regarding their probability distribution over future dates of withdrawal. As above, banks announce deposit payoff vectors (R_{i1}, R_{i2}); $i = 1, 2$ to compete for depositors, and type 1 and 2 agents face the portfolio choices described above given the announcements of banks. Hence, their portfolio behavior is essentially as described above, with one difference: now type 2 agents could, in principle, make type 1 deposits and vice versa.

It remains to describe what actions are observable here. We assume that all economic actions taken by all agents are common knowledge. The only such actions here are portfolio choices and the type of deposit selected. Hence, if type 2 agents wish to select type 1 deposits (or conversely), they must choose the same portfolio as type 1 agents. Also, under the assumption that all portfolio choices are observable, it is easy to show that each depositor need make only one deposit here.[11]

Finally, then, any bank may pursue either of two courses of action. It may announce values $(R_{11},R_{12}) \neq (R_{21},R_{22})$, hoping to induce self-selection of depositor types by deposit selected (without loss of generality, hoping to induce type 1 agents to select type 1 deposits, etc.); or it may set $(R_{11},R_{12}) = (R_{21},R_{22})$ and forgo the opportunity to discriminate by price. The former arrangement is referred to as a *separating arrangement,* and the latter is termed *pooling.* If a bank does wish to induce self-selection, its announcements must be consistent with type 1 and only type 1 agents holding type 1 deposits. Define

$$V_i[R_{k1},R_{k2},Q_1,Q_2,(S_{t+1}/S_t)] \equiv p_i U(R_{k1}\Phi_{k1} + \Phi_{k2} + Q_1\Phi_{k3})$$
$$+ (1 - p_i)U[R_{k2}\Phi_{k1} + \Phi_{k2}(S_{t+1}/S_t) + Q_2\Phi_{k3}] \text{ for } k \neq i. \quad (13)$$

Then the occurrence of self-selection requires that the following incentive compatibility conditions hold if $(R_{11},R_{12}) \neq (R_{21},R_{22})$:

$$W_i[R_{i1},R_{i2},Q_1,Q_2,(S_{t+1}/S_t)] \geq V_i[R_{k1},R_{k2},Q_1,Q_2,(S_{t+1}/S_t)], \quad (14)$$

$i = 1, 2; k = 1, 2; i \neq k$. If $(R_{11},R_{12}) = (R_{21},R_{22})$, then type 2 agents are in a sense mimicking type 1 agents, and they must make the same portfolio choices.

As before, a Nash equilibrium concept is imposed on the game played by banks here. Hence, an equilibrium under laissez-faire banking must satisfy the following:

DEFINITION. An equilibrium is a set of announcements $(R_{11},R_{12},R_{21},R_{22})$ and a sequence $\{S_t\}$ such that:

   (i) given the sequence $\{S_t\}$, no bank has an incentive to announce a different set of deposit payoff vectors [with announcements subject to (12) and (14)];

   (ii) $(R_{i1},R_{i2}); i = 1, 2$ satisfy (12);

   (iii) if $(R_{11},R_{12}) \neq (R_{21},R_{22})$, then $(R_{11},R_{12},R_{21},R_{22})$ satisfies (14) given $\{S_t\}$; and

(iv) the money market clears—that is,

$$\sum_{i=1}^{2} \theta_i \Phi_{i2}[R_{i1}, R_{i2}, Q_1, Q_2, (S_{t+1}/S_t)] = S_t M \; \forall \; t \geq 0. \tag{15}$$

As a convention, type 3 agents hold only as much money as other agents wish to sell them at the end of their first period.[12] Also, attention is confined throughout to pure strategies on the part of banks.

Some Features of Equilibrium

This section provides some heuristic characterization of features of the equilibrium discussed above. Two features, which will be familiar from Rothschild and Stiglitz (1976) or Wilson (1977), are that (a) no equilibrium need exist, and (b) if an equilibrium does exist it involves separation of type 1 and 2 agents by deposits selected. The second feature is a well-known aspect of adverse selection settings, such as this one, and so need not be discussed further. Given that any equilibrium must involve such separation, however, it will be useful to discuss determination of an equilibrium here and briefly to discuss issues concerning existence.

If an equilibrium exists, then, it must display certain features. One is that in equilibrium $R_{2j} = R_{2j}^*$; $j = 1, 2$, where it will be recalled that (R_{21}^*, R_{22}^*) solves the problem (7) subject to (5) for type 2 agents. The reason for this is as follows. First, since type 2 agents are "higher risk" agents from the point of view of a bank ($p_2 > p_1$), it is easy to show that (14) holds with strict inequality for $i = 1$. Thus, competition among banks for type 2 agents (who must be distinguishable in equilibrium) dictates that (R_{21}, R_{22}) solve (7) subject to (5) for exactly the same reasons as in Section 3. In short, then, the presence of private information does not impinge upon the equilibrium returns earned by type 2 agents (if an equilibrium exists).

Private information does impinge upon the returns earned by type 1 agents, however. To see this, suppose that $R_{1j} = R_{1j}^*$; $j = 1, 2$ held. Since $R_{11}^* = R_{12}^* = p_1 Q_1 + (1 - p_1)Q_2 > 1$, type 1 agents would hold all of their portfolios in the form of bank deposits (and similarly for type 2 agents). Then equilibrium consumption levels for type i agents (independent of the date at which consumption occurred) would be $c_i = p_i Q_1 + (1 - p_i)Q_2$. But then $c_1 > c_2$, implying that $p_2 U(c_1) + (1 - p_2)U(c_1) > p_2 U(c_2) + (1 - p_2)U(c_2)$; i.e., that (14) is violated. Hence, (14) must hold with equality in equilibrium.

This places the following restriction on (R_{11}, R_{12}). Since $R_{21}^* = R_{22}^* = p_2 Q_1 + (1 - p_2)Q_2 > 1$, type 2 agents hold only deposits in a steady state equilibrium. Since they also receive full insurance, they receive expected utility $U(R_{21}^*) = U[p_2 Q_1 + (1 - p_2)Q_2]$. Now the expected utility that these agents could realize by mimicking type 1 agents cannot exceed this level (or self-selection could not occur). Of course, if type 2 agents were to mimic type 1 agents, they would have to acquire the same portfolio as these agents. Their expected utility would then be given by $V_2[R_{11},R_{12},Q_1,Q_2,(S_{t+1}/S_t)]$ [with V_2 given by (13)], so that (14) at equality would be

$$U[p_2Q_1 + (1 - p_2)Q_2] = V_2[R_{11},R_{12},Q_1,Q_2,(S_{t+1}/S_t)]. \qquad (16)$$

This along with (5) must be satisfied by any equilibrium pair (R_{11},R_{12}). Then competition for type 1 depositors implies that the (R_{11},R_{12}) pair satisfying (16) and (5) that is most preferred by type 1 agents will be the one offered in equilibrium.

The determination of an equilibrium under laissez-faire banking (if one exists) is easy to depict graphically under the assumption that $\Phi_{12}(R_{11},R_{12},Q_1,Q_2) = 0$—or that type 1 agents do not hold money in equilibrium. This will be the case for all of the analysis below under laissez-faire banking. Henceforth, then, (S_{t+1}/S_t) will be notationally suppressed in discussions of laissez-faire banking. As will be seen momentarily, $\Phi_{13}(\ ) = 0$ will also hold. Hence, determination of an equilibrium can be depicted in figure III-2, in which R_1 and R_2 (rates of return in youth and old age) appear on the axes. The loci labeled $\pi_i = 0$ are the zero profit loci for deposit payoff vectors when type i deposits are held only by type i agents. And, finally, the loci labeled $EU_i = k_i$ are type i indifference curves in this space.

As argued above, since the rates of return offered type 2 agents are not affected by considerations of self-selection, (R_{21},R_{22}) occurs at point B in

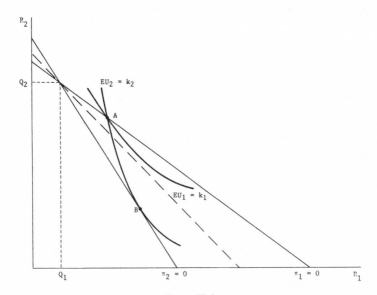

Figure III-2

the figure, where a type 2 indifference curve is tangent to the locus $\pi_2 = 0$. Then any pairs (R_{11}, R_{12}) on or below $EU_2 = k_2$ are consistent with self-selection, and such pairs along $\pi_1 = 0$ break even. The most preferred such pair (from the point of view of type 1 agents) occurs at point A, where $EU_2 = k_2$ intersects $\pi_1 = 0$. Notice, then, that $\Phi_{13} = 0$, or that type 1 agents make no use of storage themselves. This is the case since (as is readily verified) the locus $\pi_1 = 0$ and the locus $\pi_2 = 0$ intersect at the point (Q_1, Q_2). Then point A dominates storage, and also it clearly dominates convex combinations of itself and storage. Thus, no agents other than banks make use of storage opportunities.

Having discussed what an equilibrium looks like (if it exists), it is now appropriate to devote some attention to existence issues. The economy depicted in figure III-2 is one in which an equilibrium exists. To see this, note that since all banks announce the deposit payoff vectors denoted A and B, no single bank could offer a profitable deposit payoff vector that attracts any depositors. In particular, clearly no payoff vector exists that is preferred to B by type 2 agents and that earns a profit when it attracts only those agents. Also, any payoff vector that is profitable when accepted by only type 1 agents and that is preferred by such agents to A also attracts type 2 agents. Hence, if any incentive exists to offer payoff vectors other than A and B, it involves offering a payoff vector that attracts all agents (and, in particular, all agents in their population proportions). However, for such a payoff vector to (at least) break even, it must lie on or below $\bar{\pi} = 0$ [which is the locus of (R_1, R_2) pairs satisfying (12b)]. But since A is preferred to all such payoff vectors,[13] there is no alternate payoff vector that attracts any agents and that earns a profit given the agents it attracts. Hence, the situation depicted is an equilibrium.

The situation just described is reversed in figure III-3. In particular, the type 1 indifference curve through point A now intersects the locus $\bar{\pi} = 0$. Hence there are now points such as C that are preferred to A and B by all agents and that at least break even given the agents they attract. Therefore, A and B no longer constitute Nash equilibrium payoff vectors.

Figure III-4 is an enlargement of the area around point C. If any equilibrium could arise with pooling of agents, it would have to involve all banks offering a payoff vector that occurred where a type 1 indifference curve is tangent to the locus $\bar{\pi} = 0$.[14] However, no such point could be an equilibrium. In particular, if all banks were to offer C, then some bank could offer a payoff vector such as D. This offer attracts only type 1 agents. Hence, if D is selected sufficiently close to C, it earns a profit (since C breaks even when it attracts all agents). Therefore, no Nash equilibrium exists here.

Before concluding this section, let us note two things. First, no Nash equilibrium exists when competition among banks for depositors (through

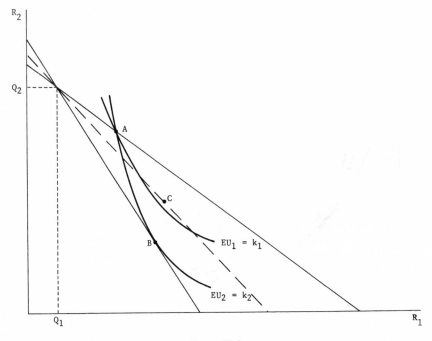

Figure III-3

deposit interest rates) prevents any bank from structuring its set of deposit interest rates in such a way that it can prevent other banks from attracting away its "best" depositors, and thereby causing it to "fail." This is the description of bank instability provided by contemporaries during all banking panics in the United States from 1857 onward. Hence, the failure of a Nash equilibrium to exist under laissez-faire banking coincides with the description of banking system instability that was current prior to 1933. Nonexistence, then, may be interpreted as instability of the banking system.[15]

Second, this instability can be overcome by the imposition of a ceiling on interest rates. In particular, let R_c be the level of R_2 associated with point C. If $R_{ij} \leq R_c \, \forall \, i, \, j$ (when nonexistence is a problem), then a Nash equilibrium (in pure strategies) always exists here.[16] Such a ceiling results in point C being an equilibrium when bank instability arises, and in the standard Nash equilibrium otherwise (since no ceiling is imposed). However, there are other regulatory interventions, such as 100 percent reserve requirements, that can also overcome existence problems. Some welfare comparison of such interventions is undertaken below.

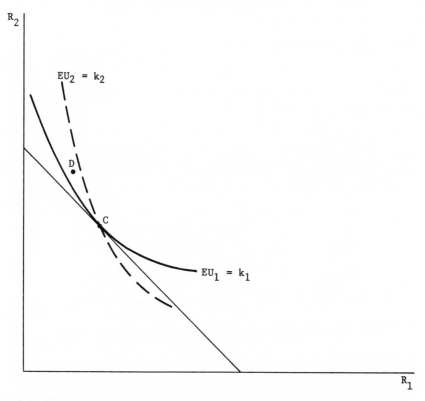

Figure III-4

4. Banking under a Quantity Theory Regime

This section examines banking when banks are required to hold 100 percent reserves against deposits in the form of noninterest-bearing government liabilities (fiat money). Throughout, the focus is on steady states, so $S_{t+1} = S_t$, and S_{t+1}/S_t is henceforth suppressed in notation. Also, to distinguish equilibrium interest rates under a quantity theory regime from laissez-faire interest rates, here (r_{i1}, r_{i2}) denotes the deposit payoff vector offered to type i agents.

The economy is exactly as described above, except now when agents deposit some units of the good with a bank, the bank uses this good to purchase money from the current old or from other banks. The assumption that all payoff vectors must at least break even individually is retained, so the analog of (12) here is

$$p_i r_{i1} + (1 - p_i)r_{i2} \leq 1; i = 1, 2, \quad \text{if} \quad (r_{11},r_{12}) \neq (r_{21},r_{22}) \quad (17a)$$

$$(\theta_1 + \theta_2)^{-1}\{(\theta_1 p_1 + \theta_2 p_2)r_{i1}$$
$$+ [\theta_1(1 - p_1) + \theta_2(1 - p_2)]r_{i2}\} \leq 1 \text{ otherwise.} \quad (17b)$$

Again, banks may attempt to induce either separation or pooling of depositors by types. The former requires

$$W_i(r_{i1},r_{i2},Q_1,Q_2) \geq V_i(r_{k1},r_{k2},Q_1,Q_2); i, k = 1, 2; i \neq k \quad (18)$$

whenever $(r_{11},r_{12}) \neq (r_{21},r_{22})$, where $W_i(\ )$ and $V_i(\ )$ are as previously defined. Finally, a Nash equilibrium concept is again imposed on the game played by banks. Hence,

DEFINITION. A steady-state Nash equilibrium is a set of announcements $(r_{11},r_{12},r_{21},r_{22})$ and a constant sequence $\{S_t\}$ such that

    (v) given the sequence $\{S_t\}$, no bank has an incentive to offer a different return vector;[17]

    (vi) the return vector satisfies (17) and (18);

    (vii) the money market clears—i.e.,

$$\sum_{i=1}^{2} \theta_i[\Phi_{i1}(\ ) + \Phi_{i2}(\ )] = S_t M \ \forall \ t \geq 0. \quad (19)$$

Equation (19) represents money market clearing since, for each unit deposited with a bank (Φ_{i1}), a unit of real balances must be acquired by the bank, so that $\Sigma\theta_i\Phi_{i1}$ represents per capita bank demand for real balances. Again, as a convention, type 3 agents only hold money sold to them by agents at the end of their first period.

The features of this equilibrium are much as they were in Section 4. Specifically, similar existence problems arise, and also any equilibrium must involve separation of types. However, there are some differences, the most important of which is that (18) can hold with strict inequality $\forall \ i, k$; or, it is possible that private information does not impinge upon the determination of equilibrium return streams.

Because this implies that a more diverse set of possible outcomes can arise in equilibrium, as an expositional device it is perhaps easiest to present an example in which private information does matter. A more general graphic analysis follows.

An Example

EXAMPLE 1. For notational purposes, let $\mu_i = \theta_i/(\theta_1 + \theta_2); i = 1, 2$. Then let $\mu_1 = .84$ and $\mu_2 = .16$. [θ_3 can be chosen to guarantee satisfaction of (10).] Preferences of type 1 and 2 agents are given by $U(c) = \ln c$, while

$p_1 = 1/5$, $p_2 = 1/2$, $Q_1 = 3/4$, and $Q_2 = 2$. For purposes of exposition, it will be useful in this first example to describe determination of a quantity theory equilibrium in some detail. This determination begins by describing how type 1 and 2 agents choose their portfolios given rates of return on their various investment opportunities. Now type i agents receive the state contingent consumption levels given by (3). Hence, the Φ_{ik}; $k = 1, 2, 3$ solve the problem

$$\max p_i \ln[\Phi_{i1}r_{i1} + \Phi_{i2} + \Phi_{i3}Q_1] + (1 - p_i) \ln[\Phi_{i1}r_{i2} + \Phi_{i2} + \Phi_{i3}Q_2] \quad (20)$$

subject to $\Sigma_{k=1}^{3}\Phi_{ik} = 1$ and $0 \le \Phi_{ik} \le 1$, where the fact that $S_{t+1} = S_t$ in steady state has been employed.

The first point of note is that $\Phi_{i1}\Phi_{i2} = 0$; $i = 1, 2$. To see this, suppose otherwise and notice that the first-order conditions associated with (20) if $\Phi_{i1}\Phi_{i2} > 0$ can be manipulated to obtain

$$\frac{r_{i1} - Q_1}{1 - Q_1} = \frac{Q_2 - r_{i2}}{Q_2 - 1}. \quad (21)$$

Equation (21), in conjunction with (17a) (recall that separation of types must result in equilibrium), implies that $r_{i2} = 1$ (and hence that $r_{i1} = 1$). Hence, for $\Phi_{i1}\Phi_{i2} > 0$ to obtain, it is necessary that banks call out return vectors identical to the return on money. Since bank deposits and real balances would then be perfect substitutes, without loss of generality $\Phi_{i2} = 0$; $i = 1, 2$ could be chosen as a normalization. In addition, since banks can call out return vectors at least weakly preferred by all agents to the return on real balances, $\Phi_{i2} = 0$; $i = 1, 2$ in equilibrium. Thus, all money is held by banks here.

Given that $\Phi_{i2} = 0$ will hold for any equilibrium set of returns on deposits, the first-order condition for selection of Φ_{i3} (which implies Φ_{i1}, since $\Phi_{i1} = 1 - \Phi_{i3}$) is

$$\frac{p_i(r_{i1} - Q_1)}{\Phi_{i3}Q_1 + (1 - \Phi_{i3})r_{i1}} = \frac{(1 - p_i)(Q_2 - r_{i2})}{\Phi_{i3}Q_2 + (1 - \Phi_{i3})r_{i2}}; i = 1, 2. \quad (22)$$

This can be manipulated to obtain

$$\Phi_{i3}(r_{i1}, r_{i2}, Q_1, Q_2) = \frac{(1 - p_i)Q_2 r_{i1} + p_i Q_1 r_{i2} - r_{i1}r_{i2}}{(Q_2 - r_{i2})(r_{i1} - Q_1)}, \quad (23)$$

where throughout an interior optimum has been assumed.

Having derived optimal portfolios, the next step is to substitute (23) (using $\Phi_{i2} = 0$ and $\Phi_{i1} = 1 - \Phi_{i3}$) into utility functions to derive the functions $W_i(\ )$ defined by:

$$W_i(r_{i1}, r_{i2}, Q_1, Q_2) = p_i \ln\{[1 - \Phi_{i3}(r_{i1}, r_{i2}, Q_1, Q_2)]r_{i1} + \Phi_{i3}(\ )Q_1\}$$

$$+ (1 - p_i) \ln\{[1 - \Phi_{i3}(\ )]r_{i2} + \Phi_{i3}(\ )Q_2\}; \, i = 1, 2. \quad (24)$$

Now for the same reasons as previously, competition among banks for deposits, and the fact that considerations of private information do not impinge upon selection of (r_{21}, r_{22}), imply that (r_{21}, r_{22}) maximizes (24) (with $i = 2$) subject to (17a). Defining $\Psi_i \equiv Q_2((1 - p_i)/p_i) + Q_1$ and $\phi_i \equiv (1/p_i) - Q_1$, and given the form of $\Phi_{i3}(\ )$ in (23), maximization of (24) subject to (17a) is equivalent to the unconstrained problem

$$\max \ln\left(\frac{Q_2}{p_2} - \Psi_2 r_{22}\right) - p_2 \ln(Q_2 - r_{22})$$

$$- (1 - p_2) \ln\{\phi_2 - [(1 - p_2)/p_2]r_{22}\} \quad (25)$$

(subject, of course, to $r_{22} \in [0,(1/1 - p_2)]$). It is tedious but straightforward to show that at any value of r_{22} such that the first-order condition for r_{22} holds with equality, the second-order condition fails. Hence, a corner solution emerges for r_{22}, and it is easy to check that type 2 agents prefer $r_{22} = 0$ to $r_{22} = (1/1 - p_2)$. Thus, if an equilibrium exists, it has $(r_{21}, r_{22}) = [(1/p_2), 0]$.[18]

Next, it can be checked that considerations of self-selection do impinge on the determination of equilibrium values for (r_{11}, r_{12}). To see this, suppose the contrary. Using (23) in (24), using (17a), and supposing that (18) holds with strict inequality implies that r_{12} would solve

$$\max \ln\left(\frac{Q_1}{p_1} - \Psi_1 r_{12}\right) - p_1 \ln(Q_2 - r_{12})$$

$$- (1 - p_1) \ln\{\phi_1 - [(1 - p_1)/p_1]r_{12}\}; \, r_{12} \in [0, 1/(1 - p_1)]. \quad (26)$$

As before, a corner solution always results with $r_{12} = 0$. Then $r_{11} = (1/p_1)$, $r_{12} = 0$ would obtain. Consider portfolio choices, then. Using (23), $\Phi_{13} = .941$ and $\Phi_{23} = .8$. Then, type 2 agents receive state contingent consumption levels

$$c_{21} = (.8)Q_1 + (.2)r_{21} = (.8)(3/4) + (.2)(1/p_2) = 1$$

$$c_{22} = (.8)Q_2 = 1.6.$$

On the other hand, if these agents were to make type 1 deposits (which would require making type 1 portfolio choices), they would receive state contingent consumption levels

$$c_{21} = (.941)Q_1 + (.059)r_{11} = (.941)(3/4) + (.059)(1/p_1) = 1$$

$$c_{22} = (.941)Q_2 = 1.882.$$

Clearly, then, type 2 agents prefer to make type 1 deposits, contradicting that (18) holds.

Then (r_{11}, r_{12}) must be chosen so that type 2 agents do not prefer mimicking type 1 agents to making type 2 deposits. Using (23) and the fact that $r_{22} = 0$, it is easy to check that (for any parameter values) if type 2 agents make type 2 deposits, then $c_{21} = 1$ and $c_{22} = \Phi_{23}(\ )Q_2$. Therefore, the utility they realize in equilibrium is given by $p_2 \ln(1) + (1 - p_2) \ln(\Phi_{23}Q_2)$. Similarly, given (23) for $i = 1$, and given that mimicking type 1 agents involves type 2 agents making the same portfolio choices as do type 1 agents, state contingent consumption for both type 1 agents and type 2 agents who make type 1 deposits is given (if $\Phi_{13} < 1$) by

$$c_{11} = \frac{p_1(Q_2 r_{11} - Q_1 r_{12})}{Q_2 - r_{12}} \tag{27a}$$

$$c_{12} = \frac{(1 - p_1)(Q_2 r_{11} - Q_1 r_{12})}{r_{11} - Q_1} \tag{27b}$$

For sorting to occur, it is necessary that

$$(1 - p_2) \ln[Q_2 \Phi_{23}(\ )] \geq p_2 \ln\left[\frac{p_1(Q_2 r_{11} - Q_1 r_{12})}{Q_2 - r_{12}}\right]$$
$$+ (1 - p_2) \ln\left[\frac{(1 - p_1)(Q_2 r_{11} - Q_1 r_{12})}{r_{11} - Q_1}\right] \tag{28}$$

(again if $\Phi_{13} < 1$). Since if (28) did not hold with equality the contradiction derived above would occur, (28) at equality and (17a) for $i = 1$ determines the set of possible (r_{11}, r_{12}) pairs. The most preferred of these for type 1 agents is the equilibrium level of (r_{11}, r_{12}) if an equilibrium exists. Finally, it has been noted that only banks hold money. Hence, (19) requires that

$$\sum_{i=1}^{2} \theta_i \Phi_{i1}(r_{i1}, r_{i2}, Q_1, Q_2) = \sum_{i=1}^{2} \theta_i[1 - \Phi_{i3}(r_{i1}, r_{i2}, Q_1, Q_2)] = S_t M \ \forall t \geq 0. \tag{29}$$

For the example, then, multiplying both sides of (28) by 2 and exponentiating both sides, the resulting equation can be manipulated to obtain

$$(1.6)(2 - r_{12})(r_{11} - 3/4) = (4/25)[4r_{11}^2 + (9/16)r_{12}^2 - 3r_{11}r_{12}]. \tag{30}$$

Using (17a), which for the parameter values of the example becomes $r_{12} = (1 - p_1)^{-1} - p_1 r_{11}/(1 - p_1) = 1.25 - (.25)r_{11}$, the expression in (30) can be solved for $r_{11} = 3.426$. Using the zero profit condition, $r_{12} = .393$. Then, $\Phi_{13}(3.426, .393, .75, 2) = .975.$[19]

Finally, it remains to say something about existence issues. The same reasoning as in the previous section implies that an equilibrium will fail to exist if there exists a pooling arrangement that type 1 agents prefer to the separating payoff vectors discussed above. The return vector under pooling most preferred by type 1 agents maximizes $W_1(r_1,r_2,Q_1,Q_2)$ subject to (17b). As was the case for separating return vectors, the most preferred return vector under pooling involves a corner solution, or sets $r_1 = \bar{p}^{-1}$, $r_2 = 0$, where $(r_1,r_2) \equiv (r_{11},r_{12}) = (r_{21},r_{22})$, and where $\bar{p} \equiv \mu_1 p_1 + (1 - \mu_1)p_2$. Then using the portfolio choices dictated by (23), and for the parameter values above, $\Phi_{13}(\bar{p}^{-1},0,Q_1,Q_2) = .9828$, which implies (common) consumption values $c_1 = (.75)(.9828) + (.0172)\bar{p}^{-1} = .8065$, and $c_2 = 2(.9828) = 1.9656$. This compares with consumption levels $c_{11} = .817$, $c_{12} = 1.96$ under the separating arrangement. Now, $p_1 \ln(.817) + (1 - p_1) \ln(1.96) = .4979 > .4976 = p_1 \ln(.8065) + (1 - p_1) \ln(1.9656)$. Thus, for this example an equilibrium exists under 100 percent reserve requirements.

Before going on to discuss a more general graphic analysis, one further point about the example is worthy of note. A 100 percent reserve requirement does not simply convert banks into "money warehouses." In particular, although banks are forced to hold portfolios consisting only of money, deposits do not bear the same returns as money. In other words, bank deposits and money do not become redundant assets under 100 percent reserves; or, put yet another way, 100 percent reserve requirements do not eliminate the importance of banks in the resource allocation process when private information is present.

A Graphic Exposition

This section presents a graphic analysis of a quantity theory equilibrium. The presentation of this analysis should then make clear that the main features of Example 1 are completely general when self-selection constraints bind on choices of values (r_{11},r_{12}) by banks. Consider figure III-5. Consumption for type i agents ($i = 1,2$) when young (c_1) appears on the horizontal axis and old-age consumption (c_2) on the vertical axis. The point labeled (Q_1,Q_2) represents consumption under autarky (returns to storage), and the remainder of the diagram is interpreted as follows. The dashed lines labeled $\pi_i = 0$ are zero profit loci for payoff vectors on deposits held (only) by type i agents. Thus, the $\pi_i = 0$ loci are combinations of (r_{i1},r_{i2}) pairs satisfying (17a). Note, in particular, that these loci intersect the horizontal axis at the points $(p_i^{-1},0)$. Finally, the loci labeled $\bar{U}_i$ are type i indifference curves.

Consider first the determination of (r_{21},r_{22}). Type 2 agents realize a return of (Q_1,Q_2) on storage, and competition will force banks to call out a return (r_{21},r_{22}) on the locus $\pi_2 = 0$. Money earns return $(1,1)$ which is where

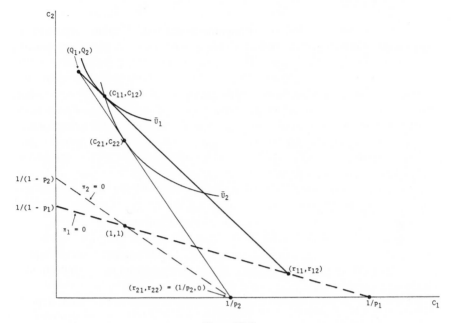

Figure III-5

$\pi_1 = 0$ intersects $\pi_2 = 0$. Suppose, then, that type 2 agents do not hold money. Their state contingent consumption levels can then be any convex combination of (Q_1, Q_2) and (r_{21}, r_{22}). The return vector (r_{21}, r_{22}) most preferred by type 2 agents, then, is the one that gives them the largest feasible consumption set. Since the relevant portion of this feasible set is just the line connecting (Q_1, Q_2) and (r_{21}, r_{22}), clearly these agents will prefer $(r_{21}, r_{22}) = (p_2^{-1}, 0)$ to all other return vectors. Hence, competition among banks produces this result in equilibrium. Notice also that the return on money $(1,1)$ lies in the interior of the feasible set for type 2 agents, so money is not held in their portfolios.

Given the announced returns on bank deposits, then, type 2 agents choose a portfolio such that a type 2 indifference curve is tangent to the feasibility frontier [the solid locus connecting (Q_1, Q_2) with $(p_2^{-1}, 0)$]. This is the point labeled (c_{21}, c_{22}), which represents the equilibrium level of state contingent consumption values for type 2 agents.

Now consider type 1 agents. It is easy to check that if $\Phi_{11}(\ ) > 0$, and if $r_{11} = p_1^{-1}$, then $c_{11} = 1$. Similarly, if $\Phi_{21}(\ ) > 0$, then $c_{21} = 1$. Hence, if $(r_{11}, r_{12}) = (p_1^{-1}, 0)$ (as type 1 agents would prefer under full information), it is clear from the diagram that $c_{12} > c_{22}$, so that (18) would be violated.[20] Hence, (r_{11}, r_{12}) must be chosen as follows. For (r_{11}, r_{12}) to be consistent with self-selection, (c_{11},c_{12}) must lie on (or below) $\bar{U}_2$. Also, the feasibility locus for type 1 agents will be the line connecting (Q_1,Q_2) and (r_{11},r_{12}). These agents will then choose a portfolio such that a type 1 indifference curve is tangent to the feasibility locus. Thus, (r_{11},r_{12}) must be chosen so that a tangency between a type 1 indifference curve and the feasibility locus occurs along $\bar{U}_2$. Such a choice then results in the state contingent consumption pair (c_{11},c_{12}) for type 1 agents as shown. Notice that (r_{11},r_{12}) will always be selected (if $\Phi_{11}(\ ) > 0$) so that r_{11} occurs to the southeast of the intersection of the line connecting (Q_1,Q_2) and $(p_2^{-1},0)$ with the locus $\pi_1 = 0$. Hence, $(1,1)$ lies strictly in the interior of the feasibility set for type 1 agents, so that again these agents do not hold real balances.

Existence issues could also be discussed here, but these are essentially the same as in the previous section. Thus a discussion of existence is omitted here.

5. A Comparison of Laissez-Faire and Quantity Theory Banking

There are a number of bases on which laissez-faire and quantity theory regimes might be compared. One is simply on the basis of a Pareto criterion, and another is on the basis of the possibility that 100 percent reserve requirements could correct problems of banking "instability." Both are considered here. Finally, it will be shown that even when 100 percent reserve requirements do overcome stability problems, there may be superior means of accomplishing this.

A Pareto Comparison: An Example

As a reader of Simons (1948) will recognize, the analysis here contains a number of elements mentioned by Simons in his arguments in favor of a 100 percent reserve regime. Nevertheless, there is no presumption here in favor of quantity theory banking on the basis of a Pareto criterion. This is now demonstrated through presentation of an example in which (except for the initial old) all agents prefer the laissez-faire regime and in which an equilibrium exists under each arrangement.

EXAMPLE 2. The economy is identical to that of Example 1, except that $\mu_2[= \theta_2/(\theta_1 + \theta_2)] = .5$. From previous arguments, under the laissez-faire equilibrium (if it exists), $R_{21} = R_{22} = p_2Q_1 + (1 - p_2)Q_2 = 1.375$. Then, the self-selection condition is

$$(1/2) \ln R_{11} + (1/2) \ln R_{12} = \ln(1.375).$$

Multiplying both sides by two, and then exponentiating both sides, the self-selection condition becomes $R_{11}R_{12} = (1.375)^2$. Also (R_{11},R_{12}) must satisfy the zero profit condition, which requires $p_1 R_{11} + (1 - p_1)R_{12} = p_1 Q_1 + (1 - p_1)Q_2$, or

$$R_{12} = [1/(1 - p_1)][p_1 Q_1 + (1 - p_1)Q_2] - [p_1/(1 - p_1)]R_{11}.$$

Solving this along with $R_{11}R_{12} = (1.375)^2$ results in $R_{11} = .973$, $R_{12} = 1.944$. These are the candidate values for a separating equilibrium. Finally, notice that this equilibrium does exist. To see this, note that the most preferred pooling arrangement for type 1 agents solves

$$\max (1/5) \ln(R_1) + (4/5) \ln(R_2) \tag{31}$$

subject to

$$\bar{p}R_1 + (1 - \bar{p})R_2 = \bar{p}Q_1 + (1 - \bar{p})Q_2, \tag{32}$$

where $\bar{p} = \mu_1 p_1 + \mu_2 p_2$. The solution has $R_1 = .89$ and $R_2 = 1.92$. (At these returns, it is easy to check that type 1 agents do not hold money; or, in other words, $\Phi_{11} = 1$.) Then clearly the candidate separating arrangement dominates any pooling arrangement (from the viewpoint of type 1 agents), so that an equilibrium exists as claimed.

Now consider a quantity theory regime. The candidate values for a separating equilibrium, which were computed in Example 1 above, were $(r_{21}, r_{22}) = (2, 0)$ and $(r_{11}, r_{12}) = (3.426, .393)$. Notice that this arrangement dominates autarky, as $\Phi_{i1} > 0$; $i = 1, 2$. Finally, an equilibrium exists here, since, as is easily checked, for $\mu_2 \geq 2/9$, the most preferred pooling arrangement for type 1 agents is the autarky arrangement. Thus, an equilibrium exists under both laissez-faire and quantity theory regimes here.

Now compute expected utilities under the laissez-faire and quantity theory arrangements. These are

$$W_2(R_{21}, R_{22}, Q_1, Q_2) = \ln(1.375)$$

$$W_2(r_{21}, r_{22}, Q_1, Q_2) = (1/2) \ln[2\Phi_{23}(\ )] = \ln(1.265)$$

$$W_1(R_{11}, R_{12}, Q_1, Q_2) = (1/5) \ln(.973) + (4/5) \ln(1.944) = .527$$

$$W_1(r_{11}, r_{12}, Q_1, Q_2) = (1/5) \ln(.817) + (4/5) \ln(1.96) = .498.$$

Thus, all agents except the initial old prefer the laissez-faire regime.[21] Then, ignoring the initial old, laissez-faire banking Pareto-dominates quantity theory banking.

Banking System Stability

It is the case, however, that even for an economy quite similar to that of Example 2, 100 percent reserve requirements can eliminate instability in the banking system. This is the point of the next example.

EXAMPLE 3. The economy is identical to that of Example 1. It has already been shown that an equilibrium exists with 100 percent reserve requirements. Also, the discussion of Example 2 computed the candidate for a separating equilibrium under laissez-faire banking. Now, however, with $\mu_2 = .16$, the solution to (31) subject to (32) has $R_1 = 1.36$ and $R_2 = 1.798$. This results in expected utility (for type 1 agents) of $p_1 \ln(1.36) + (1 - p_1) \ln(1.798) = .531 > p_1 \ln(R_{11}) + (1 - p_1) \ln(R_{12}) = (1/5) \ln(.973) + (4/5) \ln(1.944) = .527$. Hence, the situation depicted in figure III-3 exists here, and no equilibrium exists under laissez-faire banking. Given the interpretation of such nonexistence as banking instability, then, a 100 percent reserve regime can eliminate such instability, as Simons suggested.

A Comparison of Regulatory Regimes

As pointed out in Section 3, this instability could also be corrected by imposition of an interest rate ceiling. Then $(R_{i1},R_{i2}) = (1.36,1.798)$; $i = 1, 2$ would result under an appropriately set ceiling. As the situation in Example 3 under laissez-faire is depicted in figure III-3, clearly $W_i(1.36,1.798,Q_1,Q_2) > W_i(R_{i1},R_{i2},Q_1,Q_2)$; $i = 1, 2$, where (R_{i1},R_{i2}); $i = 1, 2$ are the values derived in Example 2 above. Also, as shown in the discussion of Example 2, $W_i(R_{i1},R_{i2},Q_1,Q_2) > W_i(r_{i1},r_{i2},Q_1,Q_2)$; $i = 1, 2$. Hence, ignoring the initial old,[22] the regulatory intervention of setting an interest rate ceiling Pareto-dominates that of setting 100 percent reserve requirements as a means of eliminating bank instability for this example.[23]

6. An Economy with Investment Opportunities Varying across Types

Suppose now that there is some relationship between the probability of first-period withdrawal and access to investment opportunities. In particular, a type i agent (and only a type i agent) can invest in storage that yields gross return Q_{i1} if goods are withdrawn from storage in period 1 and Q_{i2} if they are stored for two periods. Again, $Q_{i1} < 1 < Q_{i2}$; $i = 1, 2$, and all other features of the economy are as previously. Then the analysis done above goes through as previously with an obvious modification of notation and a few minor modifications of results. The most obvious of these are that now, under laissez-faire banking, type 1 agents can be forced into an autarky situation, as will be seen below, and that self-selection constraints need not bind in a quantity theory equilibrium even if type 1 agents do make deposits.

Also, this change in economic environment permits some modification of the way in which banking is interpreted here. In particular, under laissez-faire banking, banks could be thought of as accepting deposits from type i

agents and then investing in type i (storage) "projects." Hence, for a type 2 agent to claim to have a type 1 project in which a bank might invest, for instance, it is necessary that the type 2 agent also make a type 1 deposit. Notice, then, that in a sense there is now private information here about both investment opportunities and an agent's characteristics as a depositor. Thus, private information now impinges upon investment, although in a very simple way.

An example is now produced in which the following two possibilities are demonstrated: (a) type 1 agents prefer the quantity theory regime to the laissez-faire regime, and (b) money is valued under a quantity theory regime but does not have value either under laissez-faire banking or if banking is prohibited altogether. Notice, then, that in this economy there can be no role for fiat money unless there are banks (which face nontrivial reserve requirements).

EXAMPLE 4. Let preferences be as in Example 1, and let $p_1 = 1/4$, $p_2 = .35$, $Q_{21} = 1/2$, $Q_{22} = 5/2$, $Q_{11} = 9/10$, and $Q_{12} = 16/3$. There are now three cases to consider.

Laissez-faire banking. Laissez-faire banking here works largely as before. Private information does not impinge on the deposit payoff vector faced by type 2 agents. Hence, these agents receive complete insurance—or, $R_{21} = R_{22} = p_2 Q_{21} + (1 - p_2)Q_{22} = 1.8$. Notice, then, that these agents do not hold money. Also, type 2 agents receive expected utility equal to $\ln(1.8)$ under laissez-faire banking. Now $p_2 \ln(Q_{11}) + (1 - p_2) \ln(Q_{12}) = (.35) \ln(9/10) + (.65) \ln(16/3) > .588 = \ln(1.8)$. Therefore, type 2 agents would claim to be type 1 agents if they could receive even their autarky returns. Hence, type 1 agents cannot deal with banks in any laissez-faire equilibrium (if one exists). Type 1 agents might conceivably hold money, however. Let τ_1 denote the fraction of their portfolio held in storage. Then (since real balances would earn return $(1, 1)$ in steady state), τ_1 solves

$$\max_{0 \le \tau_1 \le 1} p_1 \ln[\tau_1 Q_{11} + (1 - \tau_1)] + (1 - p_1) \ln[\tau_1 Q_{12} + (1 - \tau_1)].$$

Then

$$\tau_1 = \frac{(1 - p_1)(Q_{12} - 1) - p_1(1 - Q_{11})}{(1 - Q_{11})(Q_{12} - 1)} \tag{33}$$

if the right-hand side lies in the unit interval, and $\tau_1 = 1$ if the right-hand side exceeds one. For the parameters of the example this is the case, so $\tau_1 = 1$. Finally, notice that there is some critical value μ_2^* here such that a laissez-faire equilibrium exists if $\mu_2 \ge \mu_2^*$ and fails to exist if $\mu_2 < \mu_2^*$. If a laissez-faire equilibrium does exist, money fails to have value under it.

Banking prohibited. Suppose all banking is prohibited. Then type 1 agents, as noted above, do not hold money. The analog of (33) for type 2 agents is

$$\tau_2 = \frac{(1 - p_2)(Q_{22} - 1) - p_2(1 - Q_{21})}{(1 - Q_{21})(Q_{22} - 1)} \tag{34}$$

if the right-hand side lies in the unit interval, etc., where τ_2 is the fraction of the portfolio of type 2 agents held in storage. Again, for the parameters of the example the right-hand side of (34) exceeds one, so $\tau_2 = 1$ here. Thus, even under a situation where banking is prohibited altogether, money does not have value in this economy.

Quantity theory banking. Again, quantity theory banking works much as previously. In particular, $r_{21} = p_2^{-1}$, $r_{22} = 0$. Using expression (23), then, the fraction of type 2 portfolios held in storage is

$$\Phi_{23} = \frac{(1 - p_2)Q_{22}r_{21}}{Q_{22}(r_{21} - Q_{21})} = .787.$$

Then type 2 agents receive state contingent consumption levels

$$c_{21} = (.787)(1/2) + (1 - .787)\left(\frac{1}{.35}\right) = 1$$

$$c_{22} = (.787)(5/2) = 1.9675.$$

This results in expected type 2 utility $(.65) \ln(1.9675) = .44$.

Now suppose that self-selection conditions do not bind on the determination of (r_{11}, r_{12}). Then, as previously, $r_{11} = p_1^{-1}$, $r_{12} = 0$ would result. Thus (23) would imply that

$$\Phi_{13} = \frac{(1 - p_1)r_{11}Q_{12}}{Q_{12}(r_{11} - Q_{11})} = .968.$$

Then if type 2 agents were to mimic type 1 agents, they would obtain state contingent consumption levels

$$c_1 = (.968)(1/2) + 4(1 - .968) = .612$$

$$c_2 = (.968)(5/2) = 2.42.$$

This results in expected type 2 utility $(.35) \ln(.612) + (.65) \ln(2.42) = .402$. Hence, it is incentive compatible to set $(r_{11}, r_{12}) = (p_1^{-1}, 0)$, so that private information does not affect the determination of deposit payoff vectors in a quantity theory equilibrium. Further, this implies that a quantity theory equilibrium exists here.

Several features of the example can now be noted. First, if an equilibrium exists under laissez-faire banking, the equilibrium has the feature that money does not have value. Similarly, if banking is prohibited money does not have value. Thus, a banking system with reserve requirements is a prerequisite for the valuation of fiat money here. Or, put otherwise, there can be no role in this economy for money unless there are banks. This can also be viewed as a validation of the claim that without reserve requirements the government will "lose control" of the process of money creation.

Second, if $\mu_2 < \mu_2^*$, no equilibrium exists under laissez-faire banking. Thus, 100 percent reserve requirements serve to stabilize the banking system here, as the magnitude of μ_2 is irrelevant to existence of an equilibrium under quantity theory banking.

Third, type 1 agents clearly prefer the quantity theory equilibrium to autarky (as autarky is feasible for them). Because these agents face autarky under laissez-faire banking, they therefore prefer the quantity theory regime to the laissez-faire regime. So do the initial old, since their money holdings have value under a quantity theory regime and only under such a regime. Thus, there are now agents with a preference for 100 percent reserve requirements (in contrast to the earlier examples).

7. Conclusions

Recent literature has emphasized that, in the absence of frictions, banking is not a special activity.[24] In particular, banking is not a special candidate for government regulation. To make sense of the arguments of Smith (1776) or Simons (1948), for instance, that various kinds of banking activities should be encouraged or discouraged, then, it is necessary to introduce frictions of some sort. In light of recent developments in the theory of financial intermediation, it is natural to introduce private information into a model with a real role for such intermediaries. Moreover, private information as a source of frictions seems consistent with the discussions of Smith (1776) and Simons (1948).

When there is a real role for financial intermediaries in the resource allocation process, a 100 percent reserve regime does not simply convert banks into money warehouses. Even under a 100 percent reserve regime, bank deposits and money bear different rates of return. Hence, such a proposal does not eliminate an economically meaningful role for banks. Moreover, when investors possess private information about the nature of their projects (as in Section 6 above), investors with access to the most lucrative investment opportunities may prefer a 100 percent reserve regime. Hence, economic arguments may be made in favor of such an intervention. The analysis above suggests that these need to be based on the possession of private information by both depositors (ultimate lenders) and investors (ultimate borrowers).

More generally, though, when only depositors are possessed of private information it is more difficult to construct a case for a 100 percent reserve regime. For instance, it is true that for some economies an equilibrium exists under quantity theory but not under laissez-faire banking. Moreover, this may be given an interpretation in terms of the stability of the banking system. However, there are always other regulatory interventions that result in existence of an equilibrium and that result in a Pareto-superior (except for the initial old in the model) allocation of resources. This is the case even though the model seems to possess the important features emphasized by Simons (1948) in his discussion of 100 percent reserve requirements.

Finally, one conclusion that emerges from the analysis is that it matters a great deal for different regulatory proposals who is endowed with private information. In particular, as seen in Section 6, even a very simple introduction of private information regarding access to investment opportunities changes conclusions related to the desirability of a 100 percent reserve regime. Although such an introduction has been accomplished in only the most rudimentary way here, the results strongly suggest that future analyses of the real bills-quantity theory debate should consider different possibilities regarding the presence of private information and the specific manner in which private information enters the analysis.

Notes

1. The research described in this paper was supported by the Federal Reserve Bank of Minneapolis. The views expressed herein are solely those of the author and do not necessarily represent the views of that institution or of the Federal Reserve System. I have benefited in writing this paper from discussions with David Laidler, Thomas Sargent, and Neil Wallace. None of these individuals bears responsibility for the contents, however.

2. See, e.g., Kareken and Wallace (1978) or Fama (1980).

3. Preferences of this or of similar forms are widely employed in the literature on banking with private information; see, e.g., Diamond and Dybvig (1983), King and Haubrich (1983), or Smith (1984).

4. Say, for instance, that individuals learn they will only live one period at the end of the period.

5. It is also assumed that once goods are in storage, they cannot be transferred between agents.

6. Subject to a restriction to be discussed below.

7. See, e.g., Diamond and Dybvig (1983).

8. Diamond and Dybvig (1983) or Jacklin (1983).

9. This argument requires that type 3 agents have enough resources in the aggregate so that they can lend banks enough to tide them over even if all agents (except one) choose to withdraw at the end of their initial period. The condition that would permit this (under full information) is $[(1 - p_1)\theta_1 + (1 - p_2)\theta_2](Q_2 - Q_1) \leq \theta_3$. This condition in turn implies (6).

Under private information below, an even weaker condition suffices to prevent runs, so that these can never occur in the model if the condition above is assumed.

10. See, e.g., Rothschild and Stiglitz (1976) or Wilson (1977).

11. See Smith (1984) for a formal demonstration.

12. In steady state these agents are indifferent regarding their portfolio composition, so this convention is just a device for avoiding price level indeterminacy.

13. Formally, $W_1(R_{11}, R_{12}, Q_1, Q_2) > W_1(R_1, R_2, Q_1, Q_2)$ for any values (R_1, R_2) satisfying (12b).

14. For the same reason as before, $\Phi_{i3} = 0$; $i = 1, 2$ (i.e., there is no private storage). Also, previous assumptions on parameters imply that $\Phi_{12} = 0$, i.e., type 1 agents do not hold money here. Thus, the discussion in the text is accurate.

15. A more detailed version of this argument appears in Smith (1984).

16. See Smith (1984).

17. Subject, of course, to (17) and (18).

18. The reason for this will be easy to see when a graphic version of the analysis is presented below.

19. Of course, there is always one other equilibrium in which $S_t = 0 \; \forall \; t$. Then agents face the autarky situation described in Section 3. This equilibrium is not of interest here, however, and is not discussed further.

20. This is an argument that (18) holds with equality unless some set of agents prefers autarky to making deposits under the quantity theory regime. This result depends upon the assumption of logarithmic utility, however.

21. The initial old prefer the quantity theory regime since under it their money holdings are valued; under laissez-faire, $S_t = 0 \; \forall \; t$.

22. Whose money holdings would have value under a quantity theory regime.

23. It is straightforward to show that, so long as an equilibrium exists under the quantity theory regime, this result is general in the model where all agents have identical investment opportunities.

24. See, e.g., Kareken and Wallace (1978) or Fama (1980).

References

Boyd, J. H., and E. C. Prescott. 1984. "Financial Intermediaries." Working paper 231, Federal Reserve Bank of Minneapolis.

Diamond, D. W., and P. H. Dybvig. 1983. "Bank Runs, Deposit Insurance, and Liquidity." *Journal of Political Economy* 91:401–19.

Fama, E. F. 1980. "Banking in the Theory of Finance. *Journal of Monetary Economics* 6:39–58.

Jacklin, C. J. 1983. "Information and the Choice between Deposit and Equity Contracts." Unpublished paper, Graduate School of Business, University of Chicago.

Kareken, J. H., and N. Wallace. 1978. "Deposit Insurance and Bank Regulation: A Partial-Equilibrium Exposition." *Journal of Business* 51:413–38.

King, R., and J. Haubrich. 1983. "Banking and Insurance." Unpublished paper, University of Rochester.

Rothschild, M., and J. Stiglitz. 1976. "Equilibrium in Competitive Insurance Markets: The Economics of Incomplete Information." *Quarterly Journal of Economics* 90:629–60.

Sargent, T. J., and N. Wallace. 1982. "The Real Bills Doctrine versus the Quantity Theory: A Reconsideration." *Journal of Political Economy* 90:1212–36.

Simons, H. C. 1948. *Economic Policy for a Free Society.* Chicago: University of Chicago Press.

Smith, A. [1776] 1937. *The Wealth of Nations*. Reprint. New York: Modern Library.
Smith, B. D. 1984. "Private Information, Deposit Interest Rates, and the 'Stability' of the Banking System." Working paper 228, Federal Reserve Bank of Minneapolis.
Wilson, C. 1977. "A Model of Insurance Markets with Incomplete Information." *Journal of Economic Theory* 16:167–207.

IV

Dealerships, Trading Externalities, and General Equilibrium

Sudipto Bhattacharya and
Kathleen Hagerty

A model of intermediated production-exchange equilibrium with constraints on trading capacity and "search" externalities is developed. The impact of *specialization* of agents into producers and dealers on the properties of equilibrium, in particular its uniqueness and welfare characteristics, is examined.

1. Introduction

In an important recent paper, Diamond (1982) has analyzed production-exchange equilibria in a model of search.[1] Trading "externalities" in this model arise from the specification that the likelihood of consummating trade per period is monotonically related to the proportion of agents having goods to trade. The probability of trading per period in turn feeds back to determine agents' optimal production decisions. Diamond shows that this combination of the trading externality and the feedback effect can create a multiplicity of Nash equilibria, which are ordered in welfare and employment levels by the Pareto criterion. In Diamond (1982) and Diamond and Fudenberg (1982), the static and dynamic properties of such an environment are developed and the role of macroeconomic policy in facilitating transitions to Pareto-superior equilibria, is examined in detail. These models appear to have the intent of providing a microfoundation for Keynesian macroeconomic conclusions.

The Diamond (1982) story is an abstract model of an economy in which the problems of coordinating transactions—that is, ensuring that two traders who meet have goods to exchange—are nontrivial. This is because of the time-consuming nature of the trade/matching process. Although both Diamond (1982) and Diamond and Yellin (1983) have emphasized that transactions occur only at meetings between a buyer and a seller selected at random, we believe the crucial feature is that agents who have potential gains from trade do not know whether they currently do or not. As a result, pairing among agents results in a probability of trade that is increasing in the proportion of those who have already produced goods for trade. For tractability in modeling, in particular to avoid multigood inventory problems, exchange is modeled through a convention that an agent can only consume units of a homogeneous good produced by others.

In the Diamond (1982) model, the problem of trading externalities is coupled with a strong symmetry assumption that the two trading agents are producers who, if they have goods, exchange them at an exogenously given trading ratio of unity. As an abstraction of empirically relevant phenomena that these models might intend to capture, this assumption is not entirely satisfactory. Many conceptions of trading processes result in localized markets in which agents trade with small subsets of the economy, rather than in a central, auctioneer-run Walrasian market, as a result of imperfect information or locational proximity (e.g., Townsend 1982). In addition, the "real world" is also characterized by a great deal of specialization of agents, in particular into those who produce and those who serve as dealers or intermediaries facilitating the trading process. The implications of such specialization for the qualitative properties of search equilibria with trading externalities constitute the focus of this paper. The issues of multiplicity of Pareto-ordered equilibria and welfare-optimal government intervention are of particular interest.

In our model, all trade is intermediated through dealers. A dealer's profit is determined by two factors—the price charged and the market size. Because we employ the Diamond setup, where identical commodities are exchanged, the dealer's net gain per trade is given as a bid-ask spread. The bid-ask spread is the difference between the amount of the good given to the dealer and the fraction of the good received by the producer in return. At any given time, the dealer only needs to have an inventory equaling a single unit of the good less the bid-ask spread. In addition to choosing the spreads, dealers also choose the size of their market, which in turn determines the effectiveness of the dealer as an intermediary.[2] The larger a dealer's market, the lower the level of service offered a customer. Dealers compete with each other (and potential entrants) by their choice of the spread and clientele size. We also assume that anyone can be a dealer or a producer, so the equilibrium has the feature that agents are indifferent between being a producer or a dealer.

This formulation introduces a potential role for prices in mitigating trading externalities because a producer's decision about how hard to work is now determined by two endogenously determined variables—the bid-ask spread and the probability of a trade; in Diamond's model, only the probability of a trade mattered. Dealers and producers are assumed to maximize their lifetime discounted expected utility, taking as given the terms and production decisions of one another, as well as the competitive constraints arising from potential entry. We explicitly compare the conditions for a unique equilibrium in our model with the uniqueness conditions for the symmetric-trading model of Diamond (1982). We find that the conditions are very similar.

Our model also inherits the welfare properties of Diamond (1982). It remains the case that the Pareto-supreme Nash equilibrium in our model is not ex ante incentive-efficient (Myerson 1979), and subsidization of trade can improve an equally weighted sum of expected utilities, as in Diamond (1982). Somewhat surprisingly, despite the greater complexity of our model, we are able to provide a fairly complete global characterization of such welfare-optimal interventions. This provides us with the value of the bid-ask spread and some insight into what the optimal ratio of dealers to producers should be.

The relationship of our work to several recent papers in the literature bears discussion. Diamond and Yellin (1983) have looked at the questions of equilibrium price-setting by firms in a search model with nominal money. In contrast to the assumptions regarding dealers in our model, their firms are assumed to have no price reputations, and the only trade-offs on pricing policy arise from "Clower constraints" and the distribution of money holdings among consumers. Rubinstein and Wolinsky (1984) provide a sequential, noncooperative bargaining analysis of the Diamond (1982) model. Neither endogenous specialization nor endogenous levels of productive activity that in turn affect trading frequencies are present in these models. Thus, the questions addressed in this paper are absent in the analysis discussed above.

An early paper on search equilibrium with an endogenous number of intermediaries and price-setting was that of Mortensen (1976). In his model, potential employers and employees (rationally) randomly picked one exchange to list themselves with. Exchanges cleared at the reservation price of the side in short supply, with employment equaling the minimum of labor supply and demand at the exchange. A theory of the equilibrium number of exchanges was developed by assuming that each exchange has increasing marginal costs of listing as its clientele grows and that transaction services are priced at expected marginal cost. Mortensen then showed that the number of exchanges resulting from a free-entry equilibrium with fixed costs— which minimizes the total transaction costs—exceeds the welfare-optimal number. The reason was a negative externality exerted by an additional exchange on the probability of matching at other exchanges.

In our model, with its additional feature of positive trading externality arising from an increased number of dealers on producers, we find that private Nash equilibria involve too few dealers relative to the number of dealers implied by an equally weighted (incentive-compatible) welfare optimum. However, there may exist more complicated pricing schemes that—if implementable within the context of the dealer-producer "relationship"—might restore the constrained efficiency of equilibrium.

In Section 2, we set out the basic structure of our model and derive the equations characterizing Nash equilibria, as well as the comparable equations for the Diamond (1982) model. In Section 3, the uniqueness properties of the two types of equilibria—with or without specialized dealers—are derived and contrasted. Following that, in Section 4, we elaborate upon the welfare properties of our equilibria. In Section 5, which concludes the paper, we summarize our qualifications about the results and suggest directions for future research.

2. Description of Dealership Equilibrium

Modeling Postulates

As in Diamond (1982), we assume that all agents are infinite lived, ex ante identical, and risk neutral, with preferences represented by the lifetime utility function

$$W[\{X_t\}_{t=0}^{\infty}, \{C_t\}_{t=0}^{\infty}] = \sum_{t=1}^{\infty} \left(\frac{1}{1 + R}\right)^t (x_t - c_t). \tag{1}$$

Preferences are intertemporally additive with a discount factor $1/(1 + R)$, where x_t equals the quantity of the (homogeneous) good consumed and c_t is the cost/effort expended in producing goods in period t. Agents are assumed to face identically and independently distributed stochastic production opportunities, represented by the random variable $\tilde{c}$, with distribution function $G(c)$, which has one in the interior of its support. We assume that $G(c)$ is twice-differentiable. Faced with a realization c of $\tilde{c}$, each agent can choose either to produce a unit of the good with effort c or to forsake the opportunity and wait for the next-period draw. In both Diamond (1982) and here, the optimal decision turns out to be a "reservation cost" criterion c^*.

The consumption and production opportunities of agents are constrained in two ways. First, an agent who has already produced, and thus has an inventory of one unit can *not* consume his own good, but must exchange it for goods from another agent. Second, while an agent has a good, he cannot engage in further production until he has exchanged his good and consumed the sales proceeds. (Immediate consumption is strictly optimal because the utility function is linear and additively discounted.) The assumption that production cannot resume before a trade occurs simplifies the model enormously. The producer's problem now has only two state variables—an inventory level of one or zero. If we allow production to start without a trade occurring, there will be an infinite number of state variables. This simplification captures the qualitative feature we want, which is that a producer's effort decision depends upon the likelihood of a trade.

In our model, some proportion of agents becomes dealers, and this specialization permits them to meet with a greater number of agents per period than a producer could. Each dealer has a clientele of n producing agents who trade only through this dealer. The proportion of dealers in the population is $1/(n + 1)$. We define the trading technology in any period as a situation where a dealer randomly picks a client to visit, with probability $p = 1/n$. This captures the effect that the dealer becomes a lower quality intermediary as his market size increases. The assumptions that each producer trades only through a single dealer, and that dealers visit in a memory-independent fashion, are made for the sake of tractability. The former assumption enormously simplifies the calculation of trading probabilities given production decision, and the latter implies that each producer's optimal reservation cost c^*—production opportunities with $c \leq c^*$ are accepted—is stationary.

Besides deciding on the clientele size n, and thus the periodic visit probability $p = 1/n$, each dealer also chooses the bid-ask spread $(1 - q)$; each producer surrendering one unit of his production is given q units of the dealer's inventory, and the dealer promptly consumes $(1 - q)$ units of the good surrendered. Given the terms $\{p,q\}$ offered by the dealer that a producer chooses to be affiliated with, the producer chooses the reservation cost c^* to maximize discounted expected utility. We look for a symmetric Nash equilibrium in which all producers choose the same c^* and all dealers the same $\{p,q\}$, taking the choice of one another as given. In particular, this implies for each dealer contemplating an alternative offer $\{\hat{p},\hat{q}\}$ that, given the c^* induced by $\{p,q\}$, producers must not be made worse off by accepting the terms $\{\hat{p},\hat{q}\}$. Dealers choose $\{p,q\}$ to maximize their expected discounted utility subject to this competitive constraint. A symmetric Nash equilibrium with free entry satisfies the further constraint that, given the $\{p,q\}$ that is optimal conditional on entry, and the correspondingly optimal c^*, the discounted expected utilities of dealers and producers are the same.

Before proceeding to the detailed analytical formulation of the above conceptualization, we will comment further on the nature of competition across dealers in our model (producers do not need to take any account of other producers' choices). Conditional on entry decisions by a set of dealers, and on the producers' choices to affiliate with them, in what sense do dealers compete, especially when informational or locational knowledge/adjacency reasons have been used to motivate both bounded trading capacities and dealer-producer affiliation? In essence, after affiliation, the issue of ex post bargaining between dealers and producers might arise. However, this "imperfection" is ameliorated by the fact that other (producer) agents within a given location can also become dealers. Thus, if the terms offered by a dealer in location A do not match (in producer-expected utility) the terms offered by dealers in locations B, C, D, ..., then a producer in location A can become a dealer and, by offering the terms offered by dealers in the other locations, capture the A dealer's business. This is particularly true if going into the dealership occupation involves no sunk cost advantages—for example, if the knowledge of local agents' needs or attributes has to be renewed every period.

Maximizing Behavior and Competition

We now characterize the optimal actions of producers and competitive dealers in greater detail, using basic tools of dynamic programming. At the beginning of each period, a producer is either in the state of having a good (e) or not having a good (u), where $\{e,u\}$ constitute the state variables for the lifetime discounted expected utility values, W_e and W_u. During any given period, only one of two things may happen to a producer depending on his initial state. If he has an inventory of one good, he will be visited by his dealer with probability p; this results in trade and consumption of q units at the end of the period and transition to the zero inventory state. If he has no inventory, he will be engaged in exploring productive activities, which is modeled as drawing an i.i.d. sample c from the distribution $G(c)$. If $c \le c^*$, where c^* is the producer's reservation cost criterion, then there will be production and thus transition to the positive inventory state at the end of the period.[3] Thus, the dynamic programming value function satisfies the following recursion relationships:

$$W_u = \max_{c^*} \frac{1}{(1 + R)} \left[\int_0^{c^*} [W_e - c]dG(c) + (1 - G(c^*))W_u \right] \quad (2)$$

and

$$W_e = \frac{1}{(1 + R)} [p(q + W_u) + (1 - p)W_e],$$

or, equivalently, that

$$RW_e = p\{q + W_u - W_e\}. \quad (3)$$

The first-order conditions for (2) imply that

$$c^* = W_e - W_u. \quad (4)$$

The second order conditions can easily be verified from the complete solution.

Integrating equation (2) by parts, and using equation (4), we obtain

$$RW_u = \int_0^{c^*} G(c)dc. \tag{5}$$

Subtracting (5) from (3), and substituting from (4), we have

$$(R + p)c^* = pq - \int_0^{c^*} G(c)dc. \tag{6}$$

Equation (3) itself can be simplified, using (4), to give

$$W_e = \frac{p}{R}(q - c^*). \tag{7}$$

Equations (4), (6), and either (5) or (7) fully specify (c^*, W_e, W_u) given $\{p,q\}$, the competitively available "terms," which are determined through dealer utility maximization.

The lifetime discounted expected utility of a dealer offering terms $\{p,q\}$, and facing a producer reservation cost decision c^*, is denoted as $U_D(p,q;c^*)$. In each period, in a given random visit to one of his n clients (where $p = 1/n$), the dealer expects to make a trade with probability Π, which represents his subjective expectation that the visited producer will have goods to sell. Since the dealer makes these visits without foreknowledge of the agent's current state, and without memory as to when this randomly picked agent was last visited, his "rational" subjective probability of trade Π must satisfy

$$\Pi = \sum_{i=1}^{\infty} p(1 - p)^{i-1}[\{(1 - G(c^*))^{i-1}\}\Pi$$

$$+ \{1 - (1 - G(c^*))^i\}(1 - \Pi)]. \tag{8}$$

The basis for equation (8) requires some elaboration. The term $p(1 - p)^{i-1}$ represents the probability that this agent was last visited i periods back. At the time of that visit, the producer had a good to trade with probability Π, or did not have goods to trade with probability $(1 - \Pi)$; we are restricting ourselves to stationary states.[4] If the last visit did result in a trade, then the current one will also if the person has had a "good" production draw in any of the last $(i - 1)$ periods, which has the probability $[1 - (1 - G(c^*))^{i-1}]$. Finally, since the time of last visit is not known, the sum over i is taken, to arrive at the (stationary) probability of trade in a random visit.

Equation (8) can be simplified, using basic geometric series formulas, to yield

$$\Pi = 1 - \frac{\Pi_p}{[1 - (1 - p)(1 - G(c^*))]} - \frac{(1 - \Pi)p(1 - G(c^*))}{[1 - (1 - p)(1 - G(c^*))]}$$

$$= \frac{[G(c^*) - \Pi p G(c^*)]}{[1 - (1 - p)(1 - G(c^*))]}, \tag{9a}$$

or, on cross-multiplying and simplifying,

$$\Pi = \frac{G(c^*)}{[G(c^*) + p]}. \tag{9b}$$

Given (9b), it is easy to calculate the dealer's expected utility to be

$$U_D = \frac{(1 - q)\Pi}{R} = \frac{(1 - q)G(c^*)}{R[G(c^*) + p]}. \tag{10}$$

Note that U_D is decreasing in p, ceteris paribus, because of the lower likelihood of trade in each visit when the dealer has fewer clients and visits each more frequently (on average).

Armed with the above results, we are now in a position to complete the description of our model. We noted before that each dealer, who is subject to competition from potential entrants (in every location), can only maximize his utility subject to the competitive constraint that, given producers' (symmetric) production decisions and the reservation cost c^*, producers are at least as well off with this dealer's terms as with those of any other. The analytical formulation of this constraint is greatly simplified by noting the following key feature of the producers' utility-maximizing equations.

From equations (5) and (4), it is clear that the optimized expected discount lifetime utilities produced by a set of terms $\{p,q\}$ are monotonically related to the induced reservation cost criterion c^*. Thus, producers are indifferent between terms $\{p,q\}$ and $\{\hat{p},\hat{q}\}$ if both induce the same c^*. This means, given that other dealers are offering $\{p,q\}$, the dealers' competition constraint can be characterized as profit maximization over terms $\{\hat{p},\hat{q}\}$, which induce the same c^* that $\{p,q\}$ induce.

The following definition formalizes our notion of a symmetric Nash equilibrium with free entry among dealers and producers, which arises from (potential) competition.

DEFINITION. Dealership equilibrium is a triple $\{q,p,c^*\}$ and associated expected discounted utilities $U_D(q,p;c^*)$, $W_e(c^*;q,p)$, $W_u(c^*;q,p)$, defined in equations (10), (7), (5), which satisfy the following conditions:

(i) c^* maximizes each "unemployed" producer's expected discounted utility given $\{q,p\}$, and thus satisfies equation (6);

(ii) $\{q,p\}$ maximizes $U_D(\hat{q},\hat{p};c^*)$ given c^*, subject to the condition that

$$W_U(c^*;\hat{q},\hat{p}) \geq W_U(c^*;q,p),$$

i.e., that producers are at least as well off with $\{\hat{q},\hat{p}\}$ as with $\{q,p\}$; and

(iii) a dealer's lifetime discounted expected utility equals that of a producer with a good for sale, i.e.,

$$U_D(q,p;c^*) = W_e(c^*;q,p), \tag{11}$$

given the equilibrium proportion of dealers.

Existence of Dealership Equilibrium

As we noted just before the definition of equilibrium above, competition among dealers implies that the equilibrium $\{q,p,c^*\}$ must satisfy

$$\{q,p\} = \underset{\{\hat{q},\hat{p}\}}{\arg\max}\ U_D(\hat{q},\hat{p};c^*) \tag{12}$$

subject to

$$c^* = \frac{\hat{p}\hat{q} - \displaystyle\int_0^{c^*} G(c)dc}{(R + \hat{p})} = \frac{pq - \displaystyle\int_0^{c^*} G(c)dc}{(R + p)}, \tag{6}$$

or that the productive decision induced by $(\hat{q},\hat{p})$ is the same as that induced by (q,p). An interior solution to this dealer-maximization problem (subject to competition) is readily characterized by the equality of marginal rates of substitution over $\{q,p\}$ among dealers and producers, given the productive decision c^*. Using equation (10) and (9), we have:

$$\frac{\partial U_D/\partial p}{\partial U_D/\partial q} = \frac{(1 - q)}{[G(c^*) + p]} = \frac{\partial W_e/\partial p}{\partial W_e/\partial q}$$

$$= \frac{(q - c^*)}{p} = \frac{Rq + \displaystyle\int_0^{c^*} G(c)dc}{p(R + p)} \tag{13a}$$

where the last equality follows from equation (6). This is, of course, the necessary Lagrangean condition for the optimization problem (12) subject to (6), which is also sufficient here (given c^*), since the indifference curves in $\{q,p\}$ space are linear for dealer utility U_D and strictly convex for producer utility W_e, as is readily verified. Note that producer utilities increase in $\{q,p\}$ while dealer utilities decline.

Writing equation (13a), representing condition (ii) for a dealership equilibrium in the form

$$\frac{U_D}{G(c^*)} = \frac{W_e}{p^2} \tag{13b}$$

and combining with equation (11), the (free entry) condition (iii) provides a partial characterization of the equilibrium

$$p^2 = G(c^*). \tag{14}$$

Using equations (10) and (7), equation (11) can be expressed as

$$\frac{(1 - q)G(c^*)}{R[G(c^*) + p]} = \frac{p}{R}(q - c^*). \tag{11'}$$

Substituting for $G(c^*)$ in (11') using (14), we obtain

$$\frac{(1 - q)p^2}{R(p^2 + p)} = \frac{p}{R}(q - c^*),$$

which can be simplified to give

$$\frac{(1 - q)}{(1 + p)} = (q - c^*). \tag{15a}$$

Our goal in further simplification is to substitute for both p and q in terms of (functions of) c^* in (15a), using (14) and (6), to obtain an equation for equilibrium in c^* space. As the first step, (15a) is simplified and rewritten as

$$[1 + c^*(1 + p)] = (2 + p)q. \tag{15b}$$

Substituting for q in (15b) from (6), we obtain

$$[1 + c^*(1 + p)] = \left(\frac{2}{p} + 1\right)\left[(R + p)c^* + \int_0^{c^*} G(c)dc\right], \tag{15c}$$

which, on substitution for p from (14), gives our characteristic equation

$$1 = c^* + \left(\frac{2}{\sqrt{G(c^*)}} + 1\right)\left[Rc^* + \int_0^{c^*} G(c)dc\right]. \tag{16}$$

The strategy for computing an equilibrium is thus exceedingly simple; solve equations (16), (14), and (15a) sequentially. Note that a valid ($0 < c^* \le 1$) solution with $0 < G(c^*) < 1$ results in $0 < p < 1$ by (14) and, since $c^* < q$ by (6), (15a) will indeed provide a q satisfying $0 < q < 1$; in other words, domain restrictions are not a problem. Thus, to prove existence of an equilibrium, it is sufficient to find conditions such that (16) has a solution $c^* \in (0,1)$. The following result summarizes one such set of conditions.

PROPOSITION 1. *Suppose that the distribution function $G(c)$ is continuous, with support $[0,b]$ for $b \geq 1$, and that the right derivative (density) of $G(c)$ at $c = 0$ is strictly positive, $g(0) > 0$. Then a dealership equilibrium exists with $0 < c^* < 1$.*

PROOF. Simply note that in equation (16) the right-hand side (RHS) exceeds unity at $c^* = 1$ and that as $c^* \to 0$,

$$\lim_{c^* \to 0} \text{RHS (16)} = \lim_{c^* \to 0} \frac{4\{R + G(c^*)\}}{\left\{ \dfrac{g(c^*)}{\sqrt{G(c^*)}} \right\}} = 0,$$

where the middle equality is obtained using L'Hopital's Rule and (16). Thus, since RHS (16) is a continuous function that maps $[0,1]$ onto $[0,K]$ for some $K > 1$, there exists c^*, $0 < c^* < 1$, such that RHS (16) equals 1, which is a dealership equilibrium. Q.E.D.

Before proceeding to analyze questions of uniqueness of equilibrium in Section 3, we now set out a comparable characterization of equilibrium for a model of nonintermediated search.

Equilibria without Intermediation

It is instructive to compare the equations above with those for an equilibrium in Diamond (1982), which has nonintermediated search with no (endogenous) specialization of agents. To do so, we consider a parameterized version of the Diamond model, as follows. Now all agents are producers, and producers with goods conduct direct searches for other producers with goods. If e is the fraction of producers with a good in the population, then we assume that the probability of one of these producers meeting another one of these producers in any period is given by ey, where $0 \leq y \leq 1$ is an efficiency parameter that allows for the possibility of lower meeting frequencies.

A steady-state equilibrium in Diamond's model is characterized by a pair $\{e,c^*\}$ such that, with a large number of agents, the per-period change in e, Δe, satisfies

$$\Delta e = (1 - e)G(c^*) - e^2 y = 0. \tag{17}$$

Second, given e, c^* is utility maximizing for producers. The latter problem is solved by methods similar to those we used previously, to arrive at the solution $c^*(e)$ satisfying

$$ey(1 - c^*) = Rc^* + \int_0^{c^*} G(c)dc. \tag{18}$$

Note that (18) is very similar to (6), with (ey) replacing p and 1 replacing q, the payoff net of the bid-ask spread in our model. The optimal solution for the producers also satisfies conditions identical to equations (4) and (5) in our model; now the expected discounted lifetime utility functions V_u and V_e in the zero inventory and nonzero inventory states[5] are given by

$$RV_u = \int_0^{c^*} G(c)dc \tag{19a}$$

$$c^* = V_e - V_u. \tag{19b}$$

Thus, as is intuitively clear (for Diamond's model), multiple equilibria are Pareto-ordered in welfare levels, as they are in our model; and welfare comparisons across (equilibria in) Diamond's model and ours can also be made in terms of the induced c^* alone.

To characterize the Diamond equilibria further, let us solve for e in terms of c^* in (17) to obtain

$$e(c^*) = \frac{[-G(c^*) + \sqrt{G^2(c^*) + 4G(c^*)y}]}{2y}. \tag{17'}$$

Substituting from (17') in (18) gives us the characteristic equation for the equilibria of this model:

$$1 = c^* + \frac{2\left(Rc^* + \int_0^{c^*} G(c)dc\right)}{[-G(c^*) + \sqrt{G^2(c^*) + 4G(c^*)y}]}. \tag{20}$$

Using arguments similar to those used in Proposition 1 above, it is easy to establish the following existence result.

PROPOSITION 2. *Suppose that $G(c)$ is continuous, with support $[0,b]$ for $b \geq 1$, and that the density $g(0)$ is strictly positive. Then a Diamond equilibrium exists, with $0 < c^* < 1$.*

REMARK. Diamond (1982) shows existence of an equilibrium even without the assumption that $g(0) > 0$. Indeed, if the support of $G(c)$ is $[a,b]$ for $0 < a < 1$, and $b \gg 1$, then (20) necessarily has multiple solutions, including a "low level equilibrium trap" at c^* near a. Since we choose to ignore the trivial equilibrium $c^* = 0$, we do not wish to have our investigation of uniqueness below to hinge on equilibria arbitrarily close to the infimum of the support of $G(c)$.

We now consider the issues of uniqueness of equilibrium, as well as welfare efficiency, for the two models elaborated above.

3. Intermediation and Multiplicity of Equilibria

As we noted in Section 1, our reasons for being interested in an intermediated version of the Diamond (1982) model are twofold. On the one hand, we seek to explore the issue of the optimal number of intermediaries, and thus to extend the analysis of Mortensen (1976) to a scenario with trading externalities; this analysis is pursued in Section 4. On the other hand, we also wish to inquire whether the additional price-setting ($q \neq 1$), implied by specialization and intermediation, substantially alters the (sufficient) conditions required for a unique equilibrium relative to Diamond's symmetric, unintermediated model. The motivation for this question arises from the observation that the unique Walrasian equilibrium in Diamond's setup can be attained by a single dealer with unbounded trading capacity who acts as a Stackelberg leader subject to the threat of potential entry and sets $q \rightarrow 1$, implying $c^* \rightarrow 1$, as the number of traders $N \rightarrow \infty$. It is interesting to inquire whether the augmentation of strategy spaces by the bid-ask spread, as opposed to a drastically different equilibrium concept and trading capability, also improves on the multiplicity problem.

Our results on the uniqueness question are presented successively in propositions 3–5. First, we discuss (minimally sufficient) conditions that turn out to imply uniqueness in both models for any value of R. Second, we show that the weaker sufficient condition for uniqueness obtained as $R \rightarrow 0$ is also identical for the two models (Diamond's and ours). Both these results are based essentially on contraction mapping arguments—that the right-hand sides of equations (16) and (20) are monotonically increasing in c^*. In the last result, Proposition 5, we prove the sufficiency (in our model) of intermediate conditions, for moderate levels of R relative to the (first) equilibrium $G(c^*)$, by using the prior knowledge that the first intersection in (16) is from below. We have been unable to verify that these conditions are also sufficient for uniqueness of equilibrium in Diamond's model.

PROPOSITION 3. *Suppose that the density $g(c)$ satisfies $g(c)c \leq 2G(c)$, for all $c \in (\underline{c}^*, 1]$, where $\underline{c}^*$ is the first solution to the characteristic equation for equilibrium—in other words, equation (16) or (20). Then $\underline{c}^*$ is the unique equilibrium for both the Diamond and dealership models.*

PROOF. For our intermediated dealership equilibrium, we have upon differentiating equation (16) that

$$\frac{d\,\text{RHS}(16)}{dc^*} = [1 + R + G(c^*)] + \frac{2}{\sqrt{G(c^*)}}[R + G(c^*)]$$

$$- \frac{g(c^*)c^*\left[R + \left(\int_0^{c^*} G(c)dc\right)\Big/c^*\right]}{[G(c^*)]^{3/2}}. \qquad (21)$$

Since $G(c^*)$ appears in equation (21), we know that it will be impossible to rule out multiple equilibria for arbitrary distributions because locally the value of $g(c^*)$ cannot be restricted. Since $G(c)$ is monotonically increasing and has support $[0,b]$,

$$G(c^*) \geq \frac{\displaystyle\int_0^{c^*} G(c)dc}{c^*}. \qquad (22)$$

Hence, under the assumptions posited, $d\text{RHS}(16)/dc^* > 0$ for $1 \geq c^* \geq \underline{c}^*$, and thus there is no other solution to (16).

For the unintermediated (Diamond) equilibrium solution, equation (20), we again obtain upon differentiating,

$$\frac{d\,\text{RHS}(20)}{dc^*} = 1 + \frac{2[R + G(c^*)]}{[-G(c^*) + \sqrt{G^2(c^*) + 4G(c^*)y}]}$$

$$- \frac{g(c^*)c^*\left[R + \int_0^{c^*} G(c)dc/c^*\right]\left[-1 + \dfrac{\{G(c^*) + 2y\}}{\sqrt{G^2(c^*) + 4G(c^*)y}}\right]}{[-G(c^*) + \sqrt{G^2(c^*) + 4G(c^*)y}]^2}. \qquad (23)$$

It follows again that $d\text{RHS}(20)/dc^* > 0$ for $c^* \in [\underline{c}^*,1]$, by comparing the last two terms in (23), using (22), and noting that

$$[-G(c^*) + \sqrt{G^2(c^*) + 4G(c^*)y}] > -2G(c^*) + \frac{\{2G^2(c^*) + 4G(c^*)y\}}{\sqrt{G^2(c^*) + 4G(c^*)y}};$$

or, equivalently, that

$$[G(c^*)\sqrt{G^2(c^*) + 4G(c^*)y}] > G^2(c^*),$$

which is self-evident.   Q.E.D.

REMARKS. Note that the condition posited in Proposition 3 is satisfied globally, if there exists a number $M > 0$ such that for all $c \in [0,b]$, $M \leq g(c) \leq 2M$. Alternatively, if the second derivative of $G(c)$ is negative, or $g'(c) \leq 0$, then again we have that $g(c^*)c^* \leq G(c^*)$. Examples of distri-

butions satisfying these conditions include the uniform, the negative exponential, and even the following "inverse exponential," $G(c) = (e^{Lc} - 1)$,
$L > 0$, $e^{Lb} = 2$.

The conditions identified in Proposition 3 are also "minimally sufficient,"
for arbitrary $R > 0$, without further knowledge of $G(\underline{c}^*)$. This is self-evident
in equation (23) and is obtained in (21) by evaluating only the terms proportional to R,

$$\frac{2R}{\sqrt{G(c^*)}} \left[\frac{\sqrt{G(c^*)}}{2} + 1 - \frac{(g(c^*)c^*)}{2G(c^*)} \right],$$

and noting that $\sqrt{G(\underline{c}^*)}$ could be arbitrarily close to zero for R sufficiently
large, i.e., large trading externalities.

When the intertemporal discount rate R goes to zero, the following result
summarizes sufficient conditions for uniqueness in both models.

PROPOSITION 4. *For negligibly small R there is a unique equilibrium for
the dealership and Diamond models, if $g(c)c < 4G(c)$, for $c \in$
$[\underline{c}^*,1]$ where $\underline{c}^*$ represents the first solution to equations (16) and
(20).*

PROOF. Ignoring the terms proportional to R in (21), and using equation
(22), we obtain that

$$\frac{d\,\text{RHS}(16)}{dc^*} \geq \sqrt{G(c^*)} \left[\frac{1}{\sqrt{G(c^*)}} + \sqrt{G(c^*)} + 2 - \frac{g(c^*)c^*}{G(c^*)} \right]$$

Now, for any $x \in (0,1)$, it is the case that[6]

$$Z(x) \equiv [x + 1/x] > 2.$$

Hence $d\text{RHS}(16)/dc^* > 0$, under the conditions posited, for $1 \geq c^* \geq$
$\underline{c}^*$, the unique equilibrium in the intermediated model.

For the unintermediated Diamond model, setting $R = 0$ in (23) and using
(22), we obtain, given $g(c)c \leq 4G(c)$, that

$$\frac{d\,\text{RHS}(20)}{dc^*} > \frac{2G(c^*)}{D^2} \left[\{G + 2y - \sqrt{G^2 + 4Gy}\} \right.$$

$$\left. + \{-G + \sqrt{G^2 + 4Gy}\} - \left\{-4G + \frac{4G^2 + 8Gy}{\sqrt{G^2 + 4Gy}}\right\} \right] \quad (24a)$$

where

$$D \equiv [-G(c^*) + \sqrt{G^2(c^*) + 4G(c^*)y}. \quad (24b)$$

Hence, $d\text{RHS}(20)/dc^* > 0$, provided

$$2y + 4G\sqrt{G^2 + 4Gy} > 4G^2 + 8Gy, \tag{24c}$$

which always holds[7] for $G > 0$, thus implying a unique equilibrium $\underline{c}^*$. Q.E.D.

We now consider an intermediate sufficient condition for uniqueness, which holds for our model when $G(c^*)$ is not negligible relative to R and is obtained by showing the convexity of RHS(16). This condition turns out in examples to be "intermediate" between those in propositions 3 and 4, and it thus follows that our equilibria may be unique even though Diamond's are not—at least for small enough y implying a low $\underline{c}^*$ in the unintermediated model, owing to the lower efficiency of search by nonspecialized producers.

PROPOSITION 5. *Suppose that the first solution $\underline{c}^*$ to equation (16) satisfies $[G(\underline{c}^*)]^{3/2} > 2R$ and that $G(c)$ satisfies $[(3g(c))/(2G(c))] \geq [(g'(c))/(g(c))]$ for all $c \in [\underline{c}^*, 1]$, where $g'(c)$ is the second derivative of $G(c)$. Then $\underline{c}^*$ is the unique dealership equilibrium.*

PROOF. Differentiating in (21), we obtain

$$\frac{d^2\mathrm{RHS}(16)}{dc^{*2}} = g(c^*) + \frac{2g(c^*)}{\sqrt{G(c^*)}} - \frac{2g(c^*)}{[G(c^*)]^{3/2}}[R + G(c^*)]$$

$$+ \frac{3g^2(c^*)}{2[G(c^*)]^{5/2}}\left[Rc^* + \int_0^{c^*} G(c)dc\right]$$

$$- \frac{g'(c^*)}{[G(c^*)]^{3/2}}\left[Rc^* + \int_0^{c^*} G(c)dc\right]$$

$$= \frac{g(c^*)}{[G(c^*)]^{3/2}}\left[\{G^{3/2} - 2R\} + \left\{\frac{3}{2}\frac{g}{G} - \frac{g'}{G}\right\}\left\{Rc^* + \int_0^{c^*} G(c)dc\right\}\right].$$

Hence, under the conditions posited, $d\mathrm{RHS}(16)/dc^* > 0$ for $c > \underline{c}^*$, the unique dealership equilibrium. Q.E.D.

We conclude this section with an illustration of the differences among the three uniqueness conditions developed above.

EXAMPLE. Let the support of $G(c)$ be $[0,1]$ and let

$$G(c) = (1 - \alpha)c^a + \alpha c \tag{25a}$$

$$a > 1, \alpha \in (0,1). \tag{25b}$$

Then, the conditions for Proposition 3 are met for α arbitrarily small, if $a \leq 2$, and those for Proposition 4 if $a \leq 4$. We now show that the conditions for Proposition 5 are satisfied—given $[G(\underline{c}^*)]^{3/2} \geq 2R$—provided $a \leq 3$. From (25a), we obtain that

$$g(c)/g'(c) = \frac{c}{(a-1)} + \frac{1}{[a(a-1)(1/\alpha - 1)c^{a-2}]} \tag{25c}$$

and

$$G(c)/g(c) = \frac{c}{a} + \frac{(a-1)}{[a^2(1/\alpha - 1)c^{a-2} + a/c]}. \tag{25d}$$

Hence

$$\frac{2}{3}[G/g] \leq g/g', \text{ if } \frac{3}{2a} \leq \frac{1}{(a-1)}, \text{ or } a \leq 3, \tag{25e}$$

which is the desired intermediate result.

4. Welfare, Intervention, and Externalities

Our goal in this section is to analyze the problem of a social planner who can order (or provide appropriate lump-sum subsidies for) agents to move into dealership versus producing occupations but who cannot dictate agents' c^* choices. This is in the spirit of the literature on incentive-compatible efficiency (e.g., Harris and Townsend 1981), in which it is recognized that the welfare criterion must acknowledge that a subset of the economic data is privately known by agents and not by the mechanism designer. Here, the productive agent's draw c from the distribution $G(c)$, where draws are independent across agents, plays such a role. In carrying out this analysis, our primary focus is on the relationship between the private equilibrium proportion of dealers versus that which is socially optimal. In Mortensen (1976), it is shown that the negative externality exercised by one dealer on others implies that in a (zero-profit) free-entry equilibrium, there are too many dealers. Here, unlike in Mortensen's model, the number of dealers per se (and not just their pecuniary terms) matters to agents. As a result, we obtain the reverse result that the socially optimal proportion of dealers exceeds that which results in the (best) free-entry equilibrium.

Consider a social planner dealing with N agents. He orders D to be dealers charging bid-ask spread $(1 - q)$ and $(N - D)$ to be producers. Given the resulting production decision c^*, the number of producers with a nonzero inventory at any point is E, which satisfies the steady-state equation (for large N):

$$\frac{(N - E - D)}{(N - D)} G(c^*) - \frac{ED}{(N - D)(N - D)} = 0$$

or

$$E = \frac{(N - D)^2 G(c^*)}{(N - D)G(c^*) + D}. \tag{26}$$

Equation (26) is readily reconciled with (9b) by noting that the fraction of "employed" producers is $E/(N - D) \equiv \Pi$ and that the probability of a dealer visit per period is $D/(N - D) \equiv P$.

The social planner maximizes the objective function

$$\max_{\{c^*,D\}} Z(c^*,p,q(c^*,D)) = (N - E - D)W_u + EW_e + DU_D \tag{27a}$$

where, from equations (5), (6), (7), and (10), we have

$$W_u = \int_0^{c^*} \frac{G}{R} \, dc \tag{27b}$$

$$W_e = W_u + c^* \tag{27c}$$

$$U_D = \frac{(1 - q)G(c^*)(N - D)}{R[(N - D)G(c^*) + D]} \tag{27d}$$

$$(1 - q) = \frac{D - c^*[R(N - D) + D] - (N - D)\int_0^{c^*} G(c)dc}{D} \tag{27e}$$

$$\frac{D}{N - D} = P. \tag{27f}$$

The expression for $Z^*(c^*;D;q(c^*,D))$ in (27a) can be rewritten, using (27b–e) and (28), as

$$\max_{\{c^*,D\}} Z(c^*,D,q(c^*,D))$$

$$= \frac{D(N - D)}{R[(N - D)G(c^*) + D]} \left[\int_0^{c^*} G(c)dc + (1 - c^*)G(c^*) \right]. \tag{27g}$$

Notice that we have not restricted the value of q to be less than one. This means we are allowing for the possibility that the dealers can pay $q > 1$ and recover their costs through government subsidies financed by lump-sum taxes from the producers—in other words, a two-part tariff. Because the utility functions are linear, the allocation of income between producers and dealers is clearly immaterial to the equally weighted social welfare function. Therefore, the lump-sum part of the two-part tariff does not appear in the social welfare function.[8]

An additional issue that arises with $q > 1$ being feasible is that of inventories for dealers, and these being state variables in a much more complicated (utility maximization) problem than the one we have solved. We tackle this whole set of interrelated issues by adapting the following story. Each dealer is assumed to have many clients, so that (in equilibrium) his volume of trade does not fluctuate much from (properly measured) period to period. We assume that the government can (i) collect lump-sum taxes from producers; (ii) order or persuade dealers to provide production subsidies ($q > 1$) by (iii) periodically paying dealers to replenish the predictable (purchasing power) inventory levels required for doing so; as well as, possibly, (iv) paying a (one-time) lump-sum subsidy for the opportunity cost of not being a producer. We discuss this assumption further in Section 5.

Assuming an interior solution exists, the first-order conditions are

$$\frac{\partial Z}{\partial D} = \left[\int_0^{c^*} G(c)dc + (1 - c^*)G(c^*) \right]^*$$

$$\frac{[\{(N - D)G(c^*) + D\}(N - 2D) - \{1 - G(c^*)\}D(N - D)]}{R[(N - D)G(c^*) + D]^2} = 0 \quad (28)$$

$$\frac{\partial Z}{\partial c^*} = D(N - D)\left[\{(N - D)G(c^*) + D\}\{(1 - c^*)g(c^*)\} - (N - D) \right.$$

$$\left. \times g(c^*)\left\{ \int_0^{c^*} g(c)dc + (1 - c^*)G(c^*) \right\} \right] \bigg/ R[(N - D)G(c^*) + D]^2$$

$$= 0. \quad (29)$$

The first equation yields the condition

$$G(c^*) = \frac{D^2}{(N - D)^2} = p^2. \quad (30)$$

The second equation yields the condition

$$(1 - c^*) - \frac{(N - D)}{D}\int_0^{c^*} G(c)dc = (1 - c^*) - \frac{1}{p}\int_0^{c^*} G(c)dc = 0. \quad (31)$$

Equation (30) is exactly the same as the productive efficiency condition (14) for the dealership equilibrium. This condition appears in both the dealership equilibrium and the social planner's problem because, in both cases,

(i) the marginal rates of substitution for producers and dealers are equated and (ii) the social opportunity cost of being a dealer is taken into account.

Equation (30) gives the value of p, which maximizes the number of trades per period given c^*. Combining the equations (30) and (31) gives the first-order optimality condition

$$1 = c^* + \frac{1}{\sqrt{G(c^*)}} \int_0^{c^*} G(c)dc. \tag{32}$$

The following result gives a partial characterization of the social optimum.

PROPOSITION 6. *Suppose that the distribution function $G(c)$ is continuous with support $[0,b]$ for $b \geq 1$, and the right derivative (density) or $G(c)$ at $c = 0$ is strictly positive. Then there exists a solution to the social planner's problem. If $4G(c) \geq cg(c)$ for $c \in [\underline{c}^*,1]$, where $\underline{c}^*$ is the first solution to (32), then $\underline{c}^*$ is the unique solution to the social planner's problem.*

PROOF. The existence proof is similar to that in Proposition 1, so it will not be repeated here.

To show uniqueness, it is only necessary to show that the right-hand side of (32) is monotonically increasing if $4G(c^*) \geq c^*g(c^*)$. Differentiating the right-hand side of (32) with respect to c^* gives

$$\frac{d \, \text{RHS}(32)}{dc^*} = 1 + \frac{G(c^*)}{\sqrt{G(c^*)}} - \frac{g(c^*)}{2G(c^*)\sqrt{G(c^*)}} \int_0^{c^*} G(c)dc$$

$$\geq 1 + \frac{G(c^*)}{\sqrt{G(c^*)}} - \frac{g(c^*)c^*}{2\sqrt{G(c^*)}}$$

since $c^*G(c^*) \geq \int_0^{c^*} G(c)dc$

$$\geq \frac{2\sqrt{G(c^*)} + 2G(c^*) - c^*g(c^*)}{2\sqrt{G(c^*)}}$$

since $\sqrt{g(c^*)} \geq g(c^*)$

$$\geq \frac{4G(c^*) - c^*g(c^*)}{2\sqrt{G(c^*)}} > 0. \quad \text{Q.E.D.}$$

We also obtain the following result, on the necessity of production subsidies ($q > 1$) in the social optimum.

PROPOSITION 7. *The social optimum always requires that $q > 1$ (i.e., production is subsidized).*

PROOF. From Equation (6) we have

$$q = \frac{c^*(R + p) + \displaystyle\int_0^{c^*} G(c)dc}{p}.$$

Using equation (30) gives

$$q = \frac{Rc^*}{\sqrt{G(c^*)}} + c^* + \frac{1}{\sqrt{G(c^*)}} \int_0^{c^*} G(c)dc.$$

Substituting in the social optimality condition (32) yields

$$q = \frac{Rc^*}{\sqrt{G(c^*)}} + 1 > 1. \quad \text{Q.E.D.}$$

Given equations (30), (32), and propositions 6 and 7, it is easy to compare the dealership equilibrium with the social optimum. Inspection shows that the value given by the right-hand side of (32) always lies below the value given by the right-hand side of equation (16). When the right-hand side of (32) is monotonically increasing, the social optimum c^* is clearly greater than any c^* that solves (16). Since the equation for p is the same in both cases and p is increasing in c^*, we know that the dealership equilibrium has too few dealers. We provide an illustration of these differences below.

EXAMPLE. Let $G(c)$ be uniformly distributed with support $[0,2]$ and let $R = .075$.

	Dealership Equilibrium	Social Optimum with Intermediation
c^*	.5	.77
p	.5	.62
q	.7	1.10
$e = E/N$	.22	.24
$d = D/N$	.33	.38
$u = (N - E - D)/N$	.45	.38
Average per capita utility	1.11	1.20

5. Concluding Remarks

We have examined an intermediated version of the general equilibrium, search-theoretic model of Diamond (1982) and have characterized its uniqueness and welfare properties. Many of the multiplicity of equilibria problems in the unintermediated Diamond model remain, and even the Pareto-supreme Nash equilibrium with free entry is inefficient (when only proportional pricing can be used), in the precise sense that there are too few dealers, or intermediaries—and hence too low a level of productive activity—relative to the social optimum. Indeed, these conclusions and similarities persist even when the intertemporal discount rate is small; the social optimum productivity level (for any equally weighted welfare function) is independent of this discount factor.

In addition, we found that—given the constraints of our problem—two-part tariffs would always be optimal. This solution implies that the government can be "in contact" with every individual in order to collect some fixed payment up front, even though no single dealer has this ability. The notion behind this is that our (or Diamond's) one-commodity model is only an abstraction of a multicommodity model in which a particular agent's excess demand vector (taste) changes stochastically over time, whereas dealers specialize in goods. Given statistical stability of the distribution of excess demands over goods, however, a dealer's (or society's) aggregate trade vector is "stable" over time, in equilibrium. However, the absence of long-term trading "relationships" among dealers and specific clients implies that neither a production subsidy ($q > 1$) nor collection of lump-sum charges from producers is economically feasible in a purely private dealership equilibrium.

An interesting but difficult extension of this model would be to consider the Stackelberg leader case with multiple dealers, each of whom has a finite trading capacity. As before, utility-maximizing producers would choose a level of effort c^* based on q and the likelihood of a trade, p. Profit-maximizing dealers would choose a bid-ask spread taking several different things into account. First, they would take the bid-ask spread of other dealers as given; second, they would realize that when they raise or lower their q relative to what other dealers are charging, they will gain or lose customers. For example, if they raise q, then they will gain customers up to the point where a producer is indifferent between going to them and receiving a higher q but having a lower p (since $p = 1/n$ where n is the dealer's clientele size) or going to someone else who has a lower q but a higher p. Third, they would realize that changing q also has an effect on the value of the induced level of effort c^*. This is in contrast to the equilibrium concept used in this paper, where dealers take the value of c^* as given when they choose q. Solving this problem, and investigating the limit set of equilibria as dealers' trading capacities become large, would provide a general equilibrium extension of the work of Fuchs and Laroque (1974), who look at related questions in a partial equilibrium framework.

Notes

1. We would like to thank George Akerlof, Ben Bernanke, Drew Fudenberg, Ed Prescott, John Roberts, Bill Rogerson, Michael Rothschild, Rob Townsend, and especially Peter Diamond for helpful discussions, while retaining responsibility for all errors. Sudipto Bhattacharya's research was supported by a Batterymarch Fellowship. This work was partially carried out during stays at Harvard Business School and Stanford University and was presented at the University of Minnesota Conference on Intertemporal Trade and Financial Intermediation, May 1984, sponsored by the Institute for Mathematics and Its Applications and by the Finance Department.

2. A Walrasian resolution, in which a single (social-welfare maximizing) dealer—acting as a Stackelberg leader subject to potential competition—brings about the Pareto-supreme production-exchange equilibrium, does *not* come about in our model.

3. The "zero inventory" producer is also visited by his dealer with probability p, but the visit necessarily results in no trade. As in Diamond (1982), we are also assuming that trading is time-consuming for producers, even with intermediation, and thus that *both* production and trade in the same period are not feasible.

4. Diamond and Fudenberg (1982) consider non-steady state equilibria, and the role played by out-of-steady-state beliefs ("animal spirits"), in the dynamics of transition to particular steady states.

5. The value functions V_u and V_e satisfy

$$V_e = \frac{1}{(1 + R)} \left[ey(V_u + 1) + (1 - ey)V_e \right] \qquad \text{(i)}$$

and

$$V_u = \max \frac{1}{(1 + R)} \left[(1 - G(c^*))V_u + \int_0^{c^*} (V_e - c)dG(c) \right], \qquad \text{(ii)}$$

which has the first-order condition

$$c^* = V_e - V_u. \qquad \text{(iii)}$$

Substitution in (i) gives us

$$RV_e = ey(1 - c^*), \qquad \text{(iv)}$$

and integration by parts in (ii), followed by substitution from (iii), gives

$$RV_u = \int_0^{c^*} G(c)dc, \qquad \text{(v)}$$

which, in combination with (iv) and (iii), yields

$$ey(1 - c^*) = Rc^* + \int_0^{c^*} G(c)dc. \qquad \text{(18)}$$

6. Notice that $dZ/dx = 1 - 1/x^2 = 0$ at $x = 1$, and that $d^2Z/dx^2 > 0$, implying that the *minimum* is at $x = 1$, with $Z(1) = 2$.

7. Squaring both sides in (24c), we obtain

$$(4y^2 + 16Gy + 16G^2)(G^2 + 4Gy) > (16G^4 + 64G^2y^2 + 64G^3y),$$

which follows by termwise dominance.

8. Note that two different lump-sum charges are involved: one to recover the cost of production subsidies $(q - 1)$ and another to compensate dealers for their opportunity cost of not being producers. See Hayes (1984) for an alternative justification of two-part tariffs under competition given risk-sharing externalities.

References

Diamond, P. 1982. "Aggregate Demand Management in Search Equilibrium." *Journal of Political Economy* 90:881–94.

Diamond, P., and D. Fudenberg. 1982. "An Example of Aggregate Demand Management in Search Equilibrium." Economics Department, M.I.T.

Diamond, P., and J. Yellen. 1983. "The Distribution of Inventory Holdings in a Pure Exchange Barter Search Economy." Economics Department, M.I.T.

Fuchs, G., and G. Laroque. 1974. "Continuity of Equilibria for Economies with Vanishing External Effects." *Journal of Economic Theory* 9:1–22.

Harris, M., and R. Townsend. 1981. "Resource Allocation under Asymmetric Information." *Econometrica* 49:33–64.

Hayes, B. 1984. "Competition and Two-Part Tariffs." Department of Managerial Economics and Decision Science, Kellogg Graduate School of Management, Northwestern University.

Mortensen, D. 1976. "Job Matching under Imperfect Information." In *Evaluating the Labor Market Effects of Social Programs,* edited by O. Ashenfelter and J. Blum. Princeton, N.J.: Princeton University Press.

Myerson, R. 1979. "Incentive Compatibility and the Bargaining Problem." *Econometrica* 47:61–74.

Rubinstein, A., and A. Wolinsky. 1984. "Equilibrium in a Market with Sequential Bargaining." ICERD, London School of Economics and Political Science.

Townsend, R. 1982. "Theories of Intermediated Structures." Unpublished paper, Carnegie-Mellon University.

V

Circulating Private Debt: An Example with a Coordination Problem

Robert Townsend and Neil Wallace

We use a model of pure, intertemporal exchange with spatially and informationally separated markets to explain the existence of private securities that circulate and, hence, play a prominent role in exchange. The model, which utilizes a perfect-foresight equilibrium concept, implies that a Schelling-type coordination problem can arise. It can happen that the amounts of circulating securities that are required to support an equilibrium and that are issued at the same time in informationally separated markets must satisfy restrictions not implied by individual maximization and market clearing in each market separately.

1. Introduction

A seemingly central observation for monetary economics is that some objects—often referred to as monies—appear in exchange much more frequently than other objects.[1] In this paper, we present and study a model that generates a version of this observation for private securities; in the model, some securities get traded frequently, or circulate, whereas others do not. In this and other respects, the securities in our model resemble historically observed bills of exchange.

The model that we use to explain the existence of circulating securities is one of intertemporal trade in spatially and informationally separated markets. The assumption that trade occurs in separate markets has been used by Ostroy (1973), Ostroy-Starr (1974), and Harris (1979) to model the transaction patterns of commodities and by Townsend (1980) to model that of fiat money. We use it here to model the transaction patterns of private securities. Adopting that assumption is consistent with the general view that fruitful theories of the pattern of exchange and of media of exchange require settings in which it is somehow difficult to carry out exchange.

The difficulty of carrying out exchange under our assumptions shows up in two distinct ways. One is market incompleteness: it can happen that some physically feasible and beneficial trades cannot be accomplished. This, as we will see, is an obvious implication of our assumptions and does not, therefore, require extended discussion. The other is much less obvious: it turns out to resemble the problem in a Schelling pure coordination game.

As described by Schelling (1960), a *pure coordination game* is one in which there is no communication and no conflict and in which the problem facing the players is to choose strategies that are coordinated. In our model, it can happen that the quantities of securities that are required to support an equilibrium and that are issued by individuals at the same time in spatially and informationally separated markets must satisfy restrictions not implied by individual maximization and by market clearing in each separate market. In other words, the utility-maximizing choices of quantities of securities, the strategies of individuals, are not in general unique but must somehow be coordinated across informationally separated markets if they are to be consistent with the existence of an equilibrium.

This (coordination) problem arises only in some versions of our model. In fact, there is a close connection between its appearance and that of circulating securities; the problem does not appear unless there is a role for circulating securities. In this sense, the model is consistent with the widely held view that problems—perhaps in the form of chaotic conditions—sometimes arise in credit markets with unregulated issue of private securities that play an important role in exchange.[2] Although this view is widely held, there are few, if any, other models that provide an interpretation of it.[3]

Our presentation is organized as follows. We begin in Section 2 with an introductory description of our model and of the example we use to display the coordination problem. In Section 3, we describe a somewhat general class of environments, introduce our notation, and formally describe our equilibrium concept. In Section 4, we establish for our example equivalence between our equilibrium and that implied by complete date-location contingent markets with complete participation. In Section 5, we use that equivalence to display the transaction patterns of the securities issued. Finally, in Section 6, we use it to display the coordination problem.

2. Preliminary Description: Some Example Economies

We study setups with a finite number of finite-lived people who meet deterministically at prescribed locations and at prescribed times. The example we focus on is an economy of four people who meet according to the pattern laid out in table V-1. Although the coordination problem arises only in the four-period version of this setup, in this section we also comment on the two- and three-period versions of it. In this example, at date 1, persons 1 and 2 are together at location 1, whereas persons 3 and 4 are together at location 2. Persons 1 and 4 always stay at those locations, whereas persons 2 and 3 switch locations each period.

As regards commodities or consumption goods, we assume there is one commodity for each location-date combination. Equivalently, we assume that there is one good that is indexed by location and date. The setup is pure exchange in the usual sense: goods indexed by one location-date combination cannot be transformed into goods indexed by another location-date combination; that is, there is no transportation, production, or storage technology for goods. Letting J denote the number of locations and T the number of dates, the commodity space has dimension JT. We assume that each person gets utility from commodities and has positive endowments of commodities in a proper subset whose elements correspond to the location-date combinations that the person visits. In figure V-1, we indicate by X's the subspace of the $2T$ commodity space that is relevant in the above sense for each of the persons in the four-person, four-period economy.

As regards private securities, we let the spatial separation limit trades in securities in what seems to be a natural way. First, at a particular time, a person can only trade securities with someone he or she meets. Second, although securities can be transported, they can move only with a person. Finally, we do not allow people to renege on their debts or to counterfeit others' debts. Securities or debts in our model take the form of promises to pay stated amounts of goods that are date and location specific. We assume that if the promise is presented at the relevant date and location, then it is honored.

To suggest how these rules and our spatial separation work, we briefly describe some of their implications for the table V-1 example.

If $T = 2$—that is, if the economy lasts only two periods—then no trade

Table V-1. Who Meets Whom When

Date	Location	
	1	2
1	(1,2)	(3,4)
2	(1,3)	(2,4)
3	(1,2)	(3,4)
4	(1,3)	(2,4)

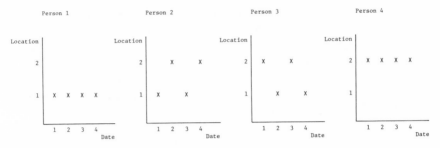

Figure V-1. Relevant commodity subspaces in the economy shown in table V-1.

is possible in the table V-1 economy under our security trading rules. For example, person 1 cannot sell a promise to person 2 because person 2 can neither redeem it at date 2 nor pass it on to person 4, who has no use for it at date 2, the assumed last date. Note in this connection that there is a complete absence of double coincidence in the table V-1, $T = 2$ example; as shown in figure V-1, for $T = 2$ no pair of persons has endowments and cares about a common two-dimensional subspace of the commodity space. From what we have just seen, the kinds of private securities we allow do not at all overcome this particular absence of double coincidence. Note, by the way, that there is potentially something to overcome in the sense that there can exist redistributions of the endowments that give rise to allocations that are Pareto-superior to the endowment allocation. Put differently, if all four people were together at some time zero and traded in complete (location and date contingent) markets, something we rule out, then the endowment would not necessarily be a competitive equilibrium.

If $T = 3$ in the table V-1 setup, our rules are consistent with some trade in private securities. It is easy to see, however, that only the following kinds of securities get traded: persons who meet at date 1 can trade debts due at date 3 when they meet again. For example, person 1 can issue a promise to pay a good at location 1, date 3, a promise that person 2 holds until he or she again meets person 1. Thus, such securities do not circulate; they do not get traded in a secondary market and are not used to make third-party payments. Corresponding to this noncirculating characteristic is the fact that such securities do no more than accomplish trades for which there is a double coincidence. For example, as is clear from figure V-1, persons 1 and 2 have a double coincidence between goods at location 1, date 1, and location 1, date 3. Note also that there remains a degree of market incompleteness in the $T = 3$ economy; in particular, the two goods at date 2 cannot be traded.

If $T = 4$ in the table V-1 economy, then our security trading rules are consistent not only with the existence of several noncirculating securities, but also with the existence of several circulating securities. At date 1, person 1 can issue to person 2 a promise to pay a good at location 1, date 4. This promise can be redeemed by being passed from person 2 to person 4 at date 2, from person 4 to person 3 at date 3, and from person 3 to person 1— the issuer—at date 4. Similarly, each of persons 2, 3, and 4 can issue at date 1 a promise of a good at date 4 at some location. Whether such securities are in fact issued is one of the questions taken up below.

3. Debt Equilibria in the General Spatial-Separation Setup

In this section, we describe the general class of economies under consideration and define a competitive debt equilibrium.

We assume an economy with G persons, each of whom lives T periods. At each time t, each person g can be paired with some other person or with no one. These pairings occur at (isolated) locations. Thus, we assume that person g is assigned to some location i at each time t and that in that location there either is or is not a single trading partner. We let there be $J \geq G/2$ locations.

If person g is in location i at time t, then he or she is endowed with some positive number of units, w_{it}^g, of the consumption good at location i, date t. For other location-date combinations, the endowment is zero. Let w^g denote the entire JT dimensional endowment vector for person g. Also let c_{it}^g denote the nonnegative number of units of location i-date t consumption of person g and let c^g denote the entire JT dimensional consumption vector for person g. Preferences of each person g are described by a utility function $U^g(c^g)$ that is continuous, concave, and strictly increasing in the T-dimensional subspace that is relevant for g.

We restrict attention to securities that can be redeemed. Thus, if d_{st}^f, which is nonnegative, denotes securities issued by person f at time s to pay d_{st}^f units of the consumption good where f will be at time t, we consider only triplets (f,s,t) with the property that there is a path or chain of pairings leading from where f is at s to where f is at t.

We let $p_{st}^f(i,u)$ be the price per unit of d_{st}^f at location i, date u, in units of good (i,u). However, we define such a price only for pairs (i,u) that potentially admit of a nontrivial trade in d_{st}^f. (This allows us to avoid having to determine a price for d_{st}^f in a market where demand and supply are identically zero and also allows us to restrict attention to positive prices.) Thus, suppose h and g meet at (i,u). We say that h is a *potential demander* of d_{st}^f at (i,u) if there is a route from h at u to f at t. We say that h is a *potential supplier* of d_{st}^f at (i,u) if there is a route from f at s to h at u. We say there is a *market* in d_{st}^f at (i,u) if and only if h is a potential demander and g is a potential supplier at (i,u), or vice versa.

We let $d_{st}^{fg}(i,u)$ be the excess demand by g at (i,u) for d_{st}^{f}. In terms of this notation, our debt trading rules are

$$\sum_{u=s}^{t} d_{st}^{ff}(\cdot,u) \geq 0 \text{ for each } f$$

$$\sum_{u=s}^{t'} d_{st}^{fg}(\cdot,u) \geq 0 \text{ for each } t' \geq s \text{ and } g \neq f \tag{1}$$

where, in each case, the locations range over those that the demander visits. The first inequality says that f must end up demanding as much as f issues, which expresses our no-reneging rule. The second says that $g \neq f$ cannot supply d_{st}^{f} without having previously acquired it. Finally, as a convention, if there is not a market in d_{st}^{f} at (i,u), we set $d_{st}^{fg}(i,u) \equiv 0$.

Then, as budget constraints for any person g, we may write

$$w_{iu}^{g} \geq c_{iu}^{g} + \sum d_{st}^{fg}(i,u)\,p_{st}^{f}(i,u), \tag{2}$$

there being T such constraints, one for each (i,u) that g visits. The summation in (2) is over all securities—all (f,s,t)—for which a market exists at (i,u).

Now, letting d^{g} denote the vector of debt demands of g over *all* securities that can be issued, a vector that has many zeros, we can now give the following definition of a debt equilibrium or of a competitive, perfect-foresight equilibrium under our security trading rules.

DEFINITION. A debt equilibrium is a specification of consumption and debt demands—c^{g} and d^{g} for each $g = 1, 2, \ldots, G$—and positive security prices, $p_{st}^{f}(i,u)$, such that

  (i) c^{g} and d^{g} maximize $U^{g}(c^{g})$ subject to (1) and (2)
  (ii) $\Sigma_{g}\,(c_{iu}^{g} - w_{iu}^{g}) = 0$ for each (i,u) and $\Sigma_{g}\,d_{st}^{fg}(i,u) = 0$ for each (i,u) and all potentially redeemable d_{st}^{f}.

Although it may seem strange to be considering competitive (price-taking) equilibrium in markets with only two traders, everything we do also holds for setups in which each of our persons is a trader type and in which there are many traders of each type.

Although we do not appeal to a general existence result in what follows, we include, in Appendix 1, a proof that every economy in our class of spatial-separation setups has a debt equilibrium. The proof draws heavily on Debreu (1959), although with modifications connected with the fact that the objects traded—the securities—are not ultimate consumption goods and are not bounded in an obvious way.

4. Debt Equilibria and Complete-Markets Equilibria

In this section we establish equivalence for the table V-1, $T = 4$ economy between the equilibrium allocations and prices of complete date-location contingent markets and the allocations and prices of debt equilibria. This proves useful in describing the transaction pattern implications of the theory and the coordination problem. We begin by showing that any complete-markets equilibrium (CME) consumption allocation can be supported by a debt equilibrium (DE).

To show that any CME can be supported by a DE in the table V-1, $T = 4$ economy, we start with a given CME. This we describe by individual consumption excess demands, $e_{it}^g \equiv c_{it}^g - w_{it}^g$, and by associated prices, s_{it} (in terms of an abstract unit of account). These constitute a CME if they satisfy:

$$\sum_i \sum_t e_{it}^g s_{it} = 0 \text{ for each } g \tag{3}$$

$$\sum_g e_{it}^g = 0 \text{ for each } (i,t) \tag{4}$$

and if, in addition, for each g, the e_{it}^g's are utility maximizing for g subject to (3).

A corresponding DE consists of positive debt prices and nonnegative, market-clearing debt quantities such that (a) the debt quantities and the given CME e_{it}^g's satisfy each person's debt budget constraints and (b) the debt quantities and the given CME e_{it}^g's are utility maximizing for each person given those debt prices.

Our first step is to produce candidate debt prices for the table V-1, $T = 4$ economy. This candidate is produced by matching the terms of trade between consumption goods implied by unconstrained trades in debts to the corresponding terms of trade given by the CME prices. Thus, for example, for person 1, $p_{14}^1(1,1)$ implies a trade between goods at location 1, date 1, and location 1, date 4. [Recall that, given our way of measuring debt quantities, $p_{14}^1(1,4) = 1$.] Thus, we let $p_{14}^1(1,1) = s_{14}/s_{11}$. In general, then, each debt price is taken to be a ratio of CME prices with the numerator corresponding to the redemption location-date and the denominator to the location-date of the current trade.

For noncirculating debts, then, our candidate is

$$(p_{13}^1(1,1), p_{13}^3(2,1), p_{24}^1(1,2), p_{24}^2(2,2))$$

$$= (p_{13}^2(1,1), p_{13}^4(2,1), p_{24}^3(1,2), p_{24}^4(2,2))$$

$$= (s_{13}/s_{11}, s_{23}/s_{21}, s_{14}/s_{12}, s_{24}/s_{22}), \tag{5}$$

whereas, for circulating debts, it is

$$
\begin{bmatrix}
p_{14}^1(1,1), p_{14}^1(2,2), p_{14}^1(2,3) \\
p_{14}^2(1,1), p_{14}^2(1,2), p_{14}^2(2,3) \\
p_{14}^3(2,1), p_{14}^3(2,2), p_{14}^3(1,3) \\
p_{14}^4(2,1), p_{14}^4(1,2), p_{14}^4(1,3)
\end{bmatrix}
=
\begin{bmatrix}
s_{14}/s_{11}, s_{14}/s_{22}, s_{14}/s_{23} \\
s_{24}/s_{11}, s_{24}/s_{12}, s_{24}/s_{23} \\
s_{14}/s_{21}, s_{14}/s_{22}, s_{14}/s_{13} \\
s_{24}/s_{21}, s_{24}/s_{12}, s_{24}/s_{13}
\end{bmatrix}.
\tag{6}
$$

We can immediately indicate that this implies that satisfaction of (a) implies satisfaction of (b). To see this, multiply the debt constraint for e_{it}^g [equation (2)] by s_{it} and sum over i and t. Using (5) and (6), the result is (3), in which debt quantities do not appear. Thus, at prices given by (5) and (6), the debt constraints for any person are at least as constraining as (3). Therefore, if we can produce market-clearing debt quantities, d_{st}^f's, which make the CME e_{it}^g's feasible choices subject to the budget constraints (2), then they are certainly utility-maximizing choices. That is, (a) implies (b).

To motivate how we produce debt quantities, recall that a CME consists of arbitrary s_{it}'s and e_{it}^g's that satisfy (3), (4), and zero restrictions for those e_{it}^g's that correspond to (i,t)'s that g does not visit. For the table V-1, $T = 4$ economy, there are $3 + 8 + 16$ *independent* constraints on the 32 e_{it}^g's. This leaves us free to choose 5 e_{it}^g's arbitrarily, but not any 5. For example, e_{11}^1 and e_{11}^2 cannot both be chosen arbitrarily because (4) and the zero restrictions imply that these sum to zero. Similarly, e_{11}^1, e_{12}^1, e_{13}^1, e_{14}^1 cannot each be chosen arbitrarily since (3) must be satisfied. We arrive at candidates for equilibrium debt quantities by finding some that satisfy constraints (1) and (2) and the relevant debt market clearing conditions for a set of e_{it}^g's that can be chosen arbitrarily.

For the table V-1, $T = 4$ economy, the following equations are the debt budget constraints, at prices satisfying (5) and (6), for five e_{it}^g's that *can* be chosen arbitrarily:

$$
(e_{21}^4, e_{22}^4, e_{11}^1, e_{12}^1, e_{13}^1)' = Ad
\tag{7}
$$

where

$$
A =
\begin{bmatrix}
s_{23}/s_{21} & 0 & 0 & 0 & 0 & 0 & -s_{14}/s_{21} & s_{24}/s_{21} \\
0 & s_{24}/s_{22} & 0 & 0 & -s_{14}/s_{22} & 0 & s_{14}/s_{22} & 0 \\
0 & 0 & s_{13}/s_{11} & 0 & s_{14}/s_{11} & -s_{24}/s_{11} & 0 & 0 \\
0 & 0 & 0 & s_{14}/s_{12} & 0 & s_{24}/s_{12} & 0 & -s_{24}/s_{12} \\
0 & 0 & -1 & 0 & 0 & 0 & -s_{14}/s_{13} & s_{24}/s_{13}
\end{bmatrix}
$$

and $d = (d_{13}^4 - d_{13}^3, d_{24}^4 - d_{24}^2, d_{13}^1 - d_{13}^2, d_{24}^1 - d_{24}^3, d_{14}^1, d_{14}^2, d_{14}^3, d_{14}^4)'$. Note that zeros in the A matrix do not denote zero debt prices, but rather that the particular debt cannot be traded at the relevant location-date combination.

Note also that the relevant debt market clearing conditions are imposed in equation (7). Thus, for example, the equilibrium demands for d_{14}^3 at dates 1, 2, and 3 are imposed in the first, second, and fifth equations of (7), respectively.

To see that there are *nonnegative* debt quantities that satisfy (7) for arbitrary s_{it}'s and an arbitrary left-hand side (LHS) of (7), consider an equivalent set of equations obtained by replacing the last equation of (7) by itself plus a multiple (s_{11}/s_{13}) of the third equation, namely

$$[e_{21}^4, e_{22}^4, e_{11}^1, e_{12}^1, e_{13}^1 + (s_{11}/s_{13})e_{11}^1]' = [A_1, A_2, A_3, A_4, A_5 + (s_{11}/s_{13})A_3]'d, \quad (8)$$

where A_i denotes the ith row of the matrix A. Note that in each of the first four equations of (8), there appears (with a nonzero coefficient) a difference between noncirculating debts that do not appear in any other equation. Thus, for any quantities of the other debts, each of the first four equations can be satisfied by choosing *nonnegative* quantities of the noncirculating debts that appear in that equation only. This allows us to choose nonnegative quantities of the circulating debts in any way that satisfies the last equation of (8), namely

$$e_{13}^1 + (s_{11}/s_{13})e_{11}^1 = (s_{14}/s_{13})(d_{14}^1 - d_{14}^3) - (s_{24}/s_{13})(d_{14}^2 - d_{14}^4). \quad (9)$$

Equation (9) is easily satisfied; if the LHS is positive (negative), it can be satisfied by setting at zero all but $d_{14}^1(d_{14}^3)$.

Given debt quantities that satisfy (8), all that remains is to show that they, (5) and (6), and the 11 other potentially nonzero CME e_{it}^g's satisfy the associated debt budget constraints. Two facts imply that they do. First, if, for any g, three debt budget constraints are satisfied at equality (as they are for person 1), then the fourth is also; note that we have already referred to the fact that (5) and (6) imply that the debt budget constraints satisfy (3). Second, we know that if g and h meet at (i,t), then the debt budget constraint for e_{it}^g is minus that for e_{it}^h. Thus, if debt prices and quantities are such that the debt budget constraint for g implies the CME e_{it}^g, then the debt budget constraint for h implies minus the CME e_{it}^g. But, by (4), this is the CME value of e_{it}^h. This concludes our argument that any CME for the table V-1, $T = 4$ economy can be supported by a DE.

The converse—that any DE consumption excess demands are also CME excess demands in the table V-1, $T = 4$ economy—is established in Appendix 2.

5. Debt Equilibrium Transaction Patterns

We now show that most table V-1, $T = 4$ environments imply, rather than just permit, the existence of several private securities that play different roles in exchange. We then describe two ways of summarizing these different roles.

The coexistence of circulating and noncirculating private debts can be demonstrated using the equivalence results of Section 4. That is, for some setups for which DEs and CMEs coincide, we now show that some CMEs can be supported *only* by DEs with both circulating and noncirculating securities.

From (9), if $e_{13}^1 + (s_{11}/s_{13})e_{11}^1 \neq 0$, then some circulating debt, d_{14}^h for some h, must be positive. Notice also that by multiplying the fifth equation of (7) by s_{13}/s_{21} and subtracting it from the first, we get an equation for $e_{21}^4 - (s_{13}/s_{21})e_{13}^1$ that contains only noncirculating debts. Thus, if a table V-1, $T = 4$ setup is such that any CME satisfies $e_{13}^1 + (s_{11}/s_{13})e_{11}^1 \neq 0$ and $e_{21}^4 - (s_{13}/s_{21})e_{13}^1 \neq 0$, then every DE for that setup displays positive amounts of both circulating and noncirculating debts.[4]

We now describe two ways of summarizing the different exchange roles played by the different objects in debt equilibria in our setups. One way is in terms of a payments matrix (see Clower 1967); the other is in terms of transaction velocities.

By a payments matrix we mean an N by N matrix, where N is the number of objects observed in a debt equilibrium, in which the (i,j)-th element is one if object i is observed to trade for object j and is zero otherwise. Thus, for a table V-1, $T = 4$ economy, N equals the number of distinct consumption goods—eight—plus the number of distinct private securities issued in an equilibrium. And, if the transaction pattern is such that each consumption good gets traded for one circulating security and one noncirculating security, then there are two nonzero elements in each row corresponding to a consumption good or to a noncirculating debt, and there are four in each row corresponding to a circulating debt. Note, by the way, that nontrivial spatial setups seem not to produce equilibria in which *one* object trades for *every* other object.

By the transaction velocity of an object, we mean the ratio of the average amount traded per date to the average stock, a pure number per unit time. For example, for a table V-1, $T = 4$ economy, the following transaction velocity pattern among objects shows up in a debt equilibrium. For a consumption good at location i, date t, the *average* stock outstanding may be taken to be the total endowment divided by 4 (at dates other than t, the stock of this good is zero), whereas the average amount traded per date is the amount traded at t divided by 4. Thus, the transaction velocity is in the interval $(0,1)$. Computed in a similar way, the transaction velocity of noncirculating debt in such an economy is $2/3$ (such debt is outstanding for three dates and the entire stock is traded at two of those dates), whereas that of circulating debt is unity (the maximum possible velocity given our choice of time unit).

Thus, either in terms of a payments matrix or in terms of the pattern of transaction velocities across objects, our setups can imply different exchange roles for different objects and, in particular, a relatively prominent exchange role for what we have been calling circulating debt.

6. The Coordination Problem

Although a debt equilibrium exists in a table V-1, $T = 4$ economy, there is a difficulty in arriving at debt quantities that achieve it. The difficulty can be described as follows.

Individual equilibrium debt demands are correspondences, not functions; that is, when faced with equilibrium debt prices, each of many vectors of debt quantities achieves a given equilibrium vector of consumption for each individual. Of course, not surprisingly, in order to be a debt equilibrium, the vectors chosen from these individual correspondences must satisfy a restriction. In particular, the quantities of circulating debts must satisfy equation (9), which we rewrite here as

$$d^1_{14} - (s_{24}/s_{14})d^2_{14} = b + d^3_{14} - (s_{24}/s_{14})d^4_{14}, \tag{10}$$

where $b = (s_{13}/s_{14})[e^1_{13} + (s_{11}/s_{13})e^1_{11}]$. Equation (10) says that a linear function of the circulating debts issued in location 1 must equal a linear function of those issued in location 2. What distinguishes this situation from others in which demands are correspondences is that if people in one location at date 1 do not observe the quantities issued in the other location at date 1, then whether a vector of debt quantities is consistent or inconsistent with equation (10) is not revealed at date 1. Corresponding to any nonnegative pair of circulating debts issued in location 1 at date 1 is a net trade of noncirculating debts in location 1 at date 1, a magnitude of $d^1_{13} - d^2_{13}$, consistent with the equilibrium date 1, location 1 consumption trade and with market clearing in the debts traded in location 1 at date 1 [see the third row of equation (8)]. A similar situation prevails in location 2 at date 1 [see the first row of equation (8)]. Only at date 2 and thereafter is it revealed whether the quantities chosen at date 1 are consistent with equation (10) and, hence, with equilibrium consumption trades at subsequent dates.

We call this difficulty a coordination problem because arriving at quantities that satisfy equation (10) calls for communication across locations, which is precluded by assumption. In that respect, our situation resembles those described by Schelling (1960) as giving rise to coordination problems. The absence of communication across locations is, by the way, consistent with one interpretation of our concept of a perfect-foresight equilibrium. That concept can be interpreted to mean that each person knows the endowments and preferences of each other person and, hence, knows the equilibrium consumption excess demands and debt prices. Such knowledge is consistent with people in one location not knowing the debt quantities issued in the other location.

Our coordination problem bears some resemblance to a result obtained by Ostroy (1973) and Ostroy-Starr (1974) in their study of the decentralization of exchange. In their model, knowledge of equilibrium prices of commodities is not enough to guide people to the trades that produce the equilibrium allocation in one round of bilateral trading if the trading rules are informationally decentralized. In our model, knowledge of current and future equilibrium prices of securities is not enough to guide people to the quantities of securities required to support an equilibrium if security transactions in other markets are not observed. Of course, both private debt in our model and money in their model alleviate a quid pro quo requirement and facilitate the attainment of equilibrium. There is a sense, though, in which the monetary exchange process is informationally centralized in their model. It requires that budget balance information be transmitted to a monetary authority or requires that there be implicit agreement about which commodity is to be used to cover budget deficits and surpluses. One interpretation of our coordination problem is that a debt equilibrium also requires centralization.

7. Concluding Remarks

As promised, we have described a class of environments that, in general, give rise to private securities that circulate. The crucial feature in our environments is separated or segmented markets among which people move over time. We have also demonstrated that in some of the environments in which circulating securities appear, a problem also appears—a problem that resembles a Schelling coordination problem. Since there is nothing particularly strange about our physical environment or our security trading rules and equilibrium concept, we think the model shows promise as an explanation for why actual credit markets appear not to work well at times. However, except for breaking down barriers to communication, the model does not suggest to us any way of solving the coordination problem.

Appendix 1

Here we prove that the debt equilibrium defined in Section 2 exists. We first prove existence with imposed arbitrary bounds on debt demands. We then argue by taking the appropriate limit that there exists some equilibrium.

Let C be the space of JT-tuples, each element of which is in $[0,w]$, where $w >$ w_{iu} for all (i,u) and where w_{iu} is the social endowment of good (i,u). Also let D be the space of n-tuples, each element of which is in $[-d,d]$, where $d > 0$ and where n is the number of elements in d^g. Note that d is the arbitrary bound on debt demands. Let P_{st}^h be the n' dimensional simplex for d_{st}^h where n' is the number of location-date combinations where there is a market for d_{st}^h and let P be the product space of the P_{st}^h's, a finite product of finite dimensional simplexes. Finally, for each $p \in P$, let $\gamma^g(p,w^g) = \{(c^g,d^g) \in C \times D$ that satisfy constraints (1) and (2)$\}$. We are now in a position to follow Debreu's (1959) proof of the existence of a standard competitive equilibrium.

Since $C \times D$ restricted by (1) and (2) is compact and convex, it follows from (1) of 4.8 of Debreu (p. 63), modified for vector constraints, that $\gamma^g(p,w^g)$ is a continuous correspondence in p. The key to this assertion is that the RHS of (2) takes on the value zero at zero consumption and debt demands. Since zero is strictly less than w_{iu}^g, the exceptional case of minimum wealth does not occur.

Now, since the bounded competitive maximization problem of g involves maximizing a continuous function on a compact set, there exists a nonempty maximizing correspondence of security demands denoted $\phi^g(p)$. By theorem 4 of Section 1.8 of Debreu (p. 19), $\phi^g(p)$ is upper semicontinuous; it is also convex. Now let $\Phi(p) = \Sigma_g \phi^g(p)$. Clearly, $\Phi(p)$ is in the space of n-tuples, each element of which is in the interval $[-Gd, Gd]$. We denote this compact, convex set by Z.

Now consider the correspondence ρ from $P \times Z$ into itself defined by $\rho(p,z) = \mu(z) \times \Phi(p)$, where $\mu(z) = \{p \in P$ that maximize $p \cdot z$ for $z \in Z\}$. Following Debreu (p. 82), $\mu(z)$ is an upper semicontinuous correspondence from Z to P with $\mu(z)$ nonempty and convex. It follows that $\rho(p,z)$ is a nonempty, upper semicontinuous, and convex correspondence on $P \times Z$, which is a nonempty, compact, and convex set. So ρ has a fixed point: namely, (p^*, z^*) such that $p^* \in \mu(z^*)$ and $z^* \in \Phi(p^*)$.

We now establish that $\Phi(p^*) = 0$. Consider the subvector of $\Phi(p^*)$ associated with a particular debt, d_{st}^h. If this subvector is not zero, then some element must be positive because constraint (1) does not permit the sum of these elements to be negative. So suppose some elements of the subvector are positive. The correspondence μ sets debt prices at positive levels for at least one of these positive elements and for no nonpositive element. This, in turn, implies that more of d_{st}^h is being demanded at positive prices over all location-dates than is being supplied at positive prices. This contradicts individual maximization for someone and, hence, implies that the subvector of $\Phi(p^*)$ associated with d_{st}^h is zero. It follows that $\Phi(p^*) = 0$. Moreover, a similar argument implies that no component of p^* can be zero.

We can now show that the consumptions implied by z^* and p^* satisfy market clearing for each (i,u). For each g, individual maximization implies that (2) holds with equality. So suppose we sum (2) at a given (i,u) over g. Then market clearing in consumptions follows from $\Phi(p^*) = 0$.

We have thus established the existence of a debt equilibrium with arbitrary, imposed debt bounds d. Doubling these bounds, one can again establish existence. Continuing in this way, one can construct a sequence of debt equilibria for economies with larger and larger debt bounds. As the associated sequence of debt equilibrium prices and consumptions has elements in the same compact space, there exists a convergent subsequence—say, with limit prices and consumptions, $\bar{p}$ and $\bar{c}^g$, respectively.

Now consider the problem confronting a typical person g in the limit economy, at prices $\bar{p}$ and no imposed debt bounds whatever. The space of feasible consumptions for such a person (the budget set at prices $\bar{p}$ projected onto the space of consumptions) is compact, and the objective function is continuous, so there exists a solution, some maximizing choice of consumptions $\hat{c}^g$. Also, by construction, $\bar{c}^g$ is feasible in the limit economy. Suppose $U^g(\hat{c}^g) > U^g(\bar{c}^g)$. Then for some kth economy associated with the convergent subsequence, with debt bounds sufficiently large and prices sufficiently close to $\bar{p}$, one can find a feasible consumption vector with utility arbitrarily close to $U^g(\hat{c}^g)$. But along the convergent subsequence, utility must converge to $U^g(\bar{c}^g)$. We have thus contradicted maximization for person g in the kth economy. Thus $U^g(\hat{c}^g) = U(\bar{c}^g)$, and $\bar{c}^g$ solves the maximization problem of person g in the limit economy. Recall that person g was arbitrary.

We have thus established that consumptions $\bar{c}^g$ are all maximizing in the limit economy. Also, by construction, the $\bar{c}^g$ satisfy market clearing in the limit economy (this was a property of each economy in the convergent subsequence, by virtue of equilibrium). It only remains then to specify market-clearing debt demands for each person g in the budget set of person g and consistent with the choice of $\bar{c}^g$. This is done as follows. First, specify person 1's debt demands in his or her budget set consistent with $\bar{c}^1$. For market clearing, let these determine the debt demands of each person with whom person 1 trades, at specified dates and locations. Next, consider person 2. If there are no debt demands that remain to be determined for this person, then we are done. To suppose otherwise is to contradict the fact that $\bar{c}^1$ and $\bar{c}^2$ are market clearing and the fact that person 1's debt demands are in the budget set of person 1. If there do remain any debts to be determined, choose these consistent with $\bar{c}^2$. Continue in this way for person 3, and so on through person G. In the end, then, we have constructed an equilibrium in the limit economy, with no bounds on debts. Recall also that the (fixed) bounds on consumptions need not be imposed in the limit economy, by the choice of the bound w.

Appendix 2

Here we prove for the table V-1, $T = 4$ economy that any debt equilibrium (DE) consumption excess demands are also complete-markets equilibrium (CME) consumption excess demands.

Since the DE e_{it}^g's are market clearing—that is, satisfy (4)—we have to show only that the debt budget constraints are equivalent to (3) for some choice of s_{it}; if we can establish that equivalence, then it follows that the DE e_{it}^g's are utility maximizing subject to (3).

The debt budget constraints for person 1 in the table V-1, $T = 4$ economy can be written

$$e_{11}^1 = -d_{13}^{11}(1,1)p_{13}^1(1,1) - d_{13}^{21}(1,1)p_{13}^2(1,1)$$
$$- d_{14}^{11}(1,1)p_{14}^1(1,1) - d_{14}^{21}(1,1)p_{14}^2(1,1)$$

$$e_{12}^1 = -d_{24}^{11}(1,2)p_{24}^1(1,2) - d_{24}^{31}(1,2)p_{24}^3(1,2)$$
$$- d_{14}^{21}(1,2)p_{14}^2(1,2) - d_{14}^{41}(1,2)p_{14}^4(1,2)$$

$$e_{13}^1 = -d_{13}^{11}(1,3) - d_{13}^{21}(1,3) - d_{14}^{31}(1,3)p_{14}^3(1,3) - d_{14}^{41}(1,3)p_{14}^4(1,3)$$

$$e_{14}^1 = -d_{24}^{11}(1,4) - d_{24}^{31}(1,4) - d_{14}^{11}(1,4) - d_{14}^{31}(1,4).$$

Let us add and subtract $d_{13}^{21}(1,1)p_{13}^1(1,1)$ on the RHS of the first equation, so that the sum $-[d_{31}^{11}(1,1) + d_{13}^{21}(1,1)]$ appears. Note that the sum $[d_{13}^{11}(1,3) + d_{13}^{21}(1,3)]$ appears in the third equation and that these sums are equal to each other because, at any debt prices, debt demands satisfy $d_{13}^{11}(1,1) = -d_{13}^{11}(1,3)$ and $d_{13}^{21}(1,1) = -d_{13}^{21}(1,3)$. Moreover, the sum $[d_{13}^{11}(1,1) + d_{13}^{21}(1,1)]$ is unconstrained (as to sign). These facts imply that the first and third equations are no more constraining than the single equation that results from substituting for that sum from the third equation into the first to produce

$$e_{11}^1 + p_{13}^1(1,1)e_{13}^1 = d_{13}^{21}(1,1)[p_{13}^1(1,1) - p_{13}^2(1,1)]$$

$$- d_{14}^{11}(1,1)p_{14}^1(1,1) - d_{14}^{21}(1,1)p_{14}^2(1,1)$$

$$- d_{14}^{31}(1,3)p_{14}^3(1,3)p_{13}^1(1,1) - d_{14}^{41}(1,3)p_{14}^4(1,3)p_{14}^4(1,3)p_{13}^1(1,1). \quad \text{(i)}$$

An exactly analogous procedure allows us to combine the second and fourth equations into the following single equation, which is no less constraining than those separate equations:

$$e_{12}^1 + p_{24}^1(1,2)e_{14}^1 = d_{24}^{31}[p_{24}^1(1,2) - p_{24}^3(1,2)] - d_{14}^{21}(1,2)p_{14}^2(1,2)$$

$$- d_{14}^{41}(1,2)p_{14}^4(1,2) - p_{24}^1(1,2)[d_{14}^{11}(1,4) + d_{14}^{31}(1,4)]. \quad \text{(ii)}$$

Now consider the first term on the RHS of (i). If the price difference that multiplies $d_{13}^{21}(1,1)$ is positive, then $d_{13}^{21}(1,1)$ is infinite. Since that cannot be an equilibrium choice, it follows that the DE prices satisfy $p_{13}^1(1,1) \leq p_{13}^2(1,1)$; that is, arbitrage is not possible for person 1 in the debts d_{13}^1 and d_{13}^2. And since an analogous manipulation of the debt budget constraint for person 2 implies the reverse inequality, it follows that DE prices satisfy $p_{13}^1(1,1) = p_{13}^2(1,1)$. In addition, exactly the same reasoning allows us to conclude that the DE prices satisfy the entire first equality of equation (5).

We now proceed to combine (i) and (ii) into a single constraint that is no less constraining than both (i) and (ii). First, add and subtract $d_{14}^{31}(1,3)p_{14}^1(1,1)$ on the RHS of (i) so that the sum $d_{14}^{11}(1,1) + d_{14}^{31}(1,3)$ appears in (i). This sum of demands is equal at any debt prices to $-[d_{14}^{11}(1,4) + d_{14}^{31}(1,4)]$, which appears in (ii). Moreover, this sum is unconstrained, implying that the equation that results from eliminating it between (i) and (ii) is no less constraining than both (i) and (ii). This single equation, which we will not write out, has the following form: a linear combination of person 1's excess demands for consumption is equal to a linear combination of person 1's debt demands.

By an argument similar to that used above to establish that DE prices satisfy the first equality of equation (5)—an argument that uses the analogues of (i) and (ii) for persons 2, 3, and 4—it follows that the DE prices must be such that the coefficient of each debt demand is zero; that is, intertemporal arbitrage among the various debts must not be possible for anyone. These restrictions on coefficients of debt demands are the ones needed to be able to choose s_{it}'s to satisfy equation (6). And such choices for s_{it}'s imply equivalence between the debt constraints and (3).

To summarize, we have indicated how to manipulate the debt budget constraints for the table V-1, $T = 4$ economy so as to establish two results. The first is that security prices in a DE for that economy are constrained so that we can choose s_{it}'s to satisfy (5) and (6). Second, with that choice of s_{it}'s, debt constraints are equivalent to (3) so that the e_{it}^h's that are utility maximizing subject to the debt constraints are also utility maximizing subject to (3). These results imply that any DE is a CME in the table V-1, $T = 4$ economy.

Notes

1. A version of this paper entitled "A Model of Circulating Private Debt" was presented at the Econometric Society Summer Meeting, Cornell University, 16–19 June 1982, and at seminars at several universities. Helpful comments from the participants of these seminars and from Alvin Roth and Allan Drazen are gratefully acknowledged. We are indebted to the Federal Reserve Bank of Minneapolis for financial support. However, the views expressed are those of the authors and not those of the Bank or the Federal Reserve System.

2. See, for example, Friedman's comments about private bank note issue and unfettered intermediation (1960, 21 and 108).

3. For two recent attempts much different from ours, see Bryant (1981) and Diamond and Dybvig (1983).

4. Coexistence of circulating and noncirculating securities can occur even if there is not a coincidence between DEs and CMEs. See Townsend and Wallace (1982) for an example.

References

Bryant, J. 1981. "Bank Collapse and Depression." *Journal of Money, Credit, and Banking* 13:454–64.
Clower, R. 1967. "A Reconsideration of the Microfoundations of Monetary Theory." *Western Economic Journal* 6:1–8.
Debreu, G. 1959. *The Theory of Value*. New York: John Wiley.
Diamond, D. W., and P. H. Dybvig. 1983. "Bank Runs, Deposit Insurance, and Liquidity." *Journal of Political Economy* 91:401–19.
Friedman, M. 1960. *A Program for Monetary Stability*. New York: Fordham University Press.
Harris, M. 1979. "Expectations and Money in a Dynamic Exchange Economy." *Econometrica* 47:1403–20.
Ostroy, J. M. 1973. "The Informational Efficiency of Monetary Exchange." *American Economic Review* 63:597–610.
Ostroy, J. M., and R. M. Starr. 1974. "Money and the Decentralization of Exchange." *Econometrica* 42:1093–113.
Schelling, T. 1960. *The Strategy of Conflict*. Cambridge, Mass.: Harvard University Press.
Townsend, R. 1980. "Models of Money with Spatially Separated Agents." In *Models of Monetary Economies*, edited by J. Kareken and N. Wallace. Federal Reserve Bank of Minneapolis.
Townsend, R., and N. Wallace. 1982. "A Model of Circulating Private Debt." Staff report 83, Federal Reserve Bank of Minneapolis.

VI

Incomplete Market Participation and the Optimal Exchange of Credit

Lawrence M. Benveniste

This paper contains a generalized version of the Townsend and Wallace model that appears in this volume. Participants in the economy trade IOUs with redemption value denoted in units of account, and the potential for traders to fully value the contracts depends on the patterns of future market participation. Each participation pattern establishes a feasible set of trading patterns through which the credit instruments must circulate in equilibrium. These patterns, and the implied credit trades that result from the simplest market-clearing trades, are used to establish whether or not the economy can carry out a complete set of credit trades. The target set of trades describes a generalized spanning condition that characterizes complete credit markets when participation is incomplete.

1. Introduction

In our modern economic system, financial intermediaries (with the aid of computers and modern communications) coordinate the exchange of credit between large numbers of seemingly anonymous individuals.[1] We are moving ever more closely to the paradigm of the Walrasian auctioneer.

However, there are limits to the information capacity of any one organization. Thousands of financial intermediaries exchange excess credit balances among themselves, and these transactions are not coordinated by a central auctioneer. In essence, we have refined the historical financial institution in which individuals traded personalized IOUs whose value was backed by a promise to repay the bearer a predetermined amount at some time in the future.

At its origin, an IOU was a promise to pay some quantity of goods or services at some future date and location. Such an outstanding debt instrument could then be exchanged by its owner for commodities so long as it was acceptable to the merchant. Of course, this would require the merchant to expect that the instrument would pay him something (either through its expenditure or direct redemption).

Townsend and Wallace (1982; *this volume*) have exposited a series of examples of Arrow-Debreu competitive economies in which the location of each consumer in every period is explicitly represented and the exchange of IOUs is the sole means for consumers to trade intertemporally. Commodities are purchased on spot markets with endowments or with new or existing IOUs—individual promises to pay commodities at some future spot—that can be used repeatedly (resold) for the purchase of commodities.

Townsend and Wallace (*this volume*) focus on a specific example in which there is enough structure in the meeting pattern for agents to finance mutually with IOUs any efficient allocation that might result from a standard competitive equilibrium, and these choices are equilibrium allocations in this new institutional structure.

This paper presents a general version of their model in which spots are identified by date and location combinations and consumers are assigned a set of spots at which they participate. In this presentation, there may be many consumers participating at any given spot. Transactions at each spot are cost-accounted in terms of a spot-specific unit of account—in other words, all commodity and debt prices at any spot are quoted as quantities of this unit of account. IOUs are commitments to pay a prespecified number of account units at some future spot, and resale prices are also so quoted.[2] With the exception of these minor variations, the model is precisely the same as in Townsend and Wallace (*this volume*).

One simple scenario illustrates how financial institutions of this form may fail to allow for the execution of Pareto-improving trades. Imagine an economy with several spot markets in various locations. All but two agents in the economy remain in the same place for their entire lives. The two "transients" move every period, never locating in the same place twice. Also, one transient is one period behind the other in all periods except the last, when they meet at a location in which they are the only participants. The front transient wants to consistently save and the rear transient wants to consistently borrow, together clearing accounts at the end. This type of trade cannot be executed because the front transient will not be able to accumulate IOUs issued by the rear transient.

The main theorem of this paper is a complete characterization of the meeting patterns for which the economy can achieve any Arrow-Debreu equilibrium allocation when consumption demand is constrained by location. To arrive at this, one naturally begins the analysis by rigging preferences so that, even with complete participation, consumers do not purchase consumption for delivery at markets that they do not visit. This ensures that an equilibrium only calls for commodity exchanges between coinhabitants of spots, and the final distribution is Pareto-optimal among those in which the total endowments at each spot are distributed only to consumers who participate at that spot.

The next step is to investigate whether the goods transactions in the contrived Arrow-Debreu market equilibrium can be carried out under the more restrictive rules. Now consumers can only purchase goods and IOUs in spot markets at prices that they know in advance.

Conditioning exchange on face-to-face meetings is not a new idea. For example, Ostroy (1973) and Ostroy and Starr (1974) study the goods exchanges that agents in an economy can accomplish through a series of bilateral meetings defined by various permutations of the agents. Theirs was an essentially atemporal economy in which a final, one-period purchase at equilibrium prices is arrived at through a series of bilateral exchanges, each leaving the participants with bundles that are equal in value to those of their original endowments. As a result, there is no room here for IOU-type arrangements.

This paper is organized as follows: Section 2 contains the fundamentals of the economy, including the descriptions of market participation, endowments, and tastes. The Arrow-Debreu equilibria are described in Section 3. Securities are introduced in Section 4, and equilibria with IOU-financed trades are presented there. Sections 5 and 6 contain the mathematical analysis, and Section 7 concludes.

2. The Model

Consumers in this economy exchange exogenously prescribed endowments of a single consumption good.[3] There are T trading periods and N market locations in each period, and the pair (t,n) represents the market at location n in period t. Markets are also called spots.

Each of the M consumers (all of whom live the full T periods) visits exactly one location in each period. For consumer h, n_t^h refers to the spot where the consumer participates in period t. For the period t, location n market, the set of participating consumers is called

$$M(t,n) = \{h : n_t^h = n\}.$$

Consumer h is endowed with $y_t^h > 0$ units of consumption at market (t,n_t^h), and his endowment at the markets (t,n) where $n \neq n_t^h$ is zero. We could also represent h's endowments as $\langle w^h(t,n), t = 1,\dots,T$ and $n = 1,\dots,N\rangle$ with

$$w^h(t,n) = \begin{cases} y_t^h & \text{if} \quad n = n_t^h \\ 0 & \text{otherwise.} \end{cases}$$

Consumer h's consumption plans are described by vectors c^h, which are TN-dimensional. Coordinate $c^h(t,n)$ describes h's consumption at location n in period t. The vector c^h allows for the representation of h's consumption anywhere; however, since consumers will only visit the prescribed locations, $c^h(t,n) = 0$ if $n \neq n_t^h$.

Despite the fact that h may never consume at unvisited locations, his preferences may include consumption at unvisited locations. So a general utility function, $u^h(c^h)$, that is defined on nonnegative TN-dimensional vectors, is called for. But then the restrictions $c^h(t,n) = 0$ if $n \neq n_t^h$ must be imposed on each consumer's demand decision to force him to "behave" according to the prescription. The equivalent restrictions can be accomplished by simply assuming that consumption at unvisited markets has no value to him. I follow the second approach, assuming that utility functions $u^h : R_+^{TN} \rightarrow R$ are

continuously differentiable, that   (U.1)

$$\partial u^h / \partial c^h(t,n) \begin{cases} = 0 & \text{if} \quad n \neq n_t^h \\ > 0 & \text{if} \quad n = n_t^h, \quad \text{and} \end{cases}$$ (U.2)

u^h is strictly quasi-concave in the variables $c^h(t,n_t^h)$, $t = 1, \ldots, T$.   (U.3)

This completes an exhaustive list of the fundamentals of this economy. The structure has been set up to facilitate the most simple competitive market interpretation, which is the subject of the next section.

3. Competitive Market Equilibrium

When exchanges in this economy are all arranged through a Walrasian auctioneer with a complete set of futures markets, as is the case in the standard Arrow-Debreu economy, the available resources (in this case, they are the available consumption goods) will be efficiently distributed; in other words, the final distribution of consumption is Pareto-optimal. We leave the description of the institutional structure of finance markets in which personal IOUs are the sole means to transfer wealth between spots until the next section. The equilibria in this section provide targets for that economy to aim for.

For the present, all consumers meet before the actual exchange of any commodities and exchange future claims for consumption. Let $p(t,n)$ be the price of a claim to a unit of consumption at (t,n) and let the complete set of prices be $\langle p(t,n), t = 1,\ldots,T \text{ and } n = 1,\ldots,N \rangle$.

Consumer h purchases a consumption plan $\langle c^h(t,n) \rangle$ that at market time consists of claims for future consumption, choosing his plan by solving the constrained demand problem described by maximizing

$$u^h(c^h) \tag{1}$$

subject to

$$\sum_{t=1}^{T} \sum_{n=1}^{N} p(t,n)c^h(t,n) \leq \sum_{t=1}^{T} \sum_{n=1}^{N} p(t,n)w^h(t,n)$$

and

$$c^h(t,n) \geq 0 \quad \text{for all} \quad n = 1, \ldots, N \quad \text{and} \quad t = 1, \ldots, T.$$

Let $\bar{c}^h$ be consumer h's choice as the solution to (1). The prices $\langle p(t,n) \rangle$ are equilibrium prices if supply equals demand for each commodity (distinguished by date and location); in other words, for $t = 1, \ldots, T$ and $n = 1, \ldots, N$,

$$\sum_{h \in M(t,n)} \bar{c}^h(t,n) = \sum_{h \in M(t,n)} w^h(t,n).$$

The actual existence of equilibrium in this economy is problematic because the endowments w^h are not strictly positive. To get around this problem, consumers must be resource related [or, using the terminology of McKenzie (1959), who originally solved this problem, the economy must be irreducible]. Because endowments are positive and preferences are monotone in the commodities that h can buy, this economy is resource related as long as $M(t,n)$ does not contain just one member.[4]

Notice that assumption (U.2) guarantees that $p(t,n) \gg 0$ in equilibrium if $M(t,n)$ is not empty.

4. Sequential Markets with IOUs

Now let us assume that markets actually take place at each spot—that all purchases and sales of goods at (t,n) occur there. The spot price of consumption at (t,n) is described by $q(t,n)$, only now the prices are in terms of a separately established unit of account at that spot.

Consumers also transact in IOUs (inside money) at each spot. Each form of IOU is marketable at each spot, although clearly only a subset of the IOUs will actually be exchanged.[5] The promise by $\bar{h}$ to pay one unit of account in period s is priced at $\pi_s^{\bar{h}}(t,n)$ in period t at location n.

The description of a consumer's purchasing story goes as follows. Upon entering the market in period t, the consumer possesses a portfolio of inside money that consists of various consumers' promises to pay units of account at future periods and knowledge of the quantities of their own previous issues and when they come due. Having arrived at the market, the consumer then (and all decisions are transacted simultaneously):

1. Redeems previous issues that become due then.
2. Sells and purchases quantities of others' inside money (although the consumer cannot sell others' IOUs short).
3. Issues various quantities of his own notes with future redemption dates.
4. Sells his endowment and purchases consumption.

The liquidity and budget constraints require each consumer to pay for goods purchases in each period with credits of the correct number of account units, and by life's end, consumers must have redeemed all outstanding notes.

In the formal description of consumer h's transactions, let $\Delta b_t^h(\bar{h},s)$ be h's purchase in period t of $\bar{h}$'s notes, each of which is a promise by $\bar{h}$ to pay one unit of account in period s (of course, at $n_s^{\bar{h}}$). Positive quantities are purchases and negative quantities are sales.

A portfolio choice by consumer h is a complete list of all IOU transactions in every period and is described by $\langle \Delta b_t^h(\bar{h},s),\bar{h} = 1,\ldots,M,s = 2,\ldots,T,$ and $t = 1,\ldots,T\rangle$. The additional restrictions on h's portfolio choices are

$$\Delta b_t^h(h,s) \le 0 \quad \text{if} \quad t < s \quad \text{and} \quad \Delta b_t^h(h,s) = 0 \quad \text{if} \quad t > s, \tag{2.1}$$

$$\Delta b_s^h(h,s) = -\sum_{t=1}^{s-1} \Delta b_t^h(h,s), \, s = 2, \ldots, T, \quad \text{and} \tag{2.2}$$

$$-\Delta b_t^h(\bar{h},s) \le \sum_{\tau=1}^{t-1} \Delta b_\tau^h(\bar{h},s) \quad \text{if} \quad \bar{h} \ne h, s \ge t \quad \text{and} \quad t = 1, \ldots, T. \tag{2.3}$$

Restriction (2.1) says that h cannot repurchase an outstanding debt before its maturity. This turns out to be superfluous to the consumer's choice here, because all bonds turn out to have identical prices in each market (i.e., common interest rates); if he chose to redeem a note prematurely, he could just as well have made the original note payoff at the earlier date. (2.2) eliminates the possibility of default—i.e., h makes good on all debts—and (2.3) restricts h from selling other consumers' notes that are not currently in his portfolio. (There is no short selling.)

A portfolio $\langle \Delta b_t^h(\bar{h},s)\rangle$ finances the nonnegative consumption plan c^h if the T liquidity constraints

$$q(t,n_t^h)(c^h(t,n_t^h) - w^h(t,n_t^h)) \le -\sum_{s=t}^{T} \sum_{\bar{h}=1}^{M} \pi_s^{\bar{h}}(t,n_t^h)\Delta b_t^h(\bar{h},s), \tag{3}$$

$t = 1, \ldots, T$, are met. The liquidity constraints in (3) are calculated in "units of account" at (t,n_t^h); the term on the right is the acquired units of account when h transacts in securities there.

Consumer h will purchase the consumption plan $\bar{c}^h$ and the portfolio $\langle \Delta \bar{b}_t^h(\bar{h},s)\rangle$ if together they satisfy the constraints in (2) and (3) and if $\bar{c}^h$ maximizes h's utility among all such choices.

The IOUs permit individual consumers to trade units of account between spots. A vector $\psi \in R_{++}^{TN}$ whose individual entries are indexed by $\psi_{t,n}$ implicitly defines nominal rates of interest if for each $\bar{h}$, his IOUs payable in period s (each paying one unit of account there) have prices $\pi_s^{\bar{h}}(t,n)$ that are given by

$$\pi_s^{\bar{h}}(t,n) = \psi_{s,n_s^{\bar{h}}}/\psi_{t,n}.^6 \tag{4}$$

The following lemma is used to aggregate the budget constraints in (3) into a single budget constraint.

LEMMA 1. *If* $\psi \in R_{++}^{NT}$ *implicitly defines the nominal rates of interest when IOUs are priced at* $\langle \pi_s^h(t,n) \rangle$, *then for any portfolio* $\langle \Delta b_t^h(\bar{h},s) \rangle$ *that satisfies (2.1) to (2.3),*

$$\sum_{t=1}^{T} \psi_{t,n_t^h} \left[\sum_{s=t}^{T} \sum_{\bar{h}=1}^{M} \pi_s^{\bar{h}}(t,n_t^h) \Delta b_t^h(\bar{h},s) \right] \geq 0. \tag{5}$$

PROOF. First rewrite the expression on the left-hand side of (5) as

$$\sum_{s=t}^{T} \sum_{\bar{h}=1}^{M} \left[\sum_{t=1}^{T} \psi_{t,n_t^h} \pi_s^{\bar{h}}(t,n_t^h) \Delta b_t^h(\bar{h},s) \right]. \tag{6}$$

Then substitute the expression for the prices in (4) for $\pi_s^{\bar{h}}(t,n_t^h t)$ so that (6) becomes

$$\sum_{s=t}^{T} \sum_{\bar{h}=1}^{M} \left[\sum_{t=1}^{T} \psi_{s,n_s^{\bar{h}}} \Delta b_t^h(\bar{h},s) \right] = \sum_{s=1}^{T} \sum_{\bar{h}=1}^{M} \psi_{s,n_s^{\bar{h}}} \left[\sum_{t=1}^{T} \Delta b_t^h(\bar{h},s) \right]. \tag{7}$$

For any $\bar{h} \neq h$,

$$\sum_{t=1}^{T} \Delta b_t^h(\bar{h},s) \geq 0,$$

and if $\bar{h} = h$,

$$\sum_{t=1}^{T} \Delta b_t^h(\bar{h},s) = 0.$$

Applying these to (7) gives (5).   Q.E.D.

If we apply Lemma 1 to the budget constraints in (3), multiplying each by $\psi_{t,n}$ and adding, the result will be

$$\sum_{t=1}^{T} \psi_{t,n_t^h} q(t,n_t^h)(c^h(t,n_t^h) - w^h(t,n_t^h)) \leq 0. \tag{8}$$

The validity of (8) confirms that any bundle c^h that h can finance with a portfolio satisfies the standard, present-value budget constraint when the prices are $p(t,n) = \psi_{t,n}q(t,n)$.

Equilibrium prices are bond prices $\langle \pi_s^{\bar{h}}(t,n) \rangle$ with implicit market interest rates given by ψ and spot prices $\langle q(t,n) \rangle$ such that, when consumers choose consumption plans $\bar{c}^h$ and portfolios $\langle \Delta \bar{b}_t^h(\bar{h},s) \rangle$, both the goods and the IOU markets clear at each location in every period. The market-clearing equations are

$$\sum_{h \in M(t,n)} \bar{c}^h(t,n) = \sum_{h \in M(t,n)} w^h(t,n) \text{ for all } n = 1, \ldots, N \text{ and } t = 1, \ldots, T \quad (9)$$

and

$$\sum_{h \in M(t,n)} \Delta \bar{b}_t^h(\bar{h},s) = 0 \quad \text{for all} \quad \bar{h} = 1, \ldots, M, s = t, \ldots, T,$$

$$\text{and all} \quad n = 1, \ldots, N \quad \text{and} \quad t = 1, \ldots, T.$$

This is the point where the model captures the restriction that the credit transactions must be completed by consumers face-to-face.

The equilibrium conditions in (9) together with the budget constraints in (8) show that an Arrow-Debreu equilibrium at prices $\langle p(t,n) \rangle$ is a sequential markets equilibrium allocation with prices $\langle q(t,n) \rangle (q(t,n) = p(t,n)/\psi_{t,n})$ if and only if there is a set of portfolio choices $\langle \Delta \bar{b}_t^h(\bar{h},s) \rangle$, $h = 1, \ldots, M$, that satisfies (2.1) to (2.3),

$$q(t,n_t^h)(w^h(t,n_t^h) - \bar{c}^h(t,n_t^h)) = \sum_{s=t}^{T} \sum_{h=1}^{M} \pi_s^{\bar{h}}(t,n) \Delta \bar{b}_t^h(\bar{h},s) \quad (E.1)$$

for $t = 1, \ldots, T$ and $h = 1, \ldots, M$, and

$$\sum_{h \in M(t,n)} \Delta \bar{b}_t^h(\bar{h},s) = 0 \quad (E.2)$$

for all $\bar{h} = 1, \ldots, M$ and $s \geq t$ and at all markets $t = 1, \ldots, T$ and $n = 1, \ldots, N$.

This equivalence can be made even simpler by the following observation: If the sequential markets achieve an equilibrium in which spot commodity prices are $\langle q(t,n) \rangle$ and IOU prices are $\langle \pi_s^{\bar{h}}(t,n) \rangle$ with implicit interest rates ψ, the identical allocation will be chosen in equilibrium when securities are priced at $\bar{\pi}_s^{\bar{h}}(t,n) \equiv 1$, spot commodity prices are $\bar{q}(t,n) = q(t,n)\psi_{t,n}$, and portfolio choices are $\langle \Delta \bar{b}_t^h(\bar{h},s) = \psi_{s,n_s^{\bar{h}}} \Delta \bar{b}_t^h(\bar{h},s) \rangle$.

To support this claim, we need only demonstrate that consumers can purchase the same bundles at the new prices and that these consumption bundles are their best choices. If $\bar{c}^h$ is the choice of consumer h originally, then for each t

$$q(t,n)(\bar{c}^h(t,n) - w^h(t,n)) \leq -\sum_{s=t}^{T} \sum_{h=1}^{M} \pi_s^{\bar{h}}(t,n_t^h) \Delta \bar{b}_t^h(\bar{h},s). \quad (10)$$

Multiplying (10) by $\psi_{t,n}$ and applying (4) to the right-hand side, we obtain

$$\bar{q}(t,n)(\bar{c}^h(t,n) - w^h(t,n)) \leq \sum_{s=t}^{T}\sum_{\tilde{h}=1}^{M} \psi_{s,n_s^{\tilde{h}}} \Delta \bar{b}_t^h(\tilde{h},s)$$

$$= \sum_{s=t}^{T}\sum_{\tilde{h}=1}^{M} \bar{\pi}_s^{\tilde{h}}(t,n_t^h)\Delta \bar{b}_t^h(\tilde{h},s). \qquad (11)$$

This demonstrates that consumers can still finance the same consumption bundles with market-clearing portfolio choices when they face these new prices. I leave it as a simple exercise for the reader to show that the budget sets are identical in both environments.

From here on, attention is restricted to equilibria in which IOUs are all priced at one unit of account in each spot, which captures every possible equilibrium allocation.

The next section focuses on the primary question: When can we be sure that an Arrow-Debreu equilibrium allocation (referred to hereafter as A-D equilibria) is also a sequential markets equilibrium allocation? Before doing this, some examples will help to illustrate the difficulties.

The first example is from Townsend and Wallace (1982).

EXAMPLE 1. The accompanying tabulation describes a pattern of consumer participation in various markets. There are four consumers, two locations, and three periods. Consumers 1 and 4 remain at the same locations (1 and 2 respectively) and consumers 2 and 3 switch locations in the second period. For this pattern, any A-D equilibrium in which consumers 1 and 3 do not consume their endowments at market (2,1) cannot be a sequential markets equilibrium. For example, if 1 purchases more than he is endowed with there, he will have to sell IOUs to cover this debt and the only bonds he can sell are his own, with a promise to redeem them in period 3, or 2's bonds payable in period 3, which he may have purchased in the first period. In both cases, consumer 3 must elect to buy them and then take them to location 2 in the next period. Since neither consumer 1 nor 2 is there to redeem these outstanding notes, the equilibrium conditions on bond exchange are violated.

Date/Location	1	2
1	12	34
2	13	24
3	12	34

Consumers may elect to consume their endowments in the second period, in which case the A-D equilibrium can be transacted sequentially. For example, if, at the prices $q(t,n) = 1$ [and $\pi_s^{\tilde{h}}(t,n) = 1$] in all markets, consumer 1 purchases an additional unit of consumption at (1,1) and consumer 2 purchases an additional unit of consumption at (3,1), consumer 1 can sell a unit of his own bonds at (1,1) payable in period 3 to consumer 2 and redeem it in period 3 from consumer 2. This portfolio choice will finance the consumption transactions.

Example 1 illustrates one of the difficulties that might arise from the constraints on the exchange of bonds. It also illustrates that, for some patterns, only a subset of A-D equilibria can be transacted sequentially. The particular difficulty there was that, in some markets, there could be absolutely no exchange of bonds that satisfies the constraints in equilibrium, so consumers cannot borrow or lend there.

The next example is slightly more complicated. We will not be able to rule out bond exchanges in any market, yet the fact that securities must circulate in set patterns to enable the issuer to redeem them will "tie" certain exchanges together. And some equilibrium exchanges cannot be transacted sequentially.

EXAMPLE 2.

Date/Location	1	2
1	12	34
2	12	34
3	13	24
4	13	24

Notice, as shown in the accompanying tabulation, that every consumer in each market has a means of financing a deficit expenditure with an IOU that can circulate to maturity. The market at (2,1) is typical in this respect: consumer 1 can pay for a deficit by using IOUs he has bought from 2 at (1,1) (which promise to pay off in the second period). Similarly, consumer 2 can pay off a deficit with 1's IOUs purchased a period earlier. This same story applies to all consumers in every market.

The problem with transacting an equilibrium sequentially here is that the restrictions on the circulating patterns of securities tie together certain transactions that cannot occur independently. For example, if consumer 1 chooses to purchase more than his endowment at (2,1), he *has* to save in the first period. The only way he can pay consumer 2 for a deficit at (2,1) is with 2's notes purchased in the first period, since consumer 2 cannot carry any of consumer 1's notes with him after this date. They simply would not be redeemable because consumer 1 is never at location 2. Purchasing 2's notes initially involves a net savings by consumer 1 in the first period.

For some specification of tastes and endowments, A-D equilibrium prices might only involve consumers 1 and 3 purchasing an additional unit of consumption in the second period and consumers 2 and 4 purchasing additional units in the third period. But we know that consumer 1 cannot buy extra consumption in period 2 without saving in the first period, so this A-D equilibrium cannot be transacted sequentially.

5. Credit Balances and Equilibrium Bond Holdings

When consumers purchase a consumption plan sequentially, they are making net additions and subtractions from their lifetime accumulated wealth (measured in units of account) in every period. Credit is marked by the purchase of bonds and debt by the sale of bonds. The possibility of transacting A-D equilibria sequentially depends on whether consumers can exchange bonds sequentially and accumulate or decumulate credit according to the pattern described by the equilibrium.

For consumer h, define a vector of *credit balances* as $e^h = \langle e_t^h, t = 1, \ldots, T \rangle$, where $e_t^h \in \mathsf{R}$ and

$$\sum_{t=1}^{T} e_t^h = 0, \tag{12}$$

and identify the entire set of these as E^h (E^h is a vector subspace of R^T).

If consumer h purchases c^h when the A-D market prices are $p(t,n)$, the vector $\langle p(t,n_t^h)(w_t^h(t,n_t^h) - c^h(t,n_t^h)), t = 1, \ldots, T \rangle$ is a member of E^h. When each of the consumers is selecting a credit balance at these prices, and equilibrium results, the chosen credit balances satisfy the additional equations

$$\sum_{h \in M(t,n)} e_t^h = 0 \quad \text{for} \quad n = 1, \ldots, N \quad \text{and} \quad t = 1, \ldots, T. \tag{13}$$

This follows immediately from the market-clearing equations by

$$\sum_{h \in M(t,n)} e_t^h = \sum_{h \in M(t,n)} p(t,n)(w^h(t,n) - c^h(t,n)) = 0.$$

We can formally represent the set of credit balances that are consistent with A-D equilibria as the subset E of the product space

$$\prod_{h=1}^{M} E^h \subseteq \mathsf{R}^{MT}.$$

A member of this set is a vector $e = (e^1, e^2, \ldots, e^M)$, and the coordinates of e numbered $(h - 1)T + 1$ through hT contain consumer h's credit balances. The set is restricted to vectors satisfying the conditions

$$\sum_{h \in M(t,n)} e_{(h-1)T+t} = 0 \quad \text{for} \quad n = 1, \ldots, N \quad \text{and} \quad t = 1, \ldots, T. \tag{14}$$

As E is a subset of a vector space that satisfies a set of homogeneous equations, E itself is a vector space whose dimension will be referred to as $\tilde{N}$. As you might expect, $\tilde{N}$ depends on how interconnected the consumers in this economy are. For example, if every consumer always stays in the same location, the dimension is higher than if consumers move around. A complete description of the dimension of this vector space is given at the end of the presentation.

Consumers finance their credit balances by buying (or perhaps selling, if they are net debtors) IOUs that are priced at one unit of account in every period. The decision by consumer h to purchase the portfolio $\langle \Delta b_t^h(\bar{h},s) \rangle$ is equivalent to the purchasing of

$$\sum_{s=t}^{T} \sum_{\bar{h}=1}^{M} \Delta b_t^h(\bar{h},s)$$

units of credit in period t. (This is a deficit if the sum is negative.) Associated with the portfolio choices $\langle \Delta b_t^h(m,s) \rangle$, $h = 1, \ldots, M$ are the credit balances

$$e_{(h-1)T+t} = \sum_{s=t}^{T} \sum_{\bar{h}=1}^{M} \Delta b_t^h(\bar{h},s). \tag{15}$$

When these portfolio choices satisfy (2.1) to (2.3) and the bond market clearing conditions (which are restated here)

$$\sum_{h \in M(t,n)} \Delta \bar{b}_t^h(\bar{h},s) = 0 \quad \text{for all} \quad \bar{h} = 1, \ldots, M \quad \text{and} \quad s \geq t$$

and at all markets $t = 1, \ldots, T$ and $n = 1, \ldots, N$, (E.2)

the vector e defined by (15) is a member of E. The equations in (12) are realized because, by the end of each consumer's life, the consumer has redeemed all of his own outstanding bonds and sold off accumulated stock of every other consumer's bonds. Equation (13) is a consequence of (E.2).

The set of credit balances in E that can be generated by (15) with portfolio choices satisfying (2.1) to (2.3) and (E.2) is not necessarily all of E. I will call this subset E_B. In Example 1 we observed, for instance, that any $e \in E$ with $e_2 \neq 0$ (consumer 1's credit in period 2) cannot be so generated.

Let us consolidate the definitions that have been introduced in this section.

The set $E \subseteq \mathbb{R}^{MT}$ is the subspace of vectors that satisfy the equations

$$\sum_{t=1}^{T} e_{(h-1)T+t} = 0 \quad \text{for} \quad h = 1, \ldots, M \tag{16}$$

and

$$\sum_{h \in M(t,n)} e_{(h-1)T+t} = 0 \quad \text{for} \quad n = 1, \ldots, N \quad \text{and} \quad t = 1, \ldots, T.$$

$\bar{N}$ refers to the dimension of E.

E_B is the subset of E consisting of the vectors e that satisfy

$$e_{(h-1)T+t} = \sum_{s=t}^{T} \sum_{h=1}^{M} \Delta b_t^h(\bar{h},s) \quad \text{for} \quad t = 1, \ldots, T \quad \text{and} \quad h = 1, \ldots, M \quad (17)$$

where $\langle \Delta b_t^h(\bar{h},s) \rangle$, $h = 1, \ldots, M$ are portfolio choices that satisfy (2.1) to (2.3) and the equilibrium conditions (E.2).

The next proposition captures the important connection between A-D equilibria and the set E_B.

First, the reader is reminded that if $\langle p(t,n) \rangle$ are A-D equilibrium prices with consumers purchasing the consumption plans $\langle \bar{c}^h \rangle$, then associated with it are credit balances represented by the vector $e \in E$ with

$$e_{(h-1)T+t} = e_t^h = p(t,n_t^h)(w^h(t,n_t^h) - \bar{c}^h(t,n_t^h)). \quad (18)$$

PROPOSITION 1. *The A-D equilibrium prices $\langle p(t,n) \rangle$ are also equilibrium prices for the sequential market economy [with $\langle \pi_s^h(t,n) = 1 \rangle$] if and only if the associated vector of credit balances, e, is in E_B.*

PROOF. Suppose consumers purchase $\bar{c}^h$ at the A-D equilibrium prices $\langle p(t,n) \rangle$, which are also equilibrium prices for the sequential market economy. To finance $\bar{c}^h$ they purchase portfolios $\langle \Delta \bar{b}_t^h(m,s) \rangle$ that satisfy (2.1) to (2.3) and (E.2) and

$$p(t,n_t^h)(w^h(t,n_t^h) - \bar{c}^h(t,n_t^h)) = \sum_{s=t}^{T} \sum_{h=1}^{M} \Delta \bar{b}_t^h(\bar{h},s). \quad (19)$$

The left-hand side of (19) is the coordinate $e_{(h-1)T+t}$ of the vector of credit balances associated with the A-D equilibrium. The right-hand side of (19) is the same coordinate entry of the vector in E_B that is derived from the portfolio choice $\langle \Delta \bar{b}_t^h(m,s) \rangle$. So (19) shows that $e \in E_B$.

Now assume that $\langle p(t,n) \rangle$ are A-D equilibrium prices with consumers purchasing $\bar{c}^h$ and $e \in E_B$. Therefore, there exist portfolio choices $\langle \Delta \bar{b}_t^h(h,s) \rangle$ that satisfy (2.1) to (2.3) and (E.2) and, in addition, since $e \in E_B$, (19) is valid. But (19) is the liquidity constraint (3) when consumers buy the consumption plans $\bar{c}^h$ and the portfolios $\langle \Delta \bar{b}_t^h(m,s) \rangle$ and the goods prices are $\langle p(t,n) \rangle$. So consumers can finance the purchases $\bar{c}^h$ in the sequential market economy when goods are priced at $\langle p(t,n) \rangle$ with portfolio choices that satisfy the constraints on bond exchanges. These are in fact the consumers' consumption demands at these prices, because any bundle that h could have bought in the sequential economy could also have been purchased in the A-D economy.   Q.E.D.

The sets E and E_B depend entirely on the sets of market participants $M(t,n)$. For any participation pattern where $E = E_B$, Proposition 1 implies that any A-D equilibrium is also an equilibrium in the sequential markets economy. This is actually a necessary condition for all A-D equilibria to be sequential markets equilibria since, if $E \neq E_B$, then for any $e \in E$ and $e \notin E_B$ there are tastes and endowments giving rise to an A-D equilibrium with this associated set of credit balances. And, by Proposition 1, this same equilibrium is not a sequential markets equilibrium.

Our next task is to have a closer look at the structure of the set E_B. To begin with, consider two sets of portfolio choices $\langle \Delta \hat{b}_t^h(\bar{h},s) \rangle$ and $\langle \Delta \bar{b}_t^h(\bar{h},s) \rangle$, both of which satisfy (2.1) to (2.3) and (E.2). The sum of these portfolio choices is

$$\Delta b_t^h(\bar{h},s) = \Delta \hat{b}_{t}^{h}(\bar{h},s) + \Delta \bar{b}_t^h(\bar{h},s)$$

and, for any scalar $\alpha \geq 0$, $\alpha \cdot \langle \Delta \hat{b}_t^h(\bar{h},s) \rangle$ is the portfolio

$$\Delta b_t^h(\bar{h},s) = \alpha \Delta \hat{b}_t^h(\bar{h},s).$$

The reader can readily verify that the resulting portfolios satisfy (2.1) to (2.3) and (E.2).

Also, if $\hat{e}$ and $\bar{e}$ are the vectors of credit balances implied by the portfolio choices $\langle \Delta \hat{b}_t^h(\bar{h},s) \rangle$ and $\langle \Delta \bar{b}_t^h(\bar{h},s) \rangle$ respectively (i.e., $\hat{e}, \bar{e} \in E_B$), then for α, $\beta \geq 0$, $\alpha \hat{e} + \beta \bar{e}$ is the vector of credit balances implied by the portfolio choices $\langle \alpha \Delta \hat{b}_t^h(h,s) + \beta \Delta \bar{b}_t^h(\bar{h},s) \rangle$.

This demonstrates that E_B is a convex cone.

The following definition is motivated by the fact that when bond exchanges satisfy the equilibrium conditions (E.2), any bond issued by a consumer must go through a specific sequence of exchanges. For example, if consumer $\bar{h}$ issues a bond in period t to be redeemed in period $\bar{s} > t$, either the original purchaser must visit the same location as $\bar{h}$ in period $\bar{s}$ and sell it there, or the bond must circulate through a series of exchanges, each between consumers at common locations, returning in period $\bar{s}$ in the hands of the final purchaser to $\bar{h}$'s location in period $\bar{s}$. (Remember that $\bar{h}$ must redeem it in period $\bar{s}$.)

For consumer $\bar{h}$'s securities with a redemption date of $\bar{s}$, a feasible circulating pattern is described by a sequence $\{(h_i,t_i), i = 1,\ldots,k\}$ that satisfies the conditions

(i) Consumers h_i and h_{i+1} are at the same location in period t_i—i.e.,   (20) $n_{t_i}^{h_i} = n_{t_i}^{h_{i+1}}$, and $h_1 = \bar{h}$;

(ii) $t_1 \leq t_2 \leq \ldots \leq t_k = \bar{s}$; and

(iii) consumer h_k visits the same location as consumer $\bar{h}$ in period $\bar{s}$.

For consumer $\bar{h}$'s bonds payable in period $\bar{s}$ there are $J(\bar{h},\bar{s})$ such circulating patterns, indexed by j. Of course, this number might be zero.

To illustrate this with an example, go back to the table in Example 1. For consumer 1's notes redeemable in period 3, the only circulating pattern is described by $\{(1,1),(2,3)\}$ and involves consumer 1 selling bonds to 2 in period 1 and consumer 2 reselling them to 1 in period 3. There are no circulating patterns for 1's bonds redeemable in the second period.

When one unit of $\bar{h}$'s bonds, redeemable in period $\bar{s}$, circulates through a given (say the jth) circulating pattern, and there is no other trade in bonds, the implied portfolio choice is described as follows: the pattern is given by $\{(h_i^j,t_i^j),i = 1,\ldots,k_j\}$. In period t_i^j, h_i^j sells the bond and h_{i+1}^j purchases it. The portfolio choices $\langle \Delta b_t^h(\bar{h},\bar{s})_j \rangle$, $h = 1, \ldots, m$ are thus described as follows:

$$\Delta b_t^h(\bar{h},\bar{s})_j = \begin{cases} -1 \text{ if } h = h_i & \text{and } t = t_i, \text{ for } i = 1, \ldots, k_j \\ 1 \text{ if } h = h_{i+1} & \text{and } t = t_i, \text{ for } i = 1, \ldots, k_j \\ 1 \text{ if } h = \bar{h} & \text{and } t = \bar{s}, \end{cases} \quad (21)$$

and the purchases and sales of all other notes are zero. This set of portfolio choices satisfies (2.1) to (2.3) and (E.2). The resulting credit balances are called $e(\bar{h},s)^j$, which is described (remember that $\pi_{\bar{s}}^h(t,n) \equiv 1$) as follows:

$$e(\bar{h},\bar{s})_{(h-1)T+t}^j = \begin{cases} 1 \text{ if } h = h_i^j & \text{and } t = t_i^j \text{ for some } i = 1, \ldots, k_j \\ -1 \text{ if } h = h_{i+1}^j & \text{and } t = t_{i+1}^j \text{ for some } i = 1, \ldots, k_{j-1} \\ & \text{or if } h = \bar{h} \text{ and } t = \bar{s}, t = s \\ 0 \text{ otherwise.} \end{cases}$$

There are

$$J = \sum_{\bar{h}=1}^{M} \sum_{s=2}^{T} J(\bar{h},\bar{s})$$

credit balance vectors such as this.

The following proposition asserts that the J credit balances described above generate the cone E_B.

PROPOSITION 2.

$$E_B = \left\{ \sum_{\bar{h}=1}^{M} \sum_{\bar{s}=2}^{T} \sum_{j=1}^{J(\bar{h},s)} \beta(\bar{h},\bar{s})^j e(\bar{h},\bar{s})^j; \beta(\bar{h},\bar{s})^j \geq 0 \right.$$

$$\left. \text{for all} \quad j = 1,\ldots,J(\bar{h},\bar{s}),\bar{h} = 1,\ldots,M \quad \text{and} \quad \bar{s} = 2,\ldots,T \right\}.$$

The proof of Proposition 2 is very simple once the following intuitive fact is established: Whenever consumers make portfolio choices in which supply equals demand for each IOU in every market, it is possible to identify quantities of each type of IOU being passed through the various circulating patterns. The formal statement of this fact is given in the following lemma, a sketch of whose proof can be found in the appendix.

LEMMA 2. *If* $\{\langle \Delta b_t^h(\bar{h},s) \rangle, h = 1,\ldots,M\}$ *are portfolio choices that satisfy* (E.2), *there are nonnegative quantities* $\{\beta(\bar{h},s)^j : \bar{h} = 1,\ldots,M,$ $s = 2,\ldots,T$ *and* $j = 1,\ldots,J(\bar{h},s)\}$ *such that for each h,*

$$\langle \Delta b_t^h(\bar{h},s) \rangle = \sum_{\bar{h}=1}^{M} \sum_{\bar{s}=2}^{T} \sum_{j=1}^{J(\bar{h},\bar{s})} \beta(\bar{h},\bar{s})^j \langle \Delta b_t^h(\bar{h},\bar{s})_j \rangle.$$

I will use this to prove Proposition 2.

PROOF. The bond purchases and sales by each consumer, when $\beta(\bar{h},\bar{s})^j$ units of security $(\bar{h},\bar{s})$ are circulated through its jth pattern, are simply

$$\beta(\bar{h},\bar{s})^j \langle \Delta b_t^h(\bar{h},\bar{s})_j \rangle = \langle \beta(\bar{h},\bar{s})^j \Delta b_t^h(\bar{h},\bar{s}) \rangle.$$

Let $\langle \Delta b_t^h(\bar{h},s) \rangle$, $h = 1, \ldots, M$ be portfolio choices that satisfy (2.1) to (2.3) and (E.2). Because of the previous observation, there are nonnegative scalars $\langle \beta(\bar{h},\bar{s})^j \rangle$ with

$$\langle \Delta b_t^h(\bar{h},s) \rangle = \sum_{\bar{h}=1}^{M} \sum_{\bar{s}=2}^{T} \sum_{j=1}^{J(\bar{h},\bar{s})} \langle \beta(\bar{h},\bar{s})^j \Delta b_t^h(\bar{h},\bar{s})_j \rangle.$$

Since the credit balances that result from a linear combination of portfolios are the same as the linear combination of the credit balances resulting from each individually, the credit balances implied by the portfolio choices $\langle \Delta b_t^h(\bar{h},s) \rangle$ are

$$\sum_{\bar{h}=1}^{M} \sum_{\bar{s}=2}^{T} \sum_{j=1}^{J(\bar{h},\bar{s})} \beta(\bar{h},\bar{s})^j e(\bar{h},\bar{s})^j.$$

This same argument can easily be reversed to complete the proof.   Q.E.D.

6. The Mathematical Solution

Now that we have a simple way to generate E_B, the mathematical condition that characterizes when $E_B = E$ is very straightforward.

THEOREM 1. *The cone* $E_B = E$ *if and only if there are nonnegative scalars* $\{\bar{\beta}(\bar{h},\bar{s})^j, j = 1,\ldots,J(\bar{h},\bar{s}), \bar{h} = 1,\ldots,M$ *and* $\bar{s} = 2,\ldots,T\}$ *that solve the equations*

$$\sum_{\bar{s}=2}^{T} \sum_{\bar{h}=1}^{M} \sum_{j=1}^{J(\bar{h},\bar{s})} \bar{\beta}(\bar{h},\bar{s})^j e(\bar{h},\bar{s})^j = 0 \tag{22}$$

and the set $\{e(\bar{h},\bar{s})^j : \beta(\bar{h},\bar{s})^j > 0\}$ contains $\bar{N}$ (the dimension of E) linearly independent vectors.

Theorem 1 is an immediate consequence of the following.

LEMMA 3. *Let $v_1, \ldots, v_n$ be vectors in R^m. The cone that is generated by these vectors is all of R^m if and only if there exist nonnegative scalars $\{\bar{\alpha}_i, i = 1,\ldots,n\}$ with*

$$\sum_{i=1}^{n} \bar{\alpha}_i v_i = 0 \tag{23}$$

and the set $\{v_i : \bar{\alpha}_i > 0\}$ contains m linearly independent vectors.

PROOF. Let

$$V = \left\{ v : v = \sum_{i=1}^{n} \alpha_i v_i, \alpha_i \geq 0, i = 1,\ldots,n \right\}$$

describe this cone and assume that there are nonnegative scalars $\{\bar{\alpha}_i\}$ that satisfy the hypothesis in (23). If $V \neq \mathsf{R}^m$, then there is a nonzero vector $w \in \mathsf{R}^m$ with

$$w \cdot \left(\sum_{i=1}^{m} \alpha_i v_i \right) \leq 0$$

for all $\{\alpha_i \geq 0, i = 1,\ldots,n\}$. In particular, $w \cdot v_i \leq 0$ for $i = 1, \ldots, n$. Using this and the relationship in (23),

$$0 = w \cdot \left(\sum_{i=1}^{n} \bar{\alpha}_i v_i \right) = \sum_{i=1}^{n} \bar{\alpha}_i (w \cdot v_i). \tag{24}$$

Since $w \cdot v_i \leq 0$, $w \cdot v_i = 0$ for all v_i with $\bar{\alpha}_i > 0$ [otherwise, (24) would be violated]. But then w is in the orthogonal complement of the subspace of R^m spanned by $\{v_i : \bar{\alpha}_i > 0\}$. This is impossible because this subspace is all of R^m. (It has enough linearly independent vectors.)

To establish the result in the other direction, assume that $V = \mathsf{R}^m$. Then, for each j, there exists a set of nonnegative scalars $\{\alpha_i^j, i = 1,\ldots,n\}$ with

$$-v_j = \sum_{i=1}^{n} \alpha_i^j v_i,$$

which can be rewritten as

$$\alpha_1^j v_1 + \ldots + (1 + \alpha_i^j) v_j + \ldots + \alpha_n^j v_n = 0. \tag{25}$$

The equations in (25) can be added together to give

$$\sum_{i=1}^{n} \bar{\alpha}_i v_i = 0 \tag{26}$$

with

$$\bar{\alpha}_i = 1 + \sum_{j=1}^{n} \alpha_i^j \geq 1.$$

Therefore, all of the $\bar{\alpha}_i > 0$. Equation (26) is the first condition that was to be shown. The second, namely that $\{v_i : \bar{\alpha}_i \neq 0\}$ has m linearly independent vectors, is valid because every $\bar{\alpha}_i > 0$ and the set of vectors $\{v_i\}$ must contain m linearly independent vectors since they span all of $\mathbf{R}^m$.   Q.E.D.

This leads to the following.

COROLLARY 1. *The cone $E_B = E$ if and only if there are portfolio choices* $\langle \Delta b_t^h(\bar{h},s) \rangle$, $h = 1, \ldots, M$ *that satisfy (2.1) to (2.3) and (E.2) with*

  (i) $\Sigma_{h=1}^{M} \Sigma_{s=t}^{T} \Delta b_t^h(\bar{h},s) = 0$ *for all $h = 1, \ldots, M$ and $t = 1, \ldots, T$, and*

  (ii) *the set of credit balances $\{e(\bar{h},\bar{s})^j\}$ that are associated with circulating patterns through which nonzero quantities are being traded contains a subset of $\tilde{N}$ linearly independent vectors.*

This follows immediately from Theorem 1 because the credit balance vector e associated with the portfolio choices $\langle \Delta b_t^h(\bar{h},s) \rangle$, $h = 1, \ldots, M$ is given by

$$e = \sum_{\bar{h}=1}^{M} \sum_{\bar{s}=2}^{T} \sum_{j=1}^{J(\bar{h},\bar{s})} \beta(\bar{h},\bar{s})^j e(\bar{h},\bar{s})^j = 0,$$

where the portfolio choices that result when the nonnegative quantities $\{\beta(\bar{h},\bar{s})^j\}$ of each security are circulated through each pattern are $\langle \Delta b_t^h(\bar{h},s) \rangle$, $h = 1, \ldots, M$.

Corollary 1 gives a very easy method to verify that the economy, which is the central example in the work of Townsend and Wallace (*this volume*), has a sequential markets equilibrium that is identical to any Arrow-Debreu equilibrium.

EXAMPLE 3. For this example (see the accompanying table), the dimension of E is 5. (The final result in this paper establishes a complete description of the dimension of E.) The first five of the following six circulating patterns generate linearly independent credit balances when one unit of the appropriate bond is traded through them. (Remember that each pair in parentheses is a consumer and a date, with that consumer selling the bond in the specified period.)

1. (1,1) (2,2) (4,3) (3,4)
2. (2,1) (1,2) (3,3) (4,4)
3. (3,1) (4,2) (2,3) (1,4)

4. (4,1) (3,2) (1,3) (2,4)
5. (1,1) (2,3)
6. (2,1) (1,3)

Date/Location	1	2
1	12	34
2	13	24
3	12	34
4	13	24

Each of the circulating patterns is for bonds issued by the initial person to be paid in the last period. For example, the first is for consumer 1's bonds payable in period 4. The pattern involves 1 selling it 2 in the market at (1,1), 2 selling it to 4 at (2,2), 4 selling it to 3 at (3,2), and 2 reselling it to 1 at (4,1).

When one unit of the appropriate bond is circulated through each pattern, the implied credit balance for each consumer is zero. Take, for example, consumer 3 in the market at (2,1). He sells 4's bond that is redeemable in period 4 and buys 2's bond that is redeemable in period 4. The reader can check that each consumer in every market buys and sells exactly the same number of bonds. This implies, by Corollary 1, that any Arrow-Debreu equilibrium can be transacted sequentially with the "correct" portfolio choices.

The last problem to be discussed is the dimension of E. Recall that E is the subspace of $\mathbf{R}^{MT}$ consisting of vectors that satisfy

$$\sum_{t=1}^{T} e_{(h-1)T+t} = 0 \quad \text{for} \quad h = 1, \ldots, M$$

and

$$\sum_{h \in M(t,n)} e_{(h-1)T+t} = 0 \quad \text{for} \quad n = 1, \ldots, N \quad \text{and} \quad t = 1, \ldots, T.$$

These equations can be rewritten (v^h, v^{tn} and $e \in \mathbf{R}^{MT}$) as

$$v^h \cdot e = 0, \, h = 1, \ldots, M$$

$$v^{tn} \cdot e = 0, \, t = 1, \ldots, T \quad \text{and} \quad n = 1, \ldots, N$$

where

$$v_j^h = \begin{cases} 1 & \text{if} \quad j = (h-1)T + t, t = 1, \ldots, T \\ 0 & \text{otherwise;} \end{cases}$$

$$v_j^{tn} = \begin{cases} 1 & \text{if} \quad j = (h-1)T + t \quad \text{and} \quad h \in M(t,n) \\ 0 & \text{otherwise.} \end{cases}$$

The dimension of E is the difference between MT and the dimension of the subspace of R^{MT} that is spanned by $\{v^h, v^{tn}; h = 1, \ldots, M, t = 1, \ldots, T,$ and $n = 1, \ldots, N\}$. It will depend on how interconnected the agents of the economy are.

The economy is *decomposable* if the markets can be divided into two (nonempty) sets A_1 and A_2 [i.e., every $(t,n) \in A_i$ for exactly one $i = 1,2$] and consumers can also be divided into two sets (one of these can be empty) Φ_1 and Φ_2 (again, each consumer h belongs to exactly one $\Phi_i, i = 1,2$) so that each consumer in Φ_i participates only in the markets in A_i.

PROPOSITION 3. *If the economy cannot be decomposed, the dimension of E is $MT - [M + NT - 1]$.*

PROOF. Establishing this result involves showing that $M + NT - 1$ of the vectors $\{v^h, v^{tn}, h = 1, \ldots, M, n = 1, \ldots, N$ and $t = 1, \ldots, T\}$ are linearly independent. First of all, this entire set of vectors is not linearly independent since

$$\sum_{h=1}^{M} v^h - \sum_{t=1}^{T} \sum_{n=1}^{N} v^{tn} = 0.$$

[This follows because each consumer in each period participates in exactly one market. For coordinate number $(h - 1)T + t$, $h \in M(t,n)$ for some (t,n), therefore $v^h_{(h-1)T+t} = 1$ and $v^{tn}_{(h-1)T+t} = 1$, and all of the other vectors have a 0 in this coordinate.]

Now, assume that

$$\sum_{h=1}^{M-1} \lambda^h v^h + \sum_{t=1}^{T} \sum_{n=1}^{N} \lambda^{tn} v^{tn} = 0 \qquad (27)$$

for scalars $\{\lambda^h, \lambda^{tn}; h = 1, \ldots, M - 1, t = 1, \ldots, T$ and $n = 1, \ldots, N\}$ not identically zero. I will show that this relationship can hold only if the economy is decomposable.

Define the sets

$$\Phi_1 = \{h : \lambda^h \neq 0\}$$

$$\Phi_2 = \{h : h \notin \Phi_1\}$$

$$A_1 = \{(t,n) : \lambda^{tn} \neq 0\} \quad \text{and}$$

$$A_2 = \{(t,n) : (t,n) \notin A_1\}.$$

If $h \in A_1$ participates in the market at (t,n), then the $(h - 1)T + t$ coordinate of (27) is

$$\lambda^h - \lambda^{tn} = 0.$$

Since $\lambda^h \neq 0$, $\lambda^m \neq 0$ and $(t,n) \in A_1$. On the other hand, if $\lambda^m \neq 0$ and $h \in M(t,n)$, the same argument establishes that $h \in A_1$.

This shows that if (27) is valid, then all of the consumers in Φ_1 participate only in the markets in A_1, and they are the only consumers who participate in these markets.

If both of the sets A_1 and A_2 are nonempty, then the economy is decomposable. The fact that the sum in (27) is for $h = 1, \ldots, M - 1$, implies that $M \not\in \Phi_1$ and therefore A_2 is nonempty (it must contain the markets in which consumer M participates).

To establish that A_1 is nonempty, assume that $\lambda^{tn} = 0$ for all of the markets (t,n). Then $\lambda^{h'} \neq 0$ for some $h' \leq M - 1$. But this implies that A_1 must contain all of the markets in which h' participates and cannot be empty.

We have established that if the economy is not decomposable, the $M + NT - 1$ vectors $\{v^h, v^{tn}, h = 1, \ldots, M - 1, t = 1, \ldots, T$ and $n = 1, \ldots, N\}$ are linearly independent.   Q.E.D.

The argument that established Proposition 3 can be used to calculate the dimension of E for any economy. The method goes as follows. Divide the set of consumers into subsets $\Phi_1, \ldots, \Phi_k$ and the set of markets into subsets $A_1, \ldots, A_k$ where the consumers who visit the markets in A_j are in Φ_j and the consumers in Φ_j visit only the markets in A_j. Construct the division in such a way that each subeconomy (consisting of the consumers Φ_j and the markets A_j) is not itself decomposable.

Each subeconomy consists of the consumers Φ_j and the markets A_j. The set of credit balances that is possible in an equilibrium for this subeconomy is a subspace E_j of $R^{M_j T}$ containing vectors $(e^{1j}, \ldots, e^{M_j})$, where $h_j \in \Phi_j$ and $e^{h_j} \in E^{h_j}$ and that satisfy the equations

$$\sum_{h_j \in M(t,n)} e_t^{h_j} = 0$$

for all markets $(t,n) \in A_j$.

By an argument that is identical to that given for Proposition 3, the dimension of E_j is $M_j T - [M_j - N_j - 1]$ where N_j is the number of markets in A_j.

Since $E = E_1 x \ldots x E_k$ (the Cartesian product), the dimension of E is the sum of the dimensions of E_j; in other words,

$$\tilde{N} = \sum_{j=1}^{k} \{M_j T - [M_j + N_j - 1]\} = MT - [M + NT - k]. \qquad (28)$$

The following example illustrates this.

EXAMPLE 4. The two subeconomies shown in the accompanying tabulation have $A_1 = \{(1,1),(2,1),(3,1)\}$ with $\Phi_1 = \{1,2\}$ and $A_2 = \{(1,2),(2,2)(3,2)\}$

and $\Phi_2 = \{3,4\}$. These are clearly not themselves decomposable economies. Since $k = 2$, according to (28), the dimension of E is

$$12 - [4 + 6 - 2] = 4.$$

Notice that when an economy is decomposable, the dimension of E increases.

Date/Location	1	2
1	1, 2	34
2	1, 2	34
3	1, 2	34

7. Conclusion

This paper has provided a complete characterization of the structures in which Arrow-Debreu equilibria can be replicated with this type of financial arrangement. This characterization was accomplished by consistently assuming a special structure on the bond prices: namely, all consumers trade at identical interest rates between spots. For some participation patterns, this need not be the case. In fact, it is possible to find patterns in which an equilibrium exists where agents purchase credit at different rates of interest because they participate in different sets of markets and cannot exploit arbitrage possibilities. Of course, such an equilibrium is not Pareto-optimal.

For their particular example, Townsend and Wallace (1982) ruled out such equilibria by arguing that arbitrage prevents them. This is not an accident. Complete market spanning—in other words, $E_B = E$—carries a tremendous amount of arbitrage power. In a future paper, I will demonstrate that complete market spanning with credit contracts that are more complex than those described herein guarantees that individual arbitrage will almost always force efficient pricing.

Appendix

The proof of lemma 2 goes as follows. First choose a specific security $(\bar{h},s)$ (referring to $\bar{h}$'s security payable in period s). We want to show that there exist quantities $\beta(\bar{h},s)^j \geq 0$, $j = 1, \ldots, J(\bar{h},s)$ of this security that, when traded through the circulating patterns, produce net purchases by each consumer that are the same as in the portfolio choices $\langle \Delta b_t^h(\bar{h},s) \rangle$. This will be sufficient to establish the result.

When consumers choose the portfolios $\langle \Delta b_t^h(\bar{h},s) \rangle$, they are in essence holding (in this case, consumer h is holding)

$$b_t^h(\bar{h},s) = \sum_{\tau=1}^{t} \Delta b_\tau^h(\bar{h},s)$$

units of security $(\bar{h},s)$ at the end of period t and

$$\Delta b_t^h(\bar{h},s) = b_t^h(\bar{h},s) - b_{t-1}^h(\bar{h},s)$$

for all t.

When $\beta(m,s)^j$ units of security $(\bar{h},s)$ are traded through its jth circulating pattern $\{(h_i^j,t_i^j),i = 1,\ldots,k_j\}$, consumer h_i^j owns them between periods t_{i-1}^j and t_i^j. For circulating pattern j, let h_t^j represent the consumer who, at the end of period t, holds any bonds that circulate through the jth pattern. In particular, $h_t^j = h_i^j$ for $t_{i-1}^j \le t < t_i^j$. (The term h_t^j is only defined for $t_1^j \le t < s$.)

We are looking for nonnegative scalars $\beta(\bar{h},s)^j$, $j = 1, \ldots, J(\bar{h},s)$ that satisfy the equations

$$b_t^h(\bar{h},s) = \sum_{\{j:h=h_t^j\}} \beta(\bar{h},s)^j, t = 1, \ldots, T \quad \text{and} \quad h = 1, \ldots, M \quad \text{with} \quad h \ne \bar{h}. \quad \text{(F.1)}$$

The right-hand side of (F.1) contains the units of security $(\bar{h},s)$ that h holds at the end of period t when $\langle\beta(\bar{h},s)^j\rangle$ units of security $(\bar{h},s)$ are traded through each pattern. These equations need only hold for $h \ne m$ since then consumer $\bar{h}$ must have sold the correct number of bonds.

Once I show that there are scalars that satisfy the equations in (F.1), the assertion will follow from the observation that if the stock of bond holdings matches those of the original portfolios, the net trades must also be the same.

The existence of these scalars is established by contradiction. Assume that for all sets of nonnegative scalars $\langle\beta(\bar{h},s)^j\rangle$, (F.1) cannot be fulfilled for all consumers in every period. Then for some consumer $\hat{h}$ in some period $\hat{t}$, there exist scalars $\langle\beta(\bar{h},s)^j\rangle$ such that (F.1) is valid for all h when $t < \hat{t}$ and all $h < \hat{h}$ when $t = \hat{t}$ and not when $h = \hat{h}$ and $t = \hat{t}$, and for which it is impossible to find scalars $\langle\beta(\bar{h},s)^j\rangle$ satisfying (F.1) for all h when $t < \hat{t}$ and for $h \le \hat{h}$ and $t = \hat{t}$.

For any scalars $\langle\beta(\bar{h},s)^j\rangle$ that satisfy (F.1) for all h when $t < \hat{t}$ and $h < \hat{h}$ in period $\hat{t}$ but not for consumer $\hat{h}$ in period $\hat{t}$, there is an implied stock holding of security $(\bar{h},s)$ by $\hat{h}$ at the end of period $\hat{t}$. The set of such holdings that can be so generated is convex (actually, an interval), and $b_{\hat{t}}^{\hat{h}}(\bar{h},s)$ is not among them. So they are either all too small or too large. In both cases, we derive a contradiction.

Take the case when they are all too small. Then there are scalars $\langle\bar{\beta}(\bar{h},s)^j\rangle$ that yield the largest value of

$$\sum_{\{j:\hat{h}=h_{\hat{t}}^j\}} \beta(\bar{h},s)^j.$$

[The amount held by $\hat{h}$ after period $\hat{t}$] among all $\langle\beta(\bar{h},s)^j\rangle$ that satisfy (F.1) for all h when $t < \hat{t}$ and $h < \hat{h}$ when $t = \hat{t}$. By assumption, the quantity

$$\bar{b}_{\hat{t}}^{\hat{h}}(\bar{h},s) = \sum_{\{j:\hat{h}=h_{\hat{t}}^j\}} \bar{\beta}(\bar{h},s)^j$$

is strictly less than $b_{\hat{t}}^{\hat{h}}(\bar{h},s)$.

The market-clearing equations (E.2) imply that

$$\sum_{h\in M(\hat{t},n_{\hat{t}}^{\hat{h}})} b_{\hat{t}}^h(\bar{h},s) = \sum_{h\in M(\hat{t},n_{\hat{t}}^{\hat{h}})} b_{\hat{t}-1}^h(\bar{h},s) \qquad \text{(F.2)}$$

if $\bar{h} \notin M(\hat{t},n_{\hat{t}}^{\hat{h}})$. Or

$$\sum_{h\in M(\hat{t},n_{\hat{t}}^{\hat{h}})} b_{\hat{t}}^h(\bar{h},s) = \sum_{h\in M(\hat{t},n_{\hat{t}}^{\hat{h}})} b_{\hat{t}-1}^h(\bar{h},s) - \Delta b_{\hat{t}}^m(\bar{h},s)$$

if $h \in M(\hat{t},n_{\hat{t}}^{\hat{h}})$.

Let

$$\bar{b}_t^h = \sum_{\{j:h=h_t^j\}} \bar{\beta}(\bar{h},s)^j \quad \text{for all} \quad h = 1, \ldots, M, h \neq \bar{h}, \quad \text{and} \quad t = 1, \ldots, T.$$

This is the implied holding of security $(\bar{h},s)$ by h in period t when $\langle \bar{\beta}(\bar{h},s)^j \rangle$ units are circulated.

The bond exchanges that occur when $\langle \bar{\beta}(\bar{h},s)^j \rangle$ units are circulated also satisfy the market-clearing equations (E.2). Therefore, if no new bonds are issued in the market, the total holdings by consumers are the same before and after the market transactions. This implies that

$$\sum_{h \in M(\hat{t},n_{\hat{t}}^{\hat{h}})} \bar{b}_{\hat{t}}^h(\bar{h},s) = \sum_{h \in M(\hat{t},n_{\hat{t}}^{\hat{h}})} \bar{b}_{\hat{t}-1}^h = \sum_{h \in M(\hat{t},n_{\hat{t}}^{\hat{h}})} b_{\hat{t}-1}^h(\bar{h},s) = \sum_{h \in M(\hat{t},n_{\hat{t}}^{\hat{h}})} b_{\hat{t}}^h(\bar{h},s)$$

if $\bar{h} \notin M(\hat{t},n_{\hat{t}}^{\hat{h}})$ or if $\Delta b_{\hat{t}}^{\hat{h}}(\bar{h},s) = 0$.

Since $\bar{b}_{\hat{t}}^{\hat{h}}(\bar{h},s) < b_{\hat{t}}^{\hat{h}}(\bar{h},s)$, there is some $h' \in M(\hat{t},n_{\hat{t}}^{\hat{h}})$ with $\bar{b}_{\hat{t}}^{h'}(\bar{h},s) > b_{\hat{t}}^{h'}(\bar{h},s)$.

The contradiction comes by noticing that any units of $(\bar{h},s)$ that h' holds after period $\hat{t}$ can be rerouted through $\hat{h}$ in period $\hat{t}$ without affecting any consumer's holdings before this nor any other consumer's possessions in period $\hat{t}$. This increases the quantity held by $\hat{h}$ after period $\hat{t}$. One can thus construct another set of scalars $\langle \bar{\beta}(\bar{h},s)^j \rangle$ that satisfies (F.1) for all h when $t < \hat{t}$ and $h < \hat{h}$ when $t = \hat{t}$ and with

$$\bar{b}_{\hat{t}}^{\hat{h}}(\bar{h},s) < \sum_{\{j:\hat{h}=h_{\hat{t}}^j\}} \bar{\beta}(\bar{h},s)^j.$$

This contradicts the maximality of $\bar{b}_{\hat{t}}^{\hat{h}}(\bar{h},s)$.

If $\bar{h} \in M(\hat{t},n_{\hat{t}}^{\hat{h}})$ and $\Delta b_{\hat{t}}^{\hat{h}}(\bar{h},s) < 0$, there must be a circulating pattern for this security $\{(h_i^j,t_i^j)\}$ with $m_2^j = \bar{h}$ and $t_1^j = \hat{t}$ (i.e., originating in period $\hat{t}$ with a trade from consumer $\bar{h}$ to consumer $\hat{h}$). But then any quantity of bonds can circulate through this pattern without affecting any other consumer's holdings before consumer $\hat{h}$ in period $\hat{t}$. By allowing the quantity of $(\bar{h},s)$ circulating through this pattern to be arbitrarily large, the maximality of $\bar{b}_{\hat{t}}^{\hat{h}}(\bar{h},s)$ can be contradicted.

A similar argument establishes a contradiction when the bond holdings of $\hat{h}$ in period $\hat{t}$ implied by scalars $\langle \beta(\bar{h},s)^j \rangle$ satisfying (F.1) for all h when $t < \hat{t}$ and $h < \hat{h}$ when $t = \hat{t}$ are all too large. Then the trick is to reroute away from $\hat{h}$ in period $\hat{t}$ to reduce the smallest of these.

Notes

1. I would like to offer a special thanks to David Cass for some very critical suggestions based on a preliminary version of this paper. I also derived significant benefits from comments by and conversations with Joe Ostroy, Jim Peck, and Karl Shell. Research support from the National Science Foundation under grant SES 83-09049 is also gratefully acknowledged.

2. IOUs are securities of the form used by Arrow (1964) except that they are personalized—in other words, backed by some consumer.

3. All of the analysis can be carried out with bundles containing a variety of commodities. I chose to work with this special case as a means of simplifying the already cumbersome notation. For the generalization, one can simply reinterpret consumption goods and prices as vectors with several components. The theorems are all the same.

4. For this case, simply ignore all of the markets (t,n) at which only one individual participates. After the other equilibrium prices are derived, the remaining goods can be priced so that the consumers are then happy with what they have.

5. Townsend and Wallace (1982; *this volume*) allow for bonds to be sold only in markets where there are potential buyers and sellers. Since in equilibrium these are the only markets in which bonds are traded, I will let the equilibrium conditions close the other markets.

6. I am using the standard concept that prices implicitly define rates of return. If ψ determines the interest rates, then one unit of account at (s,n_s^h) should cost $\psi_s^h(t,n)$ units of account of (t,n).

References

Arrow, K. 1964. "The Role of Securities in the Optimal Allocation of Risk Bearing." *Review of Economic Studies* 31:91–96.

McKenzie, L. W. 1959. "On the Existence of General Equilibrium for a Competitive Market." *Econometrica* 27:54–71.

Ostroy, J. M. 1973. "The Informational Efficiency of Monetary Exchange." *American Economic Review* 63:597–610.

Ostroy, J. M., and R. M. Starr. 1974. "Money and the Decentralization of Exchange." *Econometrica* 42:1093–1113.

Townsend, R., and N. Wallace. 1982. "A Model of Circulating Private Debt." Staff report 83, Federal Reserve Bank of Minneapolis.

VII

Dynamic Coalitions, Growth, and the Firm

Edward C. Prescott and
John H. Boyd

The implications of a dynamic coalition production technology are explored. With this technology, coalitions produce the current period consumption good as well as coalition-specific capital that is embodied in young coalition members. The equilibrium allocation is efficient and displays constant growth rates, even though exogenous technological change is not a feature of the environment. Unlike the neoclassical growth model, policies that influence agents' investment-consumption decisions affect not only the level of output but also its constant growth rate. In addition to these growth entailments, the theory has equally important industrial organization implications. Specifically, in equilibrium there is no tendency for coalition (firm) size to regress to the mean or for the distribution of coalition sizes to become more disparate.

1. Introduction

In this study, we explore the implications of a dynamic coalition production technology in an equilibrium environment.[1] There are three major implications. One is that, even without exogenous technological change, with this technology there can be sustained growth in an economy's per capita output. Economies that are identical except for their initial capital endowments grow at the same constant percentage rate; output in such economies does not tend to converge to the same level or to diverge. Another implication is that, although firm size is variable, it does not tend to regress to the mean size nor does the size distribution of firms tend to become more disparate over time. A final implication is that, in this environment, unlike in the neoclassical growth model, a policy that distorts investment-consumption decisions can affect an economy's equilibrium growth rate, not just its level of output.

Few models have been able to account simultaneously for both growth and firm size observations without resorting to exogenous technological change. Very briefly, the problem has been that to have sustained growth in per capita output, there cannot be diminishing returns to capital. But if returns to capital are not diminishing and labor is a joint input, then for any reasonable production function there are increasing returns to scale. And increasing returns are inconsistent with the existence of a competitive equilibrium.

In the environment we consider, there are no diminishing returns to investment, because of a key assumption: workers' productivities depend not only on their own human capital, but also on that of their co-workers. At any point in time, though, the rate of transformation in producing this capital and output for current consumption is nonlinear. In particular, Lucas-type adjustment costs (Lucas 1967) constrain the rate of investment. As a result, percentage growth rates rather than firm sizes are determined in equilibrium. (If this point is not clear now, it should become clear as we go through the formal analysis.)[2]

Our environment is in most ways quite standard and simple: agents are identically endowed, live two periods, and have identical utility functions, defined on consumption today and tomorrow. The environment is nonstandard, however, in at least one important way: a firm is not defined by the technology to which it has access. Rather, our firms are coalitions of agents, and, as in Lucas (1978), all have access to the same blueprint technology. In Lucas (1978), agents are endowed with different managerial capabilities, and the distribution of these capabilities determines the size distribution of firms. Our agents, in contrast, are identically endowed but may choose to accumulate human capital in differing amounts. Thus, coalitions may differ too, depending on the human capital decisions of their members.[3]

Another way our environment differs from most others is in the production technology. Here each coalition's output capability is determined by its capital and by the universally available production technology. Coalition capital is, by assumption, human capital and is partly organization specific. But it is not just "firm-specific human capital" as others have used that term.

Let us be more precise. Recall that each agent lives two periods. Coalition capital is knowledge or expertise, and when created (in its first period), it is embodied in young, inexperienced coalition members. Next period they will become old, experienced members, and the coalition's production capabilities will be expanded commensurately. Moreover, the coalition's production capability is assumed to depend not only on the expertise of each individual member; it also depends on each member's knowledge of the expertise of other coalition members, and this can only be obtained by members working together when young. In other words, coalition capital is specific not to an organization but rather to a particular group of individuals who have worked and been trained together. A parametric example is included in the next section to elucidate this feature of the model.[4]

The production technology formally specified in Section 2 attempts roughly to represent these sorts of interagent and intertemporal production relationships. Admittedly, the economy is highly stylized. It deals with a representative coalition (in all respects except size), there is neither birth nor death of coalitions, and there is no specialization of productive activity. Consequently, this study is best viewed as opening a line of inquiry that might prove useful in addressing some unresolved issues in development, industrial organization, and their intersection. We are optimistic, however, that the basic environment can be modified so that equilibrium is characterized by entry and exit of coalitions and specialization in production while still producing the key observations.

The study has three main parts. First we specify the environment, and then we define a constant growth equilibrium and present an existence and uniqueness proof. We (briefly) investigate the effect of a tax policy on the steady-state growth rate. Finally, we summarize the analysis and suggest some ways in which it might be profitably extended.

2. The Economy

Initially, there is some given number of old agents. Each period, that number of young agents is born, and they live for two periods. Thus, at all points in time there are equal numbers of young and old. Those born in period t for $t = 1, 2, \ldots$ have a utility function $u : R_+ \times R_+ \to R_+$:

$$u(y_t, z_{t+1}) = \ln y_t + \beta \ln z_{t+1}$$

where y_t is consumption when young, z_{t+1} is consumption when old, and β is a parameter, $0 < \beta < 1$. The utility function of an initial old agent is simply $\ln z_0$.

Coalition Technology for Producing an Intermediate Good

We consider first how old coalition members interact to produce services, which will be inputs for the production of the consumption good and new coalition capital. Our key result will be that a coalition can be indexed by the number M of experienced workers (or, more precisely, the measure of experienced workers) and by the expertise of each of its members k, with the coalition's output of productive services being Mk. There will be costs to splitting coalitions and no gains from mergers. (Readers not familiar with measure theory, which is used in this subsection only, may want to skip to the subsection on joint production of the consumption good and coalition capital.)

The primitive in the analysis is a *coalition,* which is a set of experienced, or old, workers. Each member of a coalition is indexed by a, the member's own expertise, and by k, the accessible expertise of other coalition members. To exploit the expertise of others, old agents must know about it; and, by assumption, this can only be true if agents worked together when young.

More precisely, a coalition is a measure on the Borel sigma algebra of R_+^2. Let Ω be the set of finite countably additive set functions defined on this sigma algebra. For set A belonging to this sigma algebra and $\omega \in \Omega$, $\omega(A)$ is the measure (number) of coalition numbers with $(a,k) \in A$.

If two coalitions ω_1, $\omega_2 \in \Omega$ *merge* to form a new coalition ω, then for all Borel sets A

$$\omega(A) = \omega_1(A) + \omega_2(A).$$

If a coalition of size M *splits* into coalitions ω_1 and ω_2 of size M_1 and M_2, respectively, then

$$\omega_i(\{x \le a, y \le k\}) = (M_i/M)\omega[\{x \le a, y \le (M/M_i)k\}]$$

for all $(a,k) \in R_+^2$. Measure ω_i is well defined because its value for this subcollection of sets uniquely determines its value for all sets in the Borel sigma algebra.

The motivation for the merging assumption is perhaps obvious: the assumption implies that the joining of two coalitions affects no member's own expertise or the expertise to which members have access. The motivation for the splitting assumption is less obvious: it implies that if some percentage of a coalition is split off, then the own expertise of the coalition members who remain is unchanged, but their access to the expertise of others is reduced by that same percentage. Together, these two assumptions imply that there are no gains from merging coalitions but that if a coalition is split, there are costs—the total output of the two resulting coalitions is strictly less than the output of the original coalition. Thus, in this economy, coalitions will not split in an equilibrium.

We assume that if all coalition members work together when young, each has accessible capital equal to the average expertise of the other members. We also assume that there is a coalition production function $\Phi : \Omega \to R_+$ that has this representation:

$$\Phi(\omega) = \int \phi(a,k)d\omega$$

where $\phi : R_+^2 \to R_+$ is strictly increasing, continuous, concave, and homogeneous of degree one. Function Φ is strictly concave in a. The value of this function Φ is the output of productive services of the coalition. Thus, we are assuming that the coalition's output of productive services is the sum of the outputs of its members. Note that, unlike the neoclassical production function, this technology does not have decreasing returns to coalition capital. Proportional increases in everyone's a and k increase the output of productive services by the same factor. This technology does, however, have diminishing returns with respect to own expertise a. The output of productive services is normalized so that

$$\phi(k,k) = k, \quad \text{for all} \quad k \in R_+.$$

An Example: The Old's Choice Problem in Producing the Intermediate Good

To clarify the motivation for the assumed intermediate input production technology, we offer an example of how time can be allocated between two types of productive activity. Here we assume that old coalition members were together when young, so their accessible expertise of others is just the average expertise of the coalition.

A given old worker's contribution to the output of productive services is a function of that worker's own expertise services and the accessed expertise services of other old agents. Old agents must decide how to allocate their time. We assume own expertise services are $(1 - \tau)a$, where $(1 - \tau)$ is the fraction of an agent's time allocated to using the agent's own expertise. Accessed expertise services of other agents are τk, where τ is the fraction of an agent's time allocated to interacting with others. An old agent's total output of productive services thus depends on the values a and k, which are determined by past decisions, and on the agent's current choice of τ. For this example, we assume individual output of productive services takes the functional form

$$B(1 - \tau)a^{\psi}(k\tau)^{(1-\psi)}, \quad \text{for} \quad 0 < \psi < 1 \quad \text{and} \quad B > 0 \tag{1}$$

where ψ and B are parameters. The optimizing τ, which depends on neither k nor a, is

$$\tau = (1 - \psi)/(2 - \psi). \tag{2}$$

Substituting (2) into (1) yields

$$BAa^{\psi}k^{(1-\psi)}, \quad \text{where} \quad A = (1 - \psi)^{(1-\psi)}(2 - \psi)^{(\psi-2)}.$$

Without loss of generality, the units in which old agents' expertise k is measured are selected so that $BA = 1$ and

$$\phi(a,k) = a^{\psi}k^{(1-\psi)} \tag{3}$$

is the output of productive services of an old worker with expertise a, who is a member of a coalition with old members who have accessible expertise k and who has chosen the optimal value of τ satisfying (2).

Completing Specification of Intermediate Good Technology

To continue the specification of the technology, we assume that all agents who work together when young receive the same a and the same k and that units are selected so that $a = k$.

Again, since splitting coalitions is costly, splits do not occur in equilibrium. Consequently, the only relevant coalitions are those in which all members have the same own and accessible expertise, and own and accessible expertises are equal. Thus, coalitions place their entire mass M on some point set $\{(k,k)\}$, where the expertise of members $k \in R_+$ indexes the set. For these measures,

$$\Phi(\omega) = Mk. \tag{4}$$

Hereafter, we restrict attention to such measures and index a coalition with k and M rather than ω. This k is the value of both the M coalition members' own expertise and their accessible expertise.

Coalition Technology for Jointly Producing the Consumption Good and Coalition Capital

There is a constant return to scale coalition production technology, which produces a composite consumption good C and tomorrow's coalition expertise Nk', which is embodied in today's young coalition members. The inputs are the productive services of the old Mk and the productive services of the young Nk. The average expertise of the old members enhances the productivity of both the young and the old members. The constraint defining the technology is

$$C \le (Mk)^{1-\alpha}(Nk)^\alpha - Mk\, h\, [(Nk')/(Mk)] \tag{5}$$

where $0 < \alpha \le 1/2$ and h is convex. Function h is strictly increasing, positive, and a continuously differentiable mapping. With N, M, and k fixed, investment in coalition capital k' is increasingly costly in terms of foregone current consumption C. Thus, this technology has the adjustment cost property, which constrains growth rates. The technology does not have diminishing returns to the accumulation of coalition capital. With N and M fixed, the set of feasible (C,k') pairs varies in direct proportion to k; that is, there are constant returns with respect to (C,k',k) if N and M are fixed.

The coalition's total output of the consumption good constrains the sum of current consumption of its young members yN and current consumption of its old members zM:

$$yN + zM \leq C \qquad (6)$$

where y and z are per capita consumption of young and old, respectively. Combining (5) and (6) and dividing by M yields the constraint

$$ny + z \leq kn^\alpha - k\, h(nk'/k)$$

where $n = N/M$ is the number of young in the coalition per old.

With the assumption that all coalitions start with the same initial k, we can deal with a representative coalition. This, however, does not require that all coalitions be the same size in terms of number of members. In addition, we make the following assumption.

ASSUMPTION: *The function h, besides being increasing and convex, satisfies*

$$h(0) = h'(0) = 0$$

and

$$h'(\delta) = \infty, \quad where \quad \delta > 1.$$

This implies

$$h : [0,\delta) \rightarrow R_+.$$

That $h'(0) = 0$ implies that the cost of the first unit of k' is zero, so in equilibrium k' will be positive. That $h'(\delta) = \infty$ means the economy cannot grow at a rate faster than $\delta - 1$.

3. Constant Growth Equilibrium

In this section, first we conjecture that there exists a constant growth equilibrium that exhibits certain properties. Then we prove that conjecture. The derivation of equilibrium is essentially recursive, which, as will be shown, guarantees that the equilibrium is unique within its class.

The existence proof has three steps. The first is to find the sequence-of-markets equilibrium for an economy (unlike ours) in which capital is not embodied in coalitions and thus is tradable. In all other ways, this economy is identical to ours. The second step is to show that the amount of capital traded in equilibrium is zero. Consequently, this equilibrium allocation is also the equilibrium allocation for our economy. In the third step, the proof is completed by demonstrating that coalitions cannot design Pareto-improving redistribution schemes between their current and future members.

We seek a constant growth equilibrium. In this context, *constant growth* means that the capital stock, the consumptions of young and old, and the real wage w_t all grow at a common (gross) rate x, while the price of new capital relative to current consumption, q, is constant. This is a growth economy without exogenous technological change. Unlike the neoclassical (balanced) growth model's steady-state growth path, which is independent of initial capital, our steady-state growth path is proportional to k_0. Summarizing the desired properties of constant growth:

$$w_t = wk_0x^t \tag{7}$$

$$y_t = yk_0x^t \tag{8}$$

$$k_t = k_0x^t \tag{9}$$

$$z_t = zk_0x^t \tag{10}$$

$$q_t = q \tag{11}$$

where w, y, and z are—like x and q—parameters to be determined.

The Old's Choice Problem

All old agents are members of coalitions. They hire young agents at the real wage w and use their labor services to produce both capital K, which is sold at price q, and the consumption good, which has a price of 1. (The consumption good is the numeraire.) For convenience, we define K as the coalition's total output of capital, now assumed to be tradable, so that $K_t \equiv n_t k_{t+1}$. Defining π as profits per coalition member, we can write the old's maximization problem as

$$\pi(k_t, w_t, q_t) = \max_{n_t, K_t \geq 0} \{k_t n_t^\alpha - w_t n_t + q_t K_t - k_t h(K_t/k_t)\}. \tag{12}$$

This implies that

$$\pi(k_t, w_t, q_t) = k_t \pi_1(w_t/k_t) + k_t \pi_2(q_t)$$

where

$$\pi_1(w_t/k_t) = \max_{n_t \geq 0} \{n_t^\alpha - (n_t w_t/k_t)\}$$

$$= [\alpha^{[\alpha/(1-\alpha)]} - \alpha^{[1/(1-\alpha)]}](w_t/k_t)^{[\alpha/(\alpha-1)]}$$

$$\equiv c_1(w_t/k_t)^{[\alpha/(\alpha-1)]}$$

and

$$\pi_2(q_t) = \max_{K_t/k_t \geq 0} \{q_t(K_t/k_t) - h(K_t/k_t)\}.$$

Solving the first-order condition $q_t = h'(K_t/k_t)$ for K_t yields

$$K_t = k_t s(q_t)$$

where $s(0) = 0$, $s(\infty) = \delta$, and the function s is both increasing and continuous. For constant growth,

$$x = K_t/k_t = s(q). \tag{13}$$

The demand for young workers is determined by the first-order condition

$$\alpha n_t^{(\alpha-1)} = w_t/k_t.$$

Along a constant growth path, $w_t/k_t = w$. Further, young labor is supplied inelastically in the quantity one per old person. Therefore,

$$w = \alpha \tag{14}$$

along a constant growth path.

The Young's Choice Problem

Using (12), we can write the young's choice problem as

$$\max_{y_t, k_{t+1} \geq 0} \{\ln y_t + \beta \ln[k_{t+1}\pi_1(w_{t+1}/k_{t+1}) + k_{t+1}\pi_2(q_{t+1})]\}$$

subject to the budget constraint

$$y_t + q_t k_{t+1} \leq w_t.$$

From (7) and (11), we know that along a constant growth path $w_t = wk_0 x^t$ and $q_t = q$. Letting $a = y_t/k_0 x^t$ and $b = k_{t+1}/k_0 x^t$, we can rewrite the young's maximization problem, again using (12), as

$$\max_{a,b \geq 0} \{\ln a + \beta \ln b + \beta \ln[c_1(wx/b)^{[\alpha/(\alpha-1)]} + \pi_2(q)]\} \tag{15}$$

subject to

$$a + qb \leq w$$

(save for an additive constant in the objective function).

The objective function is strictly concave in a and b since $0 < \alpha \leq 1/2$. The demand for b is a decreasing continuous function of q:

$$k_{t+1}/k_t = b = d(q;x,w). \tag{16}$$

From the budget constraint (holding with equality) and the definition of a,

$$y_t = k_t[w - qd(q;x,w)]. \tag{17}$$

The market parameter w has already been determined. Given this w and x, "supply curve" (13), and "demand curve" (16), determine the actual (gross) growth rate k_{t+1}/k_t as a function of the expected growth rate x. Let this equilibrium relation be denoted as

$$k_{t+1}/k_t = e(x).$$

The final step in the proof is to find the x for which expected and actual growth rates are equal. The supply of capital curve (13) is invariant to x. Increases in x, however, shift the demand function down continuously.[5] This implies that the function $e(x)$ is decreasing, continuous, and strictly positive (see fig. VII-1). Consequently, function e has a unique fixed point x^*. For growth rate x^*, the expected and actual growth rates are equal.

Nothing assumed so far guarantees that growth will be positive—that is, that $x^* > 1$. We do know, however, that any growth rate less than δ will have an investment technology h for which that growth rate is the equilibrium rate. To see this, use the demand function $x = d(q;x,d)$ to determine

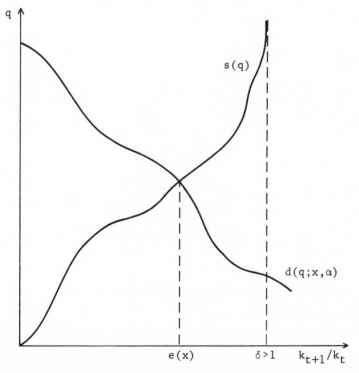

Figure VII-1. Supply of and Demand for New Capital Given the Expected Growth Rate x.

the necessary price of capital q for x to be an equilibrium value. Then select h so that $h'(x) = q$.

In summary, the balanced growth path exists. The unique equilibrium value of w^* is α from (14); the equilibrium x^* is the unique fixed point of $e(x)$; (13) uniquely determines equilibrium q^* given x^*; equilibrium y^* equals $w^* - q^*d(q^*;x^*,w^*)$ from (17); and equilibrium z^* equals $\pi_1(w^*) + \pi_2(q^*)$. This is the only equilibrium constant growth path.

Efficiency

Sometimes competitive equilibria of the sequence-of-markets variety are efficient, and sometimes they are not. In overlapping generations settings, schemes that redistribute from young to old may Pareto-improve upon the sequence-of-markets equilibrium. If this were true for our sequence-of-markets equilibrium allocation, the equilibrium concept would be inappropriate. That is, a coalition could and would institute any redistributional scheme among its current and future members that was Pareto-improving. We now show that for the constant growth equilibrium allocation, no Pareto-improving redistribution scheme exists.

A sequence-of-markets equilibrium for overlapping generations models is efficient if the present value of the sum of all generations' consumptions, calculated using the implicit interest rate, is finite. This condition is not necessary for efficiency, but it is sufficient. For our constant growth path, the implicit gross interest rate (that is, the marginal rate of substitution between consumption when young and consumption when old) is $z^*x^*/\beta y^*$. If this number exceeds x^*, the present value of the sum of all generations' consumptions is finite.

To verify the efficiency of our equilibrium, we first note from (14) that a member of generation t's consumption when young is less than or equal to $w_t = \alpha k_t$ and when old it is at least $k_t\pi_1(\alpha) = (1 - \alpha)k_t$. Thus, $y^* \leq \alpha$ and $z^* \geq 1 - \alpha$. The result that the gross interest rate exceeds x^* follows immediately once we note that $0 < \beta < 1$ and that $0 < \alpha < 1/2$. To summarize, no redistributional scheme Pareto-improves upon the constant growth equilibrium path.

Equilibrium for the Economy with Nontradable Capital

To support the allocation, the market for capital is not needed because in equilibrium capital is not traded between coalitions. The quantity of new capital produced by a coalition is precisely equal to the investment of the young who join that coalition.

Without capital markets, an initial coalition forms a plan $\{z_t, y_t, n_t, k_{t+1}\}_{t=0}^{\infty}$. For a plan to be feasible, it must satisfy two sets of conditions:

$$y_t n_t + z_t n_{t-1} \leq k_t g(n_t) - k_t h(k_{t+1} n_t / k_t), \quad \text{for} \quad t = 0, 1, 2, \ldots \quad (18)$$

$$\ln y_t + \beta \ln z_{t+1} \geq u_t^*, \quad \text{for} \quad t = 0, 1, 2, \ldots \quad (19)$$

where

$$u_t^* = \ln y_t^* + \beta \ln z_{t+1}^*$$

and where a star (*) denotes the equilibrium values of variables for the economy with tradable capital. Conditions (18) are the resource constraints, whereas condition (19) is that all generations realize at least the utility level they could have obtained if capital were traded. The initial generation of the old maximizes its utility $\ln z_0$ subject to these feasibility constraints. Clearly, $\{z_t^*, y_t^*, n_t, k_{t+1}^*\}_{t=0}^{\infty}$ satisfies (18) and (19). Further, no other feasible plan exists that yields greater z_0 than z_0^*. If one did, the star equilibrium would not be optimal.

Next we note that no future generation can profit by modifying the plan. If generation s could modify the plan subject to feasibility for all $t \geq s$ and make itself better off, again the star equilibrium would not be a Pareto optimum. A resource-feasible plan would then exist that increased generation s utility above u_s^* while providing utility levels of at least u_t^* for all other generations. Thus, no generation has an incentive to alter the star plan. This establishes that the equilibrium allocation with traded capital is also the equilibrium allocation when capital is embodied in the coalition and is not tradable.

4. The Effect of Tax Policy on the Equilibrium Growth Rate

Unlike the neoclassical growth model, this economy's balanced growth rate depends on the rate of savings by the young. Any tax policy that alters that savings rate will change the economy's growth rate forever. Increases in the tax rate on the old's incomes, for example, will reduce the economy's growth rate even if tax collections are distributed back to the old. To see this, consider the effect of a proportional tax $0 < \gamma < 1$ on the old's incomes and a lump sum transfer of π_0 to each old agent. The value of π_0 is the income tax collected per old agent, so the total amount collected equals the amount distributed. With this policy, the problem facing a young agent becomes

$$\max_{a,b \geq 0} \{\ln y + \beta \ln(1 - \gamma) + \beta \ln[bc_1(wx/b)^{[\alpha/(1-\alpha)]} + \pi_2(q)b + (\pi_0/(1 - \gamma))]\}$$

subject to

$$a + qb \leq w.$$

The effect of this policy is to reduce the marginal utility of b given x and

q. Consequently, the demand curve $d(q;x,\alpha)$ falls, implying a smaller $e(x)$ function. This in turn implies a lower equilibrium growth rate x^*.

5. Summary and Extensions

The equilibrium behavior of our economy displays three major properties. The economy experiences no exogenous technological change, yet it grows at a constant rate. It displays no tendency for coalition size to regress to a mean or for the size distribution to become more disparate over time. And, unlike the neoclassical growth model, this economy's growth rates are affected by policies that affect the savings rate. For example, a policy that decreases the savings rate also decreases forever the average rate at which the economy grows.

In the prototype structure studied here, the size distribution of coalitions is, admittedly, determined entirely by initial conditions. In a narrow sense, then, we have made no positive contribution to the theory of firm size distribution. At the same time, however, this structure does not result in the type of counterfactual entailments that have plagued most previous growth models, features such as a monopoly firm or all firms of the same size in equilibrium. Moreover, we are optimistic that our basic environment can be generalized. Introducing coalition-specific uncertainty, for example, could lead to a theory of firm size distribution that includes the birth and death of coalitions. With the approach of Lucas and Prescott (1974), the equilibrium would be an invariant distribution of coalitions jointly indexed by their size, as measured by the number of coalition members, and their coalition capital.

This structure might also prove useful in addressing a set of interesting financial questions. If physical capital and private information were added, a coalition of experienced workers would have reason to enter into recursive contracts, not only with young workers, but also with workers who supply financial capital used to purchase physical capital needed for production. Both capital and contract theory considerations might be incorporated into tractable extensions of this construct and the model then used to account for phenomena in which both considerations play important roles.

Notes

1. This paper was prepared for the Workshop on Intertemporal Trade and Financial Intermediation held 17–19 May 1984 by the Institute for Mathematics and Its Applications and the Finance Department of the University of Minnesota. We gratefully acknowledge the financial support of the Federal Reserve Bank of Minneapolis and the National Science Foundation and thank Patrick Kehoe and Thomas J. Sargent for insightful comments on an earlier draft. The views expressed herein are those of the authors and not necessarily those of the Federal Reserve Bank of Minneapolis or the Federal Reserve System.

2. Another approach is to introduce externalities that cannot be internalized within firms, as has been done by Arrow (1962) and Romer (1986). Arrow simultaneously obtains increasing industry returns and constant firm returns by having a firm's production set depend on cumulative industry output. Romer assumes individuals' productivities depend on the average human capital of other members of society as well as their own.

Lucas (1985) obtains sustained growth by assuming a standard neoclassical production function for the production of goods and an individual-specific technology for production of that individual's human capital. The latter technology has constant returns to scale, with an individual's human capital as the input and increments to that individual's human capital as the output. Unlike Romer's (1986) economy, but like ours, there is constant rather than accelerating growth.

3. We think the Lucas (1978) model is a good one of the typical small entrepreneurial firms that account for about half of the output in the United States. It may be less appropriate for the large firms that account for the other half, however; our model is perhaps more appropriate for them.

4. The notion that one component of an agent's human capital is information about co-workers (for example, what they know and what they don't know) has been stressed in recent studies of management in large corporations (Cox 1982; Kotter 1982). For managers, an important resource is knowledge of the abilities of subordinates and peers. This "networking," as it is sometimes called, may involve hundreds of people. The point is that they are specific people, so the value of this information is to a considerable extent group specific.

The productivity of a worker may also plausibly depend on the human capital of co-workers, as we assume here. For example, highly trained engineers are likely to be more productive when working with a group of similar individuals. The same holds true for such disparate professionals as, for example, artists, medical specialists, lawyers, and accountants, and even economists, who often choose to work in colonies, clinics, partnerships, and departments. Other examples abound.

Others have considered the joint production of information and output (Rosen 1972, for example). The Prescott and Visscher (1980) model of organization capital uses statistical decision theory to capture this phenomenon explicitly and analyze the resulting industry equilibrium.

5. One can easily verify that in (15) the marginal utility of a is invariant to x, whereas the marginal utility of b is decreasing in x.

References

Arrow, K. J. 1962. "The Economic Implications of Learning by Doing." *Review of Economic Studies* 29:155–73.
Cox, A. 1982. *The Cox Report on the American Corporation*. New York: Delacorte Press.
Kotter, J. P. 1982. *The General Managers*. New York: Macmillan.
Lucas, R. E., Jr. 1967. "Adjustment Costs and the Theory of Supply." *Journal of Political Economy* 75:321–34.
———. 1978. "On the Size Distribution of Business Firms." *Bell Journal of Economics* 9:508–23.
———. 1985. "On the Mechanics of Economic Development." Paper prepared for the Marshall Lectures, Cambridge University, May.
Lucas, R. E., Jr., and E. C. Prescott. 1974. "Equilibrium Search and Unemployment." *Journal of Economic Theory* 7:188–209.
Prescott, E. C., and M. Visscher. 1980. "Organization Capital." *Journal of Political Economy* 88:446–61.

Romer, P. M. 1986. "Increasing Returns and Long-Run Growth." *Journal of Political Economy* 94:1002–37.

Rosen, S. 1972. "Learning by Experience as Joint Production." *Quarterly Journal of Economics* 86:366–82.

Edward C. Prescott has been a professor of economics at the University of Minnesota since 1980. He received his Ph.D. in economics from Carnegie-Mellon University in 1966 and taught there in the 1970s. He has served as a visiting professor at the University of Chicago and at Northwestern University.

Neil Wallace, a professor of economics at the University of Minnesota since 1974, received his Ph.D. in economics from the University of Chicago. Wallace is co-editor of *Models of Monetary Economies* and contributes to various economic journals.